PARAGUAY'S
AUTONOMOUS REVOLUTION
1810–1840

PARAGUAY'S AUTONOMOUS REVOLUTION 1810–1840

Richard Alan White

UNIVERSITY OF NEW MEXICO PRESS
Albuquerque

Library of Congress Cataloging in Publication Data

White, Richard Alan, 1944—
  Paraguay's autonomous revolution, 1810–1840.

  Bibliography: p. 285.
  Includes index.
  1. Paraguay—History—1811–1870. 2. Paraguay—History—War of Independence, 1810–1811. 3. Francia, José Gaspar Rodríguez, Dictator of Paraguay, 1766–1840.
  4. Paraguay—Economic conditions. I. Title.
  F2686.W48   989.2   78-55707
  ISBN 0-8263-0486-9

© 1978 by the University of New Mexico Press. All rights reserved. Manufactured in the United States of America. Library of Congress Catalog Card Number 78-55707. International Standard Book Number 0-8263-0486-9.
First Edition.

Al pueblo paraguayo de entonces, de hoy y de siempre . . .

Contents

Maps	viii
Figures	viii
Tables	viii
Acknowledgments	ix
Introduction	1
PART 1 The Colonial Heritage	15
1. Classic Colonial Dependence	17
2. The Incorporation of the Missions	24
PART 2 The Revolutionary Process	31
3. Confronting the Metropolises	33
4. From Colony to Republic	46
5. The Establishment of the Popular Dictatorship	60
6. The Consolidation of Latin America's First Popular Regime	80
7. Popular Paraguay	99
PART 3 The Struggle for Autonomy	127
8. The Commercial Escape Valve	129
9. The Economics of Independence	152
Conclusion	166
Chronology	173
Abbreviations	177
Appendixes	179
Notes	265
Bibliography	285
Index	293

MAPS
1. South America — xii
2. Río de la Plata, 1810 — 3
3. Paraguay — 5
4. The Missions — 130

FIGURES
1. Paraguayan Exports, 1816–1820 — 83
2. Paraguayan Import Taxes, 1816–1824 — 84
3. Paraguayan National Budgets, 1816–1840 — 103
4. Paraguayan Army, 1816–1840 — 105
5. Paraguayan Taxes, 1816–1840 — 109
6. Paraguayan Taxes and Sales, 1816–1840 — 112
7. Paraguayan State Sales, 1816–1840 — 113

TABLES
1. Population of the Guaraní Missions, 1750–1801 — 26
2. State Appropriations, 1816–1840 — 95
3. Paraguayan Exports, 1826–1839 — 145

ACKNOWLEDGMENTS

In recognition of my appreciation to the people and institutions who have contributed moral, academic, technical, and financial support during the five years spent in the preparation of this work, special gratitude is owed to Lewis Hanke, who introduced me to the career of Dr. José Gaspar de Francia; to Robert N. Burr for his many years of tolerant guidance and unconditional support; to the staffs of the Archivo de Indias (Seville, Spain), the Archivo General de la Nación and the Museo Mitre (Buenos Aires, Argentina), the Archivo General de la Provincia de Corrientes (Argentina), and the Biblioteca Nacional (Rio de Janeiro, Brazil), for their professional and friendly assistance; to the Fulbright Commission, the University of California Regents Patent Fund, the University of California, Los Angeles Department of History, Research Library, and Graduate Fellowship and Assistantship Section, for the years of financial, technical, and moral support they generously provided; to Hipólito Sánchez Quell, who, during 1972 and 1973, graciously opened the Archivo Nacional de Asunción to me even while it was officially closed for extensive remodeling, and to Vicente Laguardia and Rubén Pérez, along with the other members of the archive's staff who, with professional patience and extraordinary cordiality, facilitated the investigation; to María Cristina Montaño for archival research assistance and comradely reassurance; to Efraím Cardoso, Víctor Chamorro N., Julio César Chaves, Adriano Irala Burgos, R. Antonio Ramos, and José Antonio Vázquez for their many hours of professional consultation; to Roberto S. Thompson for technical assistance and office space in the ABC newspaper building (Asunción); to John M. Michon and Robert B. Poitras for extensive technical assistance during all phases of this work; to Juan Andrés Cardozo, Kenneth Cloke, Waldo Mazelis, Mario Savio, Alexander Saxton, Allyn Sinderbrand, and James Wilkie for their extremely helpful criticisms and suggestions; to Jonathan Cobb for editing the manuscript; to Michele Burgess for typing the manuscript; to Celso Aurelio Brizuda for preparing the maps and graphs; to Joel Filártiga for contributing the frontispiece; to Domingo Laino for his years of professional consultation and technical assistance; to E. Bradford Burns for his encouragement and assistance in publishing the work; and to Henri J. M. Nouwen for his friendship and confidence.

Regardless of such enormous contributions, without which this work certainly could not have been completed, the author accepts full responsibility for all translations and any conceptual or historical shortcomings.

Map 1. South America

INTRODUCTION

The political and economic institutions that governed Spanish America during the colonial era were formulated to enrich Spain, not to promote the prosperity of America. New World silver and gold, as well as other American products, underwrote centuries of Spanish involvement in European power struggles. Spain was itself, however, an economic colony of the more industrialized countries of Europe. Consequently, to meet its chronic balance of payments deficit, Spain spent most of its New World wealth on imported manufactured goods. In this way, Spanish American riches served ultimately to finance the industrialization of the northern European nations. By achieving independence and breaking their political and economic ties to Spain, the nascent Latin American nations shifted their economic dependence from Spain to the more industrialized European nations, thereby initiating the neocolonial era.

With its new political and economic status, America's social structure also underwent change. Without altering the traditional power structure of the former colonies' class society, the native creole oligarchy assumed the dominant class position, replacing the Spanish at the top of the social pyramid. This shift in the locus of privilege and power was the principal change in the social structure brought about by the wars of independence. The basic conditions of life for the vast majority of Latin Americans remained the same; only the masters changed.

This transfer of power was neither an orderly nor a passive changing of the social guard, and nowhere in all Latin America did it take such a bloody, complex, and prolonged course as in the Río de la Plata region (map 2). For almost seventy years (1811–80), the area encompassed by the old Spanish Viceroyalty of La Plata—what today is Argentina, Bolivia, Paraguay, and Uruguay—was the scene of intermittent armed conflict among rival American groups. Following the relatively quick defeat of the Spaniards in the region, creole solidarity shattered. Although the outcome of the struggle against the Spaniards in America would not be conclusively decided for more than a decade, the power struggle among the contending creole factions in the Río de la Plata was vigorous even during this early period, bursting into civil war after 1814.

The roots of the conflict lay in the geography of the area and in the political economy of the Spanish colonial empire. Converging into the Río de la Plata as they meet the Atlantic Ocean, the Paraguay, Paraná, and Uruguay rivers form a single port of entry, which controls the entire river system and consequently access to what were then the Spanish and Portuguese provinces of the interior. From the conquest to the nineteenth century, the two empires clashed periodically over control of the port. Only the Cisplatine War (1825–28), which resulted in the creation of the buffer state of Uruguay, finally put Brazilian claims to rest.

The dominance of the port, to the detriment of the upriver provinces, also was the major point of conflict among the Spanish inhabitants of the region. To assure the interior access to the sea, an expedition from Asunción in 1580 refounded the abandoned port of Buenos Aires; but after only four decades the Spanish crown ordered it closed. Conforming to pressure from the powerful Cádiz-Panama-Lima merchants' guild, which feared the loss of its trade monopoly, the crown established a customs barrier at Córdoba (1618) and withdrew permission from its American colonies to trade with Brazil (1622). Imperial law required that all goods bound for America, with the exception of one ship per year, be sent from Spain to Panama. From there the goods had to be shipped across the isthmus, reloaded on ships bound for Peru, and then transported by mule train and oxcart across the continent to Buenos Aires. To reach Paraguay the merchandise was reloaded onto boats and transported the twelve hundred miles up the Río de la Plata to Asunción.

The continuing demands of the inhabitants of the interior prov-

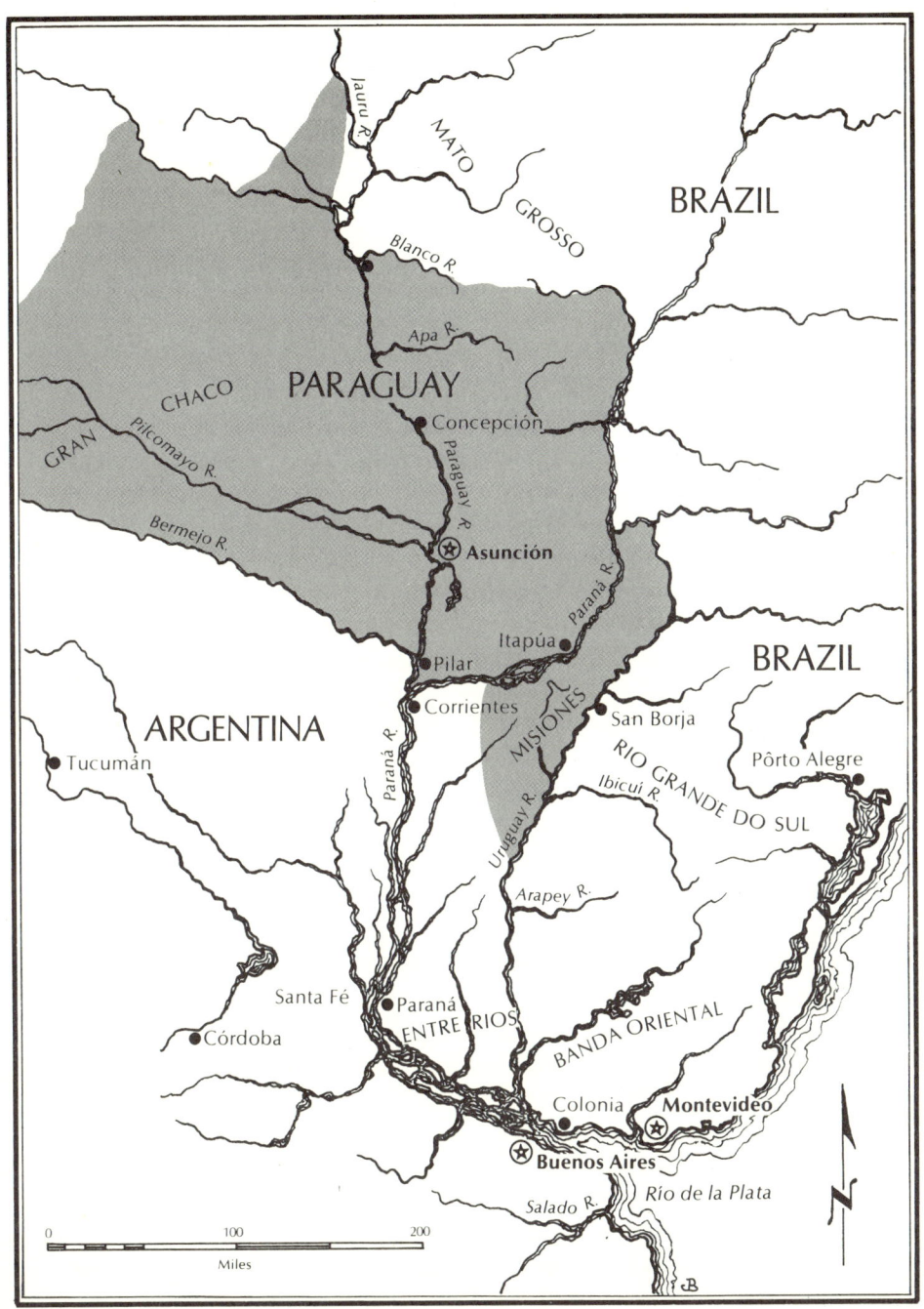

Map 2. Río de la Plata, 1810

inces and Buenos Aires (*porteños*), along with the creation of the Viceroyalty of the Río de la Plata (1776), forced the reopening of the port in 1777. Instead of serving the interior, however, Buenos Aires, the imperial administrative and commercial center of the region, wielded the power of the customs house to benefit itself and its Spanish metropolis. With the introduction of Enlightenment liberal concepts and the beginning of the independence struggle in 1810, the interior provinces hoped to gain economic parity. But at the same time that the porteños promulgated revolutionary ideas and fought for American liberation from Spain, they insisted upon maintaining their traditional position as the economic center of the Río de la Plata.

In the name of the *causa común* against Spain, Buenos Aires solicited, and received, support from the interior provinces. After the Spanish had been defeated in the Río de la Plata, the porteños sought to impose a strong central government, thereby maintaining their control over the region's economy. In opposition to this centralist (*unitario*) attempt to preserve the political and economic structure of the old viceroyalty, the autonomists (*federales*) fought for a confederation of equal provinces. Although the two factions joined to oppose Portuguese intervention in the Río de la Plata, they proceded to fight a protracted civil war among themselves. In fact, it was the struggle between the *unitarios* and the *federales* that characterized Argentina's early national history.

Paraguay constitutes the single exception to this conflict-ridden period in the region's history (map 3). Under the leadership of Dr. José Gaspar Rodríguez de Francia, this country not only maintained absolute neutrality in the bloody Río de la Plata power struggle, but, seizing political and economic independence, also enacted a radical social revolution. Although the remarkable accomplishments of the popular regime must not be considered simply another of history's "great man" stories, Francia obviously played a central role in Paraguay's profound transformation.

Born on January 6, 1766, Francia began his education at home. Later he attended the University of Córdoba, graduating in 1785 as a Master of Philosophy and Doctor of Theology. While at the university, which had been run by the more tolerant Franciscans since the expulsion of the Jesuits in 1767, he not

Map 3. Paraguay

only studied the traditional philosophers and theologians, but was also introduced to the revolutionary European and North American ideological currents of the epoch. Francia's education encompassed Saint Anselm's ontological argument and Rousseau's *Social Contract*, the moralism of Thomas Aquinas and the pragmatism of Benjamin Franklin. His years of university training and the profound influence of the Enlightenment, the North American Revolution, and the popular revolt of Túpac Amaru II in Peru all contributed to the formation of his radical philosophy. Like idealists of every epoch, Francia viewed the world around him in absolute terms, judging situtations and people as either right or wrong, good or bad.

Upon his return to Paraguay shortly after graduation, the young Doctor of Theology began teaching Latin at the Seminary of San Carlos, but was forced to resign several years later when a heated dispute erupted over his radical religious and political ideas. After reading Spanish law, Francia embarked upon a legal career that won him respect throughout Asunción. He spoke fluent Guaraní and befriended the Paraguayan peons, in whose eyes he became a protector and hero. From the poor he asked small fees, if any, while from his wealthy clients he demanded and received large sums. As John Parish Robertson, a contemporary observer, remarked, "His fearless integrity gained him the respect of all parties. He never would defend an unjust cause; while he was ever ready to take the part of the poor and the weak against the rich and the strong."[1]

Although elected dictator by the enormous representative congresses of 1814 and 1816, throughout his years in office Francia avoided the personalism which typically accompanies dictatorship. With the sole exception of Villa Franca—founded in the mid 1820s with Francia's help after floods had forced the inhabitants of Villa de Remolinos to abandon their homes[2]—he did not permit a single town, barrio, street, edifice, statue, or coin to be dedicated in his honor. Similarly, breaking a long-standing tradition, El Dictador categorically refused to accept gifts of any kind.* This policy had such a striking impact on the

---

*Because the word dictator today is strongly pejorative, it should be emphasized that during the early nineteenth century it carried no such negative connotation. The title was then used in its Roman sense—a magistrate with supreme authority elected during times of emergency—and was bestowed upon a number of the new Latin American heads of state,

people that more than twenty years after Francia's death a number of old men recalled it vividly:

> On January 6, 1817, because of El Dictador's birthday, he was given a reception [which was] obviously grander than in any other year. But he would not accept any gifts, maintaining that it was necessary to abolish that rotten Spanish practice, which was conducive to obligating the poor, who oftentimes had to make a sacrifice to comply with it.[3]

As another contemporary summarized this aspect of Francia's character, "His private fortune has not been increased by his elevation; he has never accepted a present, and his salary is always in arrear: his greatest enemies do him justice upon these points."[4]

Francia's incorruptible honesty, especially during his tenure as dictator, became proverbial. Avoiding the accumulation of any substantial personal wealth or property, he lived a modest, semisecluded bachelor's life on a fraction of the salary established for him by the popular congresses. Furthermore, as Francia left no heirs, upon his death on September 20, 1840, all of his belongings, in accordance with the laws that he had promulgated, were automatically confiscated by the state.[5]

Not suprisingly, El Dictador's radical, popular, and nationalistic policies met with growing internal and external opposition. The combined *unitario* and *federal* attacks devastated Paraguayan commerce, serving as the catalyst for the disastrous 1820 Great Conspiracy to overthrow the popular regime by the Paraguayan elites, whose privileged position had rested upon the nation's monocultural export economy. In fact, Paraguay's revolution denied the entire upper class, both Spanish and creole, their traditional social, political, and economic bases of power. Appointing new officials drawn directly from the common people, Francia did not allow the elites to hold government or military

---

including José de San Martín and Simón Bolívar. This work employs the phrase El Dictador not only because it was Francia's formal title and reflects the enormous power conferred upon him by the massive popular congresses, but also because he was often so referred to by the Paraguayan people and frequently even signed official documents simply as "El Dictador."

positions, thus prohibiting them from exercising direct power. He used a system of fines and confiscations to deny them the less direct, but equally effective, power that money commands.

Along with abolishing the elite's municipal governing council (cabildo), the revolutionary regime controlled the church and its auxiliary institutions. It banned the church's brotherhoods, closed its monasteries, and confiscated its landed estates. Nullifying the royal land grants and confiscating the property of the upper-class conspirators, Francia enacted a profound land reform which abolished the traditional latifundia land-tenure system. By the time of El Dictador's death in 1840, well over half of Paraguay's rich central region had been nationalized, scores of prosperous state ranches (estancias) had been established, and tens of thousands of people had homesteaded farms leased from the state. The private sector of the economy had to compete with the government, which, reducing taxes to a minimum, received most of its income from the sale of imported goods, livestock, and state-produced manufactured products. In addition, the state completely controlled international commerce through its own massive participation and a strictly enforced system of trade licenses.

Because Francia attacked the interests of the national and international elites—the class that has written the history of Paraguay—traditionally he has been considered the prototype of despotic tyranny. The most infamous of Latin American dictators, Francia has habitually been portrayed as a grim and somber potentate, a cruel despot with an insatiable lust for power, or simply as a vile monster; the years of his government are commonly known as Francia's "Reign of Terror." In seeking a rationale for this "modern Nero's" seemingly irrational acts, traditional historians have rarely failed to question his mental health; some have simply deemed him insane, while others, in search of more specific explanations, have claimed that the *viento del norte* (the hot and humid north wind blowing from Matto Grosso during the summer months of December, January, and February) profoundly influenced El Dictador. Presented as a sadistic and arbitrary despot unconcerned with the momentous liberation movements sweeping Latin America, Francia is accused of hermetically isolating Paraguay the better to impose his tyranny upon an intimidated nation.

These traditional interpretations stem from several contemporary sources that serve as the basis of virtually all secondary works, and from the intensive propaganda campaign conducted by disenchanted upper-class Paraguayans and Argentine opponents of Francia's radical nationalism and policy of neutrality. The earliest of these accounts, Johann Rudoph Rengger's *The Reign of Doctor Joseph Gaspar Roderick de Francia,* aside from its contempt for Francia and the masses of Paraguayans who supported him, is as objective as can be expected from an upper-class foreigner caught in the midst of a popular revolution. The Swiss doctor and his associate, Marceline Longchamps, conducted research from 1819 to 1825 concerning the natural history of Paraguay. During the last four years of their residency, a time of national crisis, Francia refused them permission to leave the country.

Another principal primary source is the work of John Parish Robertson and his brother William Parish Robertson, *Four Years in Paraguay: Comprising an Account of that Republic under the Government of the Dictator Francia,* Volumes I and II, and Volume III, entitled *Francia's Reign of Terror: Being the Continuation of Letters on Paraguay.* These two Scottish merchant adventurers arrived in Paraguay in 1812 with plans to make a fortune by establishing a trading company between Asunción and Buenos Aires. The introduction of British manufactured goods and England's enthusiastic support of the Latin American independence movements, although largely a bid to inherit the former Iberian colonies as economic dependencies, generally appealed to anticolonial Paraguayans. Consequently, the early Paraguayan governments, hoping to utilize British prestige and naval power to secure free navigation of the Río de la Plata, extended preferential treatment to the Robertsons. But in 1815, after an incident involving the Scottish merchants' representation of the porteño government, in which it became clear that England would not assure free passage of ships along the Buenos Aires–controlled river, Francia expelled the Robertsons, thus terminating their lucrative business.

Typical of the anti-Francia propaganda that issued relentlessly from Buenos Aires during El Dictador's years as head of state is the pamphlet of Frey Mariano Velazco, *Proclamation of a Paraguayan to His Countrymen.* This Buenos Aires government publication characterized Francia by his "hypochondriacal and atrabilious genius heart filled with bitterness and bile, egoistic spirit, cannibalistic thoughts, torturous ideas, unique conceit, insufferable audacity, exclusive vanity, [and] Machiavellian maneuvers."[6]

Of more consequence in the formation of anti-Francia public opinion than these few pamphlets was the campaign carried on in such Buenos Aires newspapers as *El Tribuno*, from whose October 15, 1826, issue the following quotation is taken:

> If the Dictador Francia merits any pardon it is for the vigilance with which he has confined the Protector Don José Artigas [the former leader of the Federal cause against the porteños].
>
> Nevertheless, humanity would gain much if some exterminating angel would purge the land, liberating it of these two monsters.[7]

Moreover, wild and unsubstantiated reports concerning Francia periodically swept through Europe. The first book published on the events of the Paraguayan revolution, according to its title, was written "by an individual who witnessed many of them, and obtained authentic information respecting the rest." This "authentic" account failed even to report Francia's first name correctly, referring to El Dictador as "Dr. Thomas Francia."[8] The European press was fond of entertaining its readers with sensational tales of Francia and exotic Paraguay. In a typical example dating from 1835, newspapers throughout the continent, including *Menorial Bordelais* and *L'Echo du Midi*, circulated this totally false article:

> *The Young Queen of Paraguay:* The very well known Doctor Francia, at the age of 65 [actually, Francia at this time was 69], the eccentric old man who has despotically ruled Paraguay since the emancipation of America, has just married a young French girl, the daughter of Monsieur Durand, a merchant from Bayona. . . . It is stipulated in the marriage contract that the young wife would be the successor to the political authority of her husband in case of his death without leaving a direct or legitimate heir. It is therefore very probable that a Frenchwoman one day will come to be called to govern one of the richest and most beautiful provinces of South America.[9]

By the late 1830s Francia had become so well known to European readers that Charles Darwin, commenting upon the geology and natural history of the Río de la Plata, felt obliged to malign the villain further. Although he never entered Paraguay, the young Darwin evidently could not resist the opportunity to include half a paragraph in his account of the Voyage of the Beagle inaccurately predicting that "when the old bloody-minded tyrant is gone to his long account, Paraguay will be torn by revolutions, violent in proportion to the previous unnatural calm."[10]

It should be pointed out that even the better substantiated volumes of Rengger and the Robertson brothers are not works of history per se; rather, they are personal accounts designed primarily to capture the interest of the European reading public.* Most unfortunately, historians, have uncritically accepted these works as primary sources of Paraguayan history. If read with care, Rengger and the Robertsons do, in fact, yield much valuable information.

The work of Enrique Wisner de Morgenstern, *El Dictador del Paraguay: Doctor José Gaspar Rodríguez de Francia*,[11] also deserves mention as an important source of information. Commissioned by President Francisco Solano López in 1863 to write a history of the Francia era, Wisner conducted extensive interviews and completed a rough draft the following year. But owing to Wisner's death and the chaos of the War of the Triple Alliance (1864–70), the manuscript was not edited until 1876; it was not published until 1923. Although Wisner's is by far the most objective of the early works, it contains minor factual errors and reflects the heated polemic that exploded shortly after Francia's death.

Reflecting Francia's massive support, popular poems, songs,

---

*Francia himself entered into the polemics when his article, "Notes Made in Paraguay by El Dictador Francia on the Volume of John Rengger," appeared in the August 21, 1830, issue of the Buenos Aires newspaper *El Lucero*. Insisting that Rengger's work should have been entitled *An Essay of Lies*, Francia denounced it as "stories not only accommodated to the taste of Europeans, but invented by them, in revenge for the frustration of their repeated conspiracies, machinations, and plots." A rebuttal to Francia's article, written by a countryman of Rengger's César Hipólito Bacle, appeared the following week. Reprints of Francia's article are found in Zinny, *Los gobernantes*, pp. 311–15, and in John Parish Robertson and William Parish Robertson, *Francia's Reign of Terror*, pp. 372–80. Bacle's rebuttal is reprinted in Zinny, *Los gobernantes*, pp. 315–18.

and pamphlets eulogized El Dictador and his regime.[12] The most widely circulated of the Francista literature, the funeral oration of Father Manuel Antonio Pérez,[13] was published in the Platine newspapers and translated for European readers. While the Francistas hailed El Dictador as "the savior that the Lord raised to liberate the Paraguayan people from their enemies,"[14] it was no match in intensity or effectiveness for the anti-Francia campaign conducted by the old Paraguayan oligarchy. Apparently some members of the oligarchy were not content with hysterical attacks on the memory of their archenemy; several months after Francia's death his body was stolen from the cathedral in Asunción and has not been found since.*

Francia's enemies even felt it necessary to record their attacks in his official university records. In an unfamiliar handwriting, neither dated nor signed, the following comments were added to his entry:

> Francia: Afterward he was President of the Republic of Paraguay, and a very atrocious tyrant who has bloodied the history of that country with a world wide scandal.
>
> He was a monster who tore out the entrails of his country.[15]

The oligarchy's hatred of Francia has been passed down through the generations, and he remains the subject of heated emotional arguments. To this day it is impossible to hold a rational discussion about Francia with many of the descendants of Paraguay's former upper class.

So dynamic a figure as Francia, of course, has also attracted some supporters. In a lengthy essay written in the mid 1840s, Thomas Carlyle praised Francia as a determined Latin American strongman who imposed law and order upon a tumultuous era filled with violent social contradictions.[16] In the following decade Auguste Comte, ranking El Dictador with other great American revolutionaries such as Benjamin Franklin, Símon Bolívar, and

---

*Wisner de Morgenstern, *El Dictador*, p. 170. After reviewing several accounts of the theft that were circulating at the time, Wisner concluded that most likely the Machaín family hired several men to steal the body and throw it in the Paraguay River. It is also probable that, contrary to the often accepted idea that Francia burned his personal papers shortly before his death (e.g., Chaves, *El Supremo Dictador*, p. 460), members of the oligarchy are responsible for their disappearance.

Introduction 13

Toussaint-L'Ouverture, dedicated a day in his Positivist Calendar to Francia.[17]

In our own century, despite the occasional appearance of works that attempt to vindicate Francia,[18] the Francista current remains a distinctly minority interpretation. Even the voluminous scholarly work of Julio César Chaves, and the compendium of hundreds of primary source documents brilliantly presented with an interlocking narration by José Antonio Vázquez, have had little effect in denting Francia's odious reputation. The myths about Francia have become so widely accepted that even the progressive Pablo Neruda was moved to denounce him as a "leprous king" in his short poem "El Doctor Francia."[19] From basic textbooks of Latin American history to literary works, historians still continue to propagate the traditional accepted image of Francia.[20] Typical of this attitude is the following passage from Wayne G. Broehl's 1967 introduction to Edward Lucas White's classic novel, *El Supremo:*

> A man whose very name was not to be spoken; whose spies were everywhere, even within families; who sent men to the dungeon or to the "Chamber of Truth" where torture extracted a confession and then the victim was summarily executed by firing squad or gibbet—such a man was "El Supremo." Yet this is no character lifted from a horror fiction, but a real person, a South American head of state . . . . His name was José Gaspar Rodríguez de Francia.*

In addition to the personalistic Latin American historical tradition, the historiography of this period is further complicated by a confusion between rhetorical form and historical content. Attempting to discredit Francia's regime and thereby to support their own position, Francia's enemies have utilized the rhetorical device of attacking his character. Since historians have accepted these partisan attacks as history, instead of recognizing them as historical diatribes, even the later works attack or defend Francia rather than providing an objective analysis of the epoch's history.

---

*Edward Lucas White, *El Supremo*, p. vii. As part of the image that has been created around Francia, it should be noted that the informal title of "El Supremo" ("The Supreme One"), first used by Edward Lucas White in his 1916 novel and subsequently adopted by many historians, was never used by Francia nor by any of his contemporaries.

Significantly, the original reasons for the dispute—Francia's policies—have been relegated to secondary importance.

The subject of this work is not Francia per se, nor is its purpose to vindicate El Dictador. It attempts rather to restore the historical context of this period of Paraguayan history—a uniquely important chapter in the history of the Americas directly relevant to the problems confronting their inhabitants today.

Five years of study and research in the archives of Paraguay, Spain, Argentina, and Brazil have uncovered new documentation and permitted the development of previously neglected statistical information through reconstruction of the national budgets, compilation of revenue receipts, examination of data concerning government industries, and analysis of state commercial records.

Through the incorporation of this new material, and a reevaluation of the previously existing documentation, it has been possible to define Francia's policies clearly and place them within their historical context—the political and economic forces prevalent in early nineteenth-century Paraguayan society and the Río de la Plata region. Externally, conflicts among the Spanish, Portuguese, other European interest groups, Brazilians, *unitarios*, *federales*, and Paraguayans combined to forge the changing political and economic structures of the region. Internally, the conflicts among the Spaniards, creoles, foreigners, Francia, and the Paraguayan people, although greatly influenced by rapidly developing international events, reflected the contradictions of Paraguayan class society. Even though extremely complex, this maze of interrelationships becomes comprehensible once the fundamental political and economic bases of the contending forces are clearly identified. The analysis of these forces is the history of America's first autonomous revolution.

PART 1
The Colonial Heritage

1 CLASSIC COLONIAL DEPENDENCE

Located at the periphery of the Spanish empire, Paraguay was a geographically marginal yet politically and economically integral component of the empire. Because Paraguay was a buffer state between the rival Portuguese colony of Brazil and hostile Indian nations, Paraguayans were forced to serve extended tours of military duty, which contributed to the province's severe labor shortage during the late colonial period. Of even greater consequence were the combined effects of Paraguay's export economy and its dependence on the imperial commercial system. A chainlike structure officially beginning in Spain and extending to the remote province via Panama, Lima, and Buenos Aires, this system served to depress the province's economy and appropriate a great portion of its wealth, leaving the majority of the Paraguayan people in dire poverty.

Because Paraguay was a satellite province of the Viceroyalty of Peru, and later of the Viceroyalty of La Plata (after the creation of the latter in 1776), its major political decisions and trade regulations depended upon these metropolitan centers, themselves, in turn, subservient to the interests of Spain. Consequently, Paraguay's political economy was not designed to benefit the province; its political and economic structures existed to promote the interests of American and European metropolises. There is nothing unusual about this dependent relationship, of course, for the function of an empire is to benefit the metropolis through the exploitation of its satellite colonies. What accounted for the severity of Paraguay's poverty was the misfortune of being situated at the very end of the satellite chain.

In the late eighteenth century, Paraguay's economy centered around the export of several commercial crops, including tobacco, hardwoods, sugar, honey, other sweets, and leather. But by far the most important and profitable cash crop was the Paraguayan tea, yerba maté. Noting that the region enjoyed a natural monopoly on yerba, the province's governor, Agustín Fernando Pinedo, explained to the Spanish crown in 1777:

> Yerba is collected in great quantities and is the most desired and esteemed product of Paraguay. Its commerce extends all the way to Peru and Chile, where its use is common among rich and poor alike. It is drunk in hot water much as chocolate is in Spain, but its use is far more common. Neither is moderation employed as in the use of chocolate, which is drunk two or three times a day, but yerba, which is called maté, is drunk three, four, and more times in the morning and another number of times in the afternoon. And not only by the wealthy and Europeans, but also by the very poorest people, the result of which is a great commerce. There are people so excessively fond of its use that they prefer maté to more solid substance and first spend the money that they have for this craved species.[1]

In the same report Pinedo also emphasized the central importance of the yerba trade to the Paraguayan economy, stating that, along with farming, the principal occupations "of all the inhabitants of this province, by inclination or necessity, [are] the collection of yerba in the forests where it grows . . . [and] its transportation by river in commercial vessels to Buenos Aires." In an earlier report (1773), the governor had estimated that nearly half the colony's men found employment in the collection, preparation, and transportation of yerba.[2] Felix de Azara, the famous Spanish brigadier, naturalist, and royal observer, was even more specific when he reported that of the total Paraguayan commerce of 395,108 pesos for the years 1788 to 1792, yerba alone accounted for nearly three-fourths (292,653 pesos).[3] Paraguayan trade licenses for 1800 document the export of over 2,700 tons of yerba, a vivid record of the province's single-crop economy.[4]

Paradoxically, the great demand for yerba and the ensuing commerce served to impoverish the Paraguayan people. As is typical of monocultural economies, the extreme concentration of human, natural, and capital resources in the production of the cash crop led to neglect of less profitable industry. The most notable effect of this uneven resource allocation was a chronic shortage of staple goods, resulting in high prices for their imported substitutes. As Governor Pinedo observed:

> ... cultivation is neglected, and consequently supplies of the most basic foods, such as bread, meat, and vegetables, are not established. To that one adds the absence of wine, oil, and all the rest, so that he who consumes them (which is the case with everybody) must bring them from Buenos Aires in a three- or four-month journey at excessive costs.[5]

The severe labor shortage resulting largely from the demands of the colony's political role as a buffer between Brazil and the surrounding Indian nations added to Paraguay's problems. Keeping the province in a constant state of military alertness, instead of establishing regular garrisons for its protection, the crown required male citizens to serve in the outlying forts. Including the time spent traveling to and from these distant outposts, this military obligation normally resulted in a four-to-six-month yearly tour of active duty. Moreover, the citizen-soldiers were obliged to outfit themselves with the essential clothing, horses, arms, and subsistence.[6]

As most manufacturing was prohibited by imperial law, many of these military goods had to be imported. With commerce strictly regulated by the monopolistic trade structure, regardless of considerable contraband activity, by the time imports reached Paraguay prices were exorbitant. Governor Pinedo demonstrated Paraguay's dependence upon this trade structure when he complained that "arms, powder, and munitions ... , which are brought from Europe by traders, are very expensive when they arrive at this remote province because they have had *eight and ten* sales and resales, with their price augmented each time owing to the cost of transportation and the profits to which the traders aspire."[7] Again, Paraguay suffered the consequences of its subservient satellite position in Spain's colonial empire.

Plagued by similar regulation and heavy taxation, the colony's exports were also depressed. The case of yerba clearly exemplifies Paraguay's subservience. First sent to Santa Fe and then reshipped to Buenos Aires, which served as the distribution center for Tucumán, Potosí, Chile, Lima, and Quito, yerba was subjected to both provincial and *alcabala* (sales) taxes every step of the way.[8]

Even the Free Commerce regulations of 1777 and 1778, purportedly enacted to facilitate interprovincial trade, offered little relief for Paraguay. Despite these reforms, the structure of metropolis-satellite dependency permitted the continued appropriation of the province's wealth, although now covertly, through a series of detrimental credit relationships. Referring to the yerba trade, Governor Pinedo reported:

> The causes of the bankruptcy and backwardness of commerce of this product, and of the others of this province, consists primarily in that, owing to its poverty, there is not a single merchant who trades with his own capital. The goods that they bring are borrowed on very expensive credit in Buenos Aires, and with the obligation of paying 8 percent interest upon all that remain in the marketplace where they are deposited, which is usually a year or a year and a half; experience has shown that those who bring goods to Paraguay have not finished paying for them in six, eight, ten, or more years. And so they arrive here with this heavy burden and the consideration of risking losses. With the intention of making up these losses, covering the expenses of bringing the products from Buenos Aires, and making the profit which he seeks, the merchant sets exorbitant prices and entrusts his goods to a yerba merchant, who has nothing of his own. And the yerba merchant, looking to sell them, brings them to who? To the miserable peons whose nakedness and misery forces them to offer what they can not pay. In substance they don't have food or instruments or tools with which to collect the yerba. And, so that they can work, they all buy or rent from the yerba merchant, who charges such an exorbitant price that these miserable ones can't pay even half (better to say a third) of their debt, because they are not paid a daily wage or a monthly salary. They buy their clothes and food, and rent the tools with which they work, all on credit. And not having enough time to be able to pay off the debt with their personal labor, they return once again naked, and still indebted, and in need of going still further into debt.[9]

From the governor's description, the chain of economic dependence stands in relief. The peons, without their own means of production, were dependent on the yerba merchants for tools, clothing, and subsistence. The yerba merchants, while effectively serving as a "metropolis" for the peons, functioned in turn as dependent "satellites" in relation to the Paraguayan merchants, from whom they received goods on credit. Likewise, the Paraguayan merchants functioned as satellites dependent upon the Buenos Aires merchants who lent them operating capital. And this dependency chain of exploitation did not end in the American metropolis of Buenos Aires.

In a futile attempt to convince the crown that it would be in the interest of all involved to correct the conditions devastating his province, Pinedo analyzed the economic chain and warned that

> From the losses that the yerba merchants suffer from the peons result the losses of the merchants who trade in this province. And from these losses arise the losses of the merchants of Buenos Aires who extend credit to them, and from the losses of the Buenos Aires merchants the losses of Cadiz. . . . And from the losses of the merchants of Cadiz, innumerable people of that domain [Spain], who in turn put their wealth in that trade, lose their money. From this manner of commerce, which necessarily causes the miserable naked peon of the Paraguayan yerbales to receive goods which he cannot pay for, bankruptcy will result to the first one who puts his wealth in that line of business in Cadiz, where the products flow.[10]

In this manner, the economic satellite-metropolis structure continued. The merchants of Buenos Aires, in order to acquire the goods which they sold to the Paraguayan merchants, depended upon their metropolis, the merchants of Cadiz and their financial backers.*

Understandably, Governor Pinedo, viewing this phenomenon

---

*For the sake of simplicity, the links of the Spanish commercial capitalists with the industrial capitalists of other European nations, although functionally a continuation of the dependence chain, will not be examined in this work. For a discussion and bibliographical essay of this topic, see Barbara H. Stein and Stanley J. Stein, *The Colonial Heritage of Latin America*.

from the most exploited periphery of the empire, incorrectly projected the poverty he saw surrounding him to the entire structure. Had he substituted the concept of profit, rather than loss, in his analysis, he would have presented a more accurate account of the functioning of the commercial system. For not only was each satellite exploited by its metropolis at every link of the chain, but each in turn functioned as a metropolis profiting from the exploitation of its respective satellite.

The exception to this chainlike mechanism of appropriation was the Paraguayan peon, whose labor initially produced the wealth, and who therefore had no satellite to exploit. The duplicity began with the yerba merchants. For, even while subjected to the exploitative credit conditions of their metropolis—the Paraguayan merchants—the yerba merchants reaped a profit from exploiting their satellite—the peons. The same held true for the Paraguayan merchants, who were exploited by the usurious interest rates and high prices they were forced to pay for the goods they received from their metropolis—the Buenos Aires merchants; for if they did not accept the terms of the Buenos Aires merchants, the Paraguayan merchants would not have been in a position to profit from the exploitation of their satellite—the yerba merchants. The same relationship applied at the next link of the chain. The Buenos Aires merchants reaped profits from their metropolitan position vis-à-vis the Paraguayan merchants, while at the same time serving as the source of profit for the merchants of Cadiz. In this manner, each metropolis extracted a profit from the exploitation of its respective satellite. This was a necessity, for if they did not do so, they could not have stayed in business.

Paraguay's monocultural economy, and resulting commerce, depended upon this world market system. Along with the expense of fulfilling the military obligations imposed by its political buffer role, the profits appropriated at each link of the economic dependence chain consumed the province's wealth. Although Governor Pinedo did not correctly portray contemporary commercial capitalism, he evidently understood its effects on the province when he prophetically stated, "The system that the merchants are now beginning to observe, while at the same time that it is less ruinous for them, causes, and will continue to cause in the future, more miserable and unclothed people."[11]

More than twenty years later the new governor of Paraguay informed the crown that, out of a population of nearly 100,000 people, "more than 50,000 souls live in total poverty . . . suffering with patience the terrible effects of nakedness, misery, and oppression."[12]

Clearly, as long as Paraguay's political economy remained dependent, Governor Pinedo's dismal prediction was destined to prove true.

2 | THE INCORPORATION OF THE MISSIONS

For 160 years the Jesuits administered the Guaraní Missions of Paraguay. Established in 1607, the first Missions (also called *reducciones* or *pueblos de misiones*) included only a few hundred inhabitants. By 1767, the year the monarch expelled the Jesuits from Spanish domains, these initial settlements had proliferated; thirty stable and prosperous pueblos flourished, incorporating approximately a hundred thousand Guaraní. After just a few decades of civil administration, however, and as a direct consequence of the incorporation of the Missions into Paraguay's political economy, the pueblos were reduced to pale shadows of their former selves. The majority of the people had fled, production had plummeted, and abandoned structures lay in decay.

During the administration of the Jesuits, the Missions escaped the grinding poverty of the rest of Paraguay. They, too, functioned as a buffer zone with the attendant military obligations, but the burden upon Mission inhabitants was considerably lighter. The wider geographical spread of the pueblos greatly reduced travel time, since many of the inhabitants lived closer to the outposts. Moreover, the Missions enjoyed special royal permission to manufacture their own arms and munitions, which minimized their expenditures for military supplies.

In order to pay the annual royal tribute, to continue regular contributions to the Jesuit central treasury in Spain, and to import the few goods they could not produce themselves, the Missions grew yerba and tobacco for export. They had, in fact, succeeded in cultivating the yerba tree, so rather than collecting the leaves through arduous, time-consuming expeditions into the hinterland, as was normally done, they simply harvested their own crop.[1] In addition, the Jesuits commanded sufficient wealth to finance their own commercial operations, and thereby avoided the added expense and dependency of relying upon the credit merchants.

Unlike those of the rest of Paraguay, the Missions' human, natural, and capital resources were not overconcentrated in the export sector of the economy. Like most missionary-directed groups, the Guaraní raised a balanced variety of crops and animals to meet the staple requirements of their semiisolated communities. This policy not only fulfilled the immediate needs of the people, but, just as important, eliminated the necessity of relying upon expensive imported substitutes. In short, Jesuit missionary priorities and commercial policies maintained a nearly autonomous socioeconomic unit minimally affected by the political and economic forces of dependent Paraguay.

The traditionally hostile relations between colonists and missionaries are important for an understanding of the Missions' history after the expulsion of the Jesuits. Frustrated in their attempts to exploit the labor of the Guaraní, the colonists had not forgotten that royal authorities had used Guaraní soldiers to crush the bloody Paraguayan Comuneros Revolt of the 1720s. The Missions' partial tax exemption in the yerba trade further aroused colonial resentment. Not surprisingly, the Spanish colonists did all they could to discredit the Jesuits, spreading rumors of hidden gold mines and of a Jesuit conspiracy to create an independent state in the wilds of South America.

While this kind of local agitation offered a pretext for expulsion, it was eighteenth-century absolutism that provided the political rationale for expulsion. The expulsion of the Jesuits from the Portuguese (1759), French (1763), and Spanish (1767) colonies reflected the political philosophy of enlightened despotism. Elimination of the semiautonomous Jesuit communities strengthened colonial administrations and further centralized political power in the hands of the European monarchs. Moreover, it permitted confiscation of the considerable Jesuit wealth in land, slaves, and means of production, which were desperately needed to finance the extensive reforms of "enlightened" absolutism. Confronted by such powerful opposition, without allies to champion their cause, the last of the Jesuits left America by 1768.

In order to continue the collection of the annual tribute plus the *diezmo* (a 10 percent tithe), the crown appointed the governor of Buenos Aires, Francisco de Paula Bucareli, to organize a new administration for the Missions. Despite his elaborate measures, however, the new system simply did not work.[2] In striking contrast to the steady growth of the Missions during the last decades of the Jesuit administration, the first decades of civil administration were marked by rapid depopulation. The magnitude of this exodus can be seen in table 1, showing population statistics for the thirteen Paraguayan settlements.[3]

TABLE 1. Population of the Guaraní Missions, 1750–1801

	1750	1764	1767	1784	1801	
Ana	4,778	4,001	4,400	1,700	1,200	
Candelaria	2,031	2,817	3,600	1,700	1,200	
Corpus	3,976	4,280	4,000	2,500	2,300	
Cosme	1,449	2,206	3,300	1,200	800	
Ignacio Guasú	2,251	3,139	2,100	800	700	
Ignacio Mirî	2,520	3,074	3,100	600	700	
Itapúa	3,276	4,308	4,600	2,800	2,100	
Jesús	1,899	2,301	2,900	1,200	800	
Loreto	3,276	4,937	3,200	1,300	1,000	
Maria de Fe	4,296	4,716	3,300	800	1,000	
Rosa	2,524	2,031	2,400	1,200	1,200	(1796)
Santiago	3,968	2,712	3,600	2,700	1,300	
Trinidad	2,629	2,946	2,600	1,100	900	
	38,873	43,468	43,100	19,600	15,200	

Under civil administration, rather than continuing to be a source of revenue for the crown, the Missions actually became a liability. The governor of Buenos Aires, Juan José de Vertiz, in his report of March 21, 1784, informed the king that the Mission treasury showed a deficit of 67,000 pesos.[4] By 1795, owing to nonpayment of the annual tribute and *diezmo*, the Missions had incurred "the enormous arrear and indebtedness of 247,189 pesos to the royal treasury."[5]

Attempting to evaluate and arrest this degeneration during the decades following the expulsion, the crown insistently solicited reports from various officials. As part of the attempt to gather information, the intendants were initially instructed to make yearly visits and reports on the missions.[6] The following summary of the exhaustive report of the intendant of Paraguay, Joaquín de Alós, compiled in 1788 after an extensive inspection tour of the missions, reveals the conditions he found.

> The account books of the administrators had fallen into disorder and confusion. The warehouses were empty of primary goods. Agricultural industry almost abandoned. The tobacco factories inactive. Industry and many crafts without maestros or directors. Commerce ruinous to the communities. The rents of community lands ridiculously low. The cattle herds decimated. No general distribution of clothing since 1768. Food was scarce. The tributes less than half since 1772. The populations of the pueblos were minimal. The education of the youth unattended. The many buildings ruined and deteriorated.[7]

In the text and appendices of his report, Alós elaborated upon these observations. Because of the new administrators' practice of illegally selling much of the Missions' livestock to neighboring estancias in Paraguay, Corrientes, and Entre Rios, during the first year of the civil administration the cattle herds decreased by 20 percent (from 516,371 to 412,169), and by 1788 by over 50 percent (to 243,906).[8] At the same time, the arbitrary distribution of community lands to favored Spaniards at token rents completely displaced many Mission inhabitants.

In reference to this theft of community wealth, Viceroy Avilés in 1799 reported that "the administrators . . . require the Indians to work under the pretext that the products are for the community, but they never dress them."[9] After conducting a complete inspection of the Missions earlier the same year, Felix de Azara explained the situation even more explicitly, stating that "many local administrators steal, entering in their books that they have harvested, for example, 1,000 arrobas of yerba or cotton when there are actually 1,500, which is easy as there is no audit. . . ."[10]

Alós inspected all of the thirty pueblos, and in each he found the people's clothing in miserable condition; in many cases the inhabitants had no clothes at all. In a lengthy appendix he included specific observations of each pueblo. A typical report said, "I am affirming that these natives have not had a general distribution of clothing since the expulsion of the Regulars, and that they continue to be in need of it."[11] At the conclusion of each report Alós ordered the administrator in charge to issue clothing to the inhabitants immediately. Evidently the orders were not taken seriously for, writing eleven years later, Azara reported, "As for what I have seen and inspected, I believe I can positively say that not a single pueblo has been given a complete set of clothing, not even once, since the expulsion of the Jesuits, and I emphasize . . . that I do not exaggerate."[12]

Needless to say, the Guaraní did not willingly participate in their own exploitation. According to Viceroy Avilés, only "their habit of submission, their natural gentleness, and the fear of the whip . . . makes them work."[13] Practicing a form of resistance traditionally interpreted as "laziness," the Mission inhabitants became "very skillful in eluding the obligations imposed upon them . . . [by] . . . lying, tricks, maneuvering, conspiracy, feigning illness, and hiding themselves."[14]

The civil administrative system turned the Missions' balanced economy into a replica of Paraguay's monocultural economy. As in the rest of Paraguay, the dearth of staples could be directly attributed to the disproportionate concentration of resources in the production of yerba. The neglect of agriculture, and the resulting depletion of grain supplies, was so severe that Alós noted that "they seem reserved for sowing time rather than to feed the common people."[15] In the words of the intendant,

> This abandonment of agriculture is due to the fact that the administrators have viewed this industry as the least consistent with trade and commerce, so it has been badly put off, and they have resolved to pursue the production of yerba, without considering the severe damage to the community. . . .[16]

This reorientation of the economy is the key to the impoverishment of the Missions. The civil administrators and merchants, motivated by shortsighted self-interest, confiscated much of the accumulated wealth of the missions and, by responding to market opportunities, redirected their resources to emphasize maximum production of yerba, thereby transforming a balanced economy into a monocrop economy. Under civil administration, the missions were subjected to, and soon dominated by, the same economic forces and priorities responsible for the impoverishment of the rest of Paraguay.

It must be recognized that culpability did not rest with individual exploiters alone, for their actions were more symptomatic than causal. That is, although the administrators were the overt agents of oppression and thus directly responsible for much of the Missions' plight, their actions were only possible within the context of the larger political economy of the Spanish colonial empire, and therefore must be recognized as effects of that larger structure. Indeed, the impoverishment of the Missions is only superficially attributable to the corrupt acts of individuals; the root cause lies in the incorporation of the missions as a superexploited appendage of dependent Paraguay.

PART 2
The Revolutionary Process

3 CONFRONTING THE METROPOLISES

Reflecting the deterioration of the Spanish empire, Iberian control and protection of the Río de la Plata had been drastically weakened by 1810. As early as 1806, a British expedition under the command of Sir Home Popham had been able to force its way into Buenos Aires. Significantly, it was the creoles, not the Spanish, who finally expelled the invaders. The Spanish viceroy, Rafael de Sobremonte, fled to the interior, leaving the city's colonial militia in the hands of the creole officer Santiago Liniers. After the defeat of the British, the porteño cabildo deposed Sobremonte and elected Liniers viceroy in his place. The following year a second expedition of 10,000 British soldiers, this time commanded by General John Whitelocke, occupied Montevideo and attacked Buenos Aires. Again it was the creole Liniers who successfully defended the city, forcing the British to withdraw.

Even though the British had suffered two military defeats, they succeeded in stimulating the porteños' growing demands for free trade outside the confines of the Spanish empire. During the months of British occupation, the inhabitants of the Río de la Plata experienced the benefits of direct trade with England. British merchants willingly paid twice the accustomed price for the region's principal exports of hides and tallow, at the same time selling woolen ponchos manufactured in Manchester for one-third the price of the native Tucumán products.[1]

Events in Europe further undermined Spanish authority in America. In 1808 Napoleon's armies had invaded the Iberian Peninsula and captured the Spanish monarch, Ferdinand VII. In an attempt to end the Bourbon dynasty but not the Spanish monarchy Napoleon named his brother, Joseph Bonaparte, the new king of Spain. A popular insurrection disrupted this plan, however, and led to the establishment of local juntas loyal to Ferdinand. In turn, the cabildos of Buenos Aires and Asunción voted to recognize the authority of the most prestigious of these juntas—the Junta Superior de España e Indias (Seville)—and pledged allegiance to the imprisoned Bourbon monarch, but the dissolution of the Junta Superior the following year temporarily cut America's ties to the Bourbon crown. The Buenos Aires cabildo, perhaps buoyed by the recent victories over some of the finest British soldiers, seized this opportunity to break away from Spain's commercial monopoly and assume direction of its own affairs. On May 25, 1810, the porteño cabildo deposed Viceroy Baltasar Hidalgo de Cisneros, who had been appointed by the Junta Superior the previous year, and established the Provisional Junta of the Río de la Plata to "govern in the name of Ferdinand VII."

In a move to maintain their dominant position in the economy of the region, the porteños announced their intention of retaining the political structure of the viceroyalty. The Provisional Junta immediately issued a proclamation of its authority "unto the Provinces of our dependency and even beyond to the most distant frontiers if it is possible."[2] The Buenos Aires cabildo sent a similar circular to all provinces of the Viceroyalty of La Plata.[3]

Realizing that the Paraguayan royalists would put forth strong opposition, the Buenos Aires junta, in what proved a disastrous decision, sent Colonel José Espinola to deliver the cabildo's declaration and further to explain the goals of the porteño revolt. Espinola, "the living person most hated by the Paraguayans" because he was the "principal instrument of [former] Governor Lázaro de Rivera's violence,"[4] quickly alienated both the Spanish and creole elites. After assuming the title Paraguayan Commander of Arms, he stopped in the southern border town of Pilar just long enough to force the local cabildo to pledge allegiance to the porteño junta.[5] Continuing on to Asunción, Espinola received cordial treatment from Governor Bernardo de Velasco until the news from Pilar arrived, after which he was ordered into exile in the north. But rather than traveling to Concepción, Espinola managed to escape and returned to

Buenos Aires, where he greatly exaggerated the size and power of the porteñista faction in Paraguay.

At the time of the 1810 revolt in Buenos Aires, Paraguay was under the firm control of the Spaniards. They occupied the highest political and military positions, and "the trade of Paraguay was chiefly in the hands of the old Spaniards."[6] Yet owing to the traditional Paraguayan animosity toward Buenos Aires, Governor Velasco and the ultraroyalist Asunción cabildo found it easy to rally Paraguayan support against the porteños. The association of the notorious Espinola with the porteños, and the fear of new military drafts,[7] also served to solidify Paraguayan support against this latest, and most blatant, expression of porteño dominance. But the principal reason for the unified opposition to porteño pretensions was Paraguay's peripheral position with the Spanish empire, in a political and economic cul-de-sac. There was no powerful or entrenched creole class whose socioeconomic position was advantageously based upon, or tied to, the colonial structure.* Consequently at this historical moment the antagonisms in Paraguay between creoles and Spaniards were temporarily overshadowed by their common opposition to the porteños.

But even though the enemy was clearly defined, not all Paraguayans were in agreement was to what course of action to follow. At the July 24, 1810, meeting of the *cabildo abierto* (an "open" assembly of local notables) convened by Governor Velasco and the royalist cabildo to deliberate upon the recent developments, a radical creole Doctor of Theology and lawyer shocked the Asunción elites by dismissing as irrelevant any debate over who should be recognized as sovereign of Paraguay. José Gaspar Rodríguez de Francia, greatly influenced by En-

---

*In general, the farther a colony was from the center of the empire, the more it was exploited. The progress of the South American liberation movements, beginning at the peripheries of the empire and working their way steadily to the military and administrative center (Peru), dramatically illustrates this principle. In the south, it was Paraguay that first declared its independence from Spain, as well as from its American metropolis, Buenos Aires, proclaiming itself a republic in 1813. Next came the United Provinces of the Río de la Plata (1816), and with the defeat of the Spanish in the Platine region, José de San Martín crossed the Andes into Chile (1817), whence he later sailed north to attack the last Spanish stronghold, Peru (1820). Likewise in the north Venezuela began by declaring its independence (1811). For nearly a decade Simón Bolívar's armies fought to liberate New Granada (1820), after which they moved south into Peru (1823).

lightenment philosophy, argued that since Spain no longer possessed the power to govern, sovereignty naturally reverted to the people; therefore, Paraguay should declare its independence rather than continue as a dependency of a porteño-controlled central government.[8] In his address to the assembly, Francia insisted,

> The only questions that should be discussed in this assembly and decided by a majority vote, are how we should defend and maintain our independence against Spain, against Lima, against Buenos Aires, and against Brazil; how we should maintain internal peace; how we should foster the public prosperity and the well-being of all the inhabitants of Paraguay. In short, what form of government we should adopt for Parguay.[9]

Not surprisingly, the 200 local Spanish and creole "notables" rejected such radical propositions. Instead, they rebuffed the porteños by approving the more conservative royalist resolutions to recognize the authority of the Supreme Regency Council in Spain, while at the same time pledging fraternal relations with the Buenos Aires government and the other provinces of the viceroyalty. More important, the cabildo abierto resolved to raise an army for the defense of the province, noting that Portugal was looking for a chance "to swallow this precious and coveted province," and already had its troops on the banks of the Uruguay River.[10] To coordinate the military preparations, the cabildo abierto created a War Junta of selected royalist officials headed by the ranking Spanish officer, Colonel Pedro Gracia.[11]

This resolution clearly reflected the conservative interests of the Spanish elite for, as events were shortly to prove, the new army could be used to resist porteño as well as Portuguese domination. But inherent in the Spaniards' plan to defend their privileged position was a contradiction which would shortly result in the collapse of this initial unity. Spain's continual involvement in European wars during the eighteenth century had made nearly impossible the deployment of Spanish armies to defend its American possessions, which increasingly became the targets of English military adventures as the colonial era came to a close. The Bourbon monarchs had therefore adopted the policy of enlarging local militias, at first to augment and later, particularly during the Napoleonic Wars, to replace Spanish troops in many American colonies. Thus, any military force raised to defend Paraguay threatened to fall under creole command.

When the porteños learned that their declaration of authority had been rebuffed by the July 24 assembly, they enacted a series of punitive measures, which included isolating the province by blockading all river traffic and sending secret emissaries into Paraguay to provoke an uprising.[12] Beginning in September 1810, small porteño plots began to be uncovered, first in Asunción, then, shortly afterward, in Concepción, Itá, and Yaguarón.[13] At the same time, Buenos Aires militarily pursued its ambition to perpetuate the viceroyalty as a unit under its control. In an attempt to secure the Banda Oriental (Uruguay), the porteños attacked the Spanish stronghold at Montevideo; in order to confront the royalist armies sent from the Viceroyalty of Peru, they dispatched an army to the interior northern provinces. Still believing Espinola's report of strong porteño support in Paraguay, even though the expected creole revolt had failed to materialize, they confidently sent General Manuel Belgrano with a small army to force the province into submission.

In early December the porteño "liberation" army, consisting of 1,100 well-armed and disciplined soldiers, crossed the Paraná River into Paraguay—only to find the countryside deserted.[14] The reports of a large porteñista element had proved to be false, and Belgrano was forced to concede that his proclamation to the Paraguayans that "the army of Buenos Aires does not have any other objective in its coming than to liberate you from your oppression" had not had "any effect whatsoever."[15]

Moving northward, the porteño army finally encountered the Paraguayan forces at Paraguarí; on January 19, 1811, Belgrano launched a spearhead attack which initially dispersed the center division of the Paraguayan defenses. Believing the battle lost, Governor Velasco, Colonel Gracia, and most of the Spanish high command fled the battleground toward Asunción. In a counterattack, however, the creole officers, led by Manuel Cavañas, Fulgencio Yegros, and others, were able to turn the tide and defeat the invading army.[16] The creole officers, many of whom had served in the defense of Buenos Aires four years earlier, when Viceroy Sobremonte had prematurely fled the battlefield,[17] once again saw their Spanish superiors abandon their commands.

When the first Spanish officers arrived in Asunción with the news of the porteño "victory," the city's wealthy royalists packed themselves and their possessions onto seventeen huge riverboats in preparation for an escape downriver to the Spanish stronghold of Montevideo. Later, Governor Velasco, learning that the porteños had actually been defeated, returned to his headquarters at Yaguarón in an attempt to resume command of military operations.[18]

Meanwhile, the Paraguayan forces, now under the field command of the creole officers, cautiously pursued the slowly retreating porteño army and on March 9, 1811, once again defeated Belgrano's forces at the battle of Tacuarí. Hearing of the new victory, Velasco set out personally to conduct the porteño capitulation, but, to his dismay, by the time he reached Tacuarí there was no capitulation to conduct.

During the months of retreat, officers of the two armies had constantly exchanged friendly notes. After the battle of Tacuarí, many of the officers, some of them personal acquaintances from their campaigns in Buenos Aires and Montevideo against the British, openly fraternized and discussed the goals of the porteños' anti-Spanish revolt. Through these discussions the Paraguayan creoles came to realize that Spanish dominance was coming to an end; that they, not the Spaniards, held the real power in their province. In a remarkable gesture of sympathy toward their counterparts, the Paraguayans permitted Belgrano, after he had promised never again to conduct hostilities against Paraguay, to leave the province with his troops and arms intact.[19] Rather than leaving immediately, the porteño general bestowed gifts and money upon the Paraguayans and continued the discussions until the imminent arrival of Velasco forced his retirement across the Paraná River, where he made camp in the Missions.[20] At this time the creole officers' plot to seize power from the Spanish first took form. Significantly, the Paraguayan officers, representing many of the oldest and most prestigious creole families of the province, planned simultaneous uprisings on May 25, the anniversary of the porteño revolt.[21]

Late in 1807 Prince Regent João and the Portuguese court, transported by the British fleet, fled to America to escape Napoleon's army as it approached Lisbon. Stopping in Salvador de

Bahia, the Lusitanian regent abolished the colonial commercial restrictions and opened the Brazilian ports to world trade. This allowed England to dominate the increasing foreign commerce, thus superseding Portugal as the economic metropolis. The new dependency, formalized by the treaties of 1810, so completely established British domination that, in the opinion of the resident Swedish ambassador, Brazil had become a colony of Great Britain.[22] Surrounded by Portuguese ministers and institutions, João administered the empire from Rio de Janeiro.

As João's wife, Carlota Joaquina de Bourbon, was the sister of the dethroned Spanish monarch Ferdinand VII, the royal couple assumed the role of defending the interests of both the Spanish and Portuguese monarchies in the Americas. Yet these royal pretensions mainly served to further historic Portuguese (rather than Spanish) designs upon the vaguely defined frontier region of the Banda Oriental.[23] In recognition of the strategic importance of this region, in 1680 the Portuguese established the Colônia do Sacramento on the left bank of the Río de la Plata in an attempt to open up and protect their southern interior provinces. Insisting upon maintaining control over the river network, the only inland water route to its rich Peruvian silver mines, Spain made every effort to expel the Portuguese. By the beginning of the nineteenth century the Banda Oriental, after being shuffled back and forth between Spanish and Portuguese domination, was still a disputed area. With the outbreak of the creole revolt against the Spanish in the Río de la Plata, Brazil once again sought to ensure that the river would remain open to its vessels, thereby guaranteeing its commerce and communication with the enormous province of Mato Grosso, situated at the headwaters of the Paraguay River north of Asunción. Alarmed by the porteño military expeditions into the Banda Oriental and Paraguay, Brazil took advantage of the turmoil and increased its efforts to penetrate the Río de la Plata. Under the command of the captain general of the neighboring province of Rio Grande do Sul, Diego de Souza, Portuguese troops invaded the Banda Oriental.

Meanwhile, the Spaniards in Asunción, realizing that royal authority was on the verge of collapse, moved to secure their deteriorating position. When they learned of the cordiality that had been accorded Belgrano, a cordiality that from the royalist point of view approached treason, Velasco and the cabildo realized that the creole army could not be trusted. The Paraguayan creoles now seemed to constitute the principal threat to Spanish control of the province. Consequently, even though Belgrano was just across the river with his army intact, Velasco dispersed the creole officers and sent most of the soldiers home without paying them for their eight months of service.[24]

The royalists, facing growing dissatisfaction from the Paraguayan creoles as well as the possibility of another invasion from the porteño army, frantically accelerated their efforts to gain loyal reinforcements. Besieged by porteño forces, the Spanish viceroy in Montevideo, Francisco Xavier Elio, was unable to send help. In an unabashed appeal to ruling-class solidarity against the insurgents, the Paraguayan royalists appealed to the Portuguese forces for the desperately needed reinforcements. In the north, from Matto Grosso, their missives did not even elicit a reply, but from the southern town of San Borja, Diego de Souza dispatched his personal envoy, Lieutenant José de Abreu, to negotiate the terms of Portuguese imperial military aid.[25]

After being detained for three weeks in Itapúa by Fulgencio Yegros, who at this time was serving as lieutenant governor of the Missions, Abreu finally arrived in Asunción, to the delight of the royalists. Following several days of conversations with Governor Velasco, who assured the Portuguese emissary that he was eager "to put himself at the feet of the Serenísima Señora doña Carlota as he did not recognize any other successor to the crown and domain of Spain,"[26] Abreu addressed the cabildo on May 11, 1811. He frankly informed the royalists that the price of Portuguese military aid would be the formal recognition of the Portuguese queen's claim to the Spanish throne.[27] Two days later the cabildo unanimously agreed to these terms, gratefully accepting General Souza's protection, which they prophesied would "make the insurgents and their infamous satellites tremble, seeing us under a shield that, with its forces and power, will render useless their treacherous suggestions and seductions, which are their most fearsome arms. . . ."[28]

Far from improving their precarious position, the royalists' acceptance of Portuguese military aid served only to precipitate their downfall.[29] The night after the cabildo's resolution, creole officers, incensed by this new example of foreign domination and fearing discovery of the original coup plans, decided to take the situation into their own hands. Led by Captain Pedro Juan Caballero and Lieutenant Vicente Ignacio Iturbe, the Asunción officers preempted the original plot and staged their own coup.

The activity at the barracks alarmed the royalists, many of whom—including most of the cabildo members, the bishop, and numerous other clergy and civilians—sought refuge at the governor's house. Velasco's only resistance to the coup consisted of sending a small troop of Spanish militia to surround the barracks. They, however, were quickly dispersed by creole gunfire.[30]

Although this bloodless coup is known in Paraguayan history as the May 14 and 15 Independence Revolution, its objectives were hardly revolutionary. The creole officers did not want to depose Governor Velasco or to declare independence; they wanted only to temper the royalists' actions, prevent Portuguese military intervention, and put the province in a more congenial relation to Buenos Aires.[31] As their first act, the creole officers released those who had been imprisoned by the cabildo for participating in the various porteño conspiracies.[32] In a note to Velasco which emphasized that Paraguay would not be turned over to the Portuguese, the barracks demanded that Velasco surrender all arms together with the keys to the treasury and the cabildo house; furthermore, the officers declared "that the Governor shall continue governing, but in association with two Deputies sent from this barracks."[33] Velasco, surrounded by cannons trained on his house, recognized the hopelessness of the situation. After burning his confidential papers, he capitulated to the creoles' demands.[34]

On the morning of May 15, the officers, along with some civilian participants, met to select the two deputies. As the military representative they chose Lieutenant Colonel Juan Valeriano de Zevallos, who, although a Spaniard by birth, had been a vocal and active participant in the anti-Spanish revolt.[35] To represent the civilians they chose the most experienced, qualified, and respected creole—Doctor Francia. Notified of his selection at his chacra (country residence), Francia immediately came to the barracks and in the first few hours changed the direction of the new government's relation to Buenos Aires. Vetoing the plan of the leading porteño civilian conspirator, Pedro Somellera, who wanted to send an envoy immediately to Buenos Aires, Francia limited communications to a written summary of the recent events, delaying until a future date the dispatch of a special emissary who would deal with the porteños as diplomatic equals.[36] Clearly demonstrating the autonomous direction of, and Francia's leadership in, the new Paraguayan government, the triumvirate's *bando* of May 17 stated unequivocally that the province would not be left "to the command, authority, or disposition of the province of Buenos Aires, nor of any other, and much less subjugate itself to any foreign potency."[37]

The new government, anxious to avoid a hostile reaction from its neighboring superpowers—Buenos Aires and Brazil—released all prisoners captured at the battles of Paraguarí and Tacuarí and evacuated its troops from Corrientes, which had been occupied the previous month.[38] Similarly, José de Abreu was permitted to leave Paraguay after being entrusted with a letter for General Souza. Appealing to the Portuguese policy of preventing the unification of the crumbling viceroyalty under Buenos Aires control, the triumvirate requested arms and munitions for its own defense against porteño designs to absorb the province.[39] Souza diplomatically replied that he found himself in the embarrassing position of being unable to fulfill the request without prior authorization from the Portuguese court, although he hoped shortly to offer support not only from his own province but also from Mato Grosso.[40]

But as Spanish political authority in Paraguay quickly collapsed, no aid was forthcoming from the Portuguese. Velasco, considering the end of Spanish power in America inevitable, continued to conspire with agents of the Portuguese court to establish its authority in Paraguay. When the creoles discovered the conspiracy, they expelled the former governor from the triumvirate, and to further solidify their power they relieved all Spanish officers of their commands (with the exception of Zevallos) and suspended the royalist cabildo.[44]

Portuguese reaction to the events in Paraguay was determined by regional considerations. The first priority of the Portuguese imperial forces in the Río de la Plata was to secure control of the Banda Oriental while impeding porteño hegemony over the area. Therefore, the Portuguese empire took a relatively soft line toward Paraguay in the following years. In turn, not even the Portuguese-aided Indian raids from the semiautonomous province of Matto Grosso in the north,[42] nor the sporadic clashes between the Paraguayans and the Portuguese in the Missions—such as the bombardment of the Pueblo of Santo Tomé in May 1812[43]—were sufficient to provoke Paraguay into declaring war. As long as Paraguay maintained its policy of neutrality and nonintervention, Brazil recognized the advantages of avoiding open hostilities which might force Paraguay into an alliance with Buenos Aires.

The major issue among the Paraguayan creoles centered upon the province's relationship with Buenos Aires. Many creoles wanted some form of immediate union with Buenos Aires. They feared that continued resistance to the demands of the metropolis would precipitate another porteño blockade, which in turn would cause economic stagnation or even another invasion of the province. Yet all shared a common animosity toward and distrust of Buenos Aires which made them sympathetic to the minority position led by Francia, who insisted that if Paraguay did enter into a union with the porteños it must be upon the basis of a confederation—that is, a union of equal provinces. To settle this and other major questions—the province's relationship with Buenos Aires, the fate of the royalist cabildo, and the form of government to rule Paraguay[44]—a general assembly was called for June 17, 1811.

Even before the assembly convened, the new government demonstrated that although it would attempt not to antagonize Buenos Aires in external matters, it would not tolerate interference in Paraguay's internal affairs. Only two weeks before the assembly, Francia and Zevallos, in what would become a common procedure, undermined the strength of the porteño faction by arresting Somellera and several other leading porteñistas.[45]

Although Francia had attempted to include representatives from the outlying towns and countryside, most of the 251 delegates to Paraguay's first general assembly were members of Asunción's creole elite.[46] Francia, again drawing upon his Enlightenment ideology, set the tone for the assembly in his opening speech:

> The province of Paraguay, returning from the lethargy of its slavery, has recognized and recovered its rights, today finding itself in total liberty to care for and direct itself and its own happiness. . . . Arms and force may very well suffocate and strangle these rights, but do not extinguish them, for natural rights are not prescribable. . . . All men are born free. . . . [47]

The following day Mariano Antonio Molas presented a resolution, bearing obvious marks of Francia's influence, which was accepted by the assembly. Velasco was permanently deposed and the royalist cabildo disbanded "for having abandoned the city, embarking with its armament and leaving it wholly indefensible after the battle of Paraguarí."[48] To govern the province, the assembly created a five-man junta, authorizing it to maintain an adequate army and appoint a new cabildo composed exclusively of creoles.

Those appointed to the new junta were drawn from all sectors of the creole elite. Representing the military and large landowners were Fulgencio Yegros as president and general commander of arms, and Pedro Juan Caballero; representing the clergy was Frey Francisco Javier Bogarín; and representing Asunción's creole social elite was Fernando de la Mora. Francia was chosen more or less as a representative-at-large, in recognition of his outstanding personal merits and popular reputation.

The assembly suspended recognition of the regency in Spain (while continuing to recognize no other sovereign than Ferdinand VII, of course) until a relationship of "friendship, good harmony, and correspondence with the city of Buenos Aires and the other confederated provinces" could be reached. Naming Francia to conduct these negotiations at the forthcoming general congress called by Buenos Aires, the assembly emphasized that such a union was desirable "in order to form a society founded on principles of justice, equity, and equality. . . ." Reflecting Francia's strong influence, the resolution detailed the conditions under which Paraguay would participate in a confederation of Platine states. In Latin America's first genuine expression of federalism, Paraguay insisted that it would govern itself until the general congress could be convened in Buenos Aires; that the porteños cease collecting the export duty on Paraguayan yerba (though consenting to a small, temporary tax due to the port's unusual defense costs); that the tobacco monopoly be abolished to permit unrestricted trade of the product; and, finally, that any decisions reached at the general congress "will not obligate this province until ratified by a full and general assembly of its inhabitants."[49]

Assuming the leading position in the Paraguayan junta, Francia presented these demands to the Buenos Aires junta in a note of July 20, 1811. To prevent the porteños from overlooking the significance of such principles as "equity and equality," Francia stated emphatically:

> Without any doubt, when the Supreme Power is abolished or deteriorated, its representation falls, or is naturally recast in the entire nation. All people therefore consider themselves, in a manner, participating in the attributes of sovereignty . . . the people, reassuming their primitive Rights, find themselves all in equal condition.

Justifying Paraguayan resistance to Belgrano's army, Francia explained that the province had only defended itself against "the rigors of a new slavery with which it felt itself threatened." It would be foolish, he continued, to presume that Paraguay would "submit to a foreign expedient and make its fate dependent upon another's will. In such a case nothing more would be accomplished, nor obtained from its sacrifices, than exchanging one set of chains for another—than changing masters."[50]

The events leading to the July 20 note demonstrate Francia's astute political leadership. By not forcing the issue of the province's formal independence at this time, Francia's "compromise" resolution of a conditional union between Paraguay and Buenos Aires avoided a polarization of the porteñista and nationalist sentiments among the province's creole elite. Unlike any other province of the old viceroyalty, Paraguay had, in only a few months, severed the ties with both its metropolises.

4 | FROM COLONY TO REPUBLIC

Even though Paraguayans displayed remarkable solidarity in opposing external domination, during the twenty-seven months that the junta governed the province (from July 1811 to October 1813) they did not escape the power struggle among the various sectors of the creole elite. In the wake of the deposed Spanish government, the internal composition of provincial politics was still in flux. Yet since throughout the colonial period trade had been overwhelmingly in the hands of the Spaniards, who were now effectively excluded from the political process, the absence of a powerful, firmly entrenched creole commercial element greatly simplified the process of political solidification in Paraguay.

In most other respects the struggle for power in Paraguay resembled that of its counterparts throughout Latin America. While the church was one of the factions vying for power, the principal conflict centered around the roles that the military and the civilian government would occupy in the new order. During this initial period of creole self-government, the military, exercising a monopoly on coercive force, unquestionably held the real power. For example, it was Fulgencio Yegros, the most prestigious of the military officers, who officially led the new junta; likewise, in naming the new Asunción cabildo, the junta assigned the two top positions to military officers.[1]

On August 1, 1811, Francia resigned from the junta in protest against the military's dominance of governmental affairs.[2] The withdrawal of its most popular and active member, the man entirely in charge of foreign affairs and delegate-elect to the upcoming general congress in Buenos Aires, completely disrupted the functioning of the new government. In light of the complex international developments confronting Paraguay, the members of the junta (with the exception of Frey Bogarín, with whom Francia had the most serious political differences)[3] actually begged him to return.[4] Several days later the commander of the barracks, Antonio Tomás Yegros, also pleaded for Francia's return, "seeing that without Your Mercy there is nothing done in the government...."[5] From his chacra at Ibaray, Francia seized this opportunity to attack the weakest and most conservative element of the creole elite, the church, through its representative in the government, Frey Bogarín. Francia announced that he would return on the condition that Bogarín be expelled from the junta.[6]

In a vivid demonstration of where the real seat of power lay, it was the barracks, not the junta or the cabildo, that made the crucial political decision to accede to Francia's demand. On September 2, 1811, the commander of the barracks informed the cabildo that Bogarín would be immediately removed from office in order to spare the people of Paraguay the ruin which was threatened by the "separation of the most useful member of the government junta ... [for] ... even in the countryside it is known that there is disgust, or little satisfaction."[7] The cabildo wrote to inform Francia of the decision the same day and, noting the clamor from "the barracks and the public," also pleaded with him to return: "You are begged with the greatest fervor ... because it is firmly believed that in the anguish and torment now threatening ... you will be the mediator who will calm and placate everything."[8]

The following day, September 3, Francia agreed to resume his post, but not without first warning the cabildo of the dangers of military intervention: "The Señores Officers of the Barracks are not alone the people of the province.... What would the junta and the province be if at any time the Officers prevailed at arms ...? Can you ensure that in the future they will not raise their hand?" Francia concluded, "It is necessary that you find a way of ensuring that the Officers restrict themselves to their duty [and] reduce themselves to [that] complete subordination which the tranquillity, union, good order, and defense of the province require."[9]

Francia returned to the government in early September with his power and prestige greatly enhanced. He had forced all parties to recognize that his participation in the complex and rapidly developing turns of Paraguayan politics was a pressing necessity. Significantly, both the military and the cabildo recognized not only his paramount importance within the government, but also the widespread popular support that Francia already commanded, which in the coming years would prove to be of even greater consequence. Although Francia certainly had not won a decisive victory over the military, he had taken the first step. He had demonstrated his indispensability to the junta and eliminated its most conservative member.

The junta, now including Francia, was forced to put aside its internal divisions for a time in order to cope with a threat to its very existence, and to prepare for the upcoming negotiations with Buenos Aires. Several weeks earlier the royalists had begun spreading rumors that the province was about to be turned over to Buenos Aires, which planned to draft Paraguayans into its armies and appropriate money for its treasury; that as the royalist forces had recently won a decisive victory in Alto Peru, the collapse of the anti-Spanish movement throughout South America was imminent; and that the continued Spanish blockade of Paraguayan commerce would result in the prolonged stagnation and, ultimately, in the ruin of the economy.[10] Indeed, it had been nearly sixteen months since a shipment of yerba had left Asunción.[11] By mid September royalist activites had grown to include a plot to overthrow the junta and reinstate Velasco as governor. The government, however, warned of the conspiracy, by leaks, rumors, and betrayals, uncovered the complicity of several members of the military (along with a member of the "patriotic" cabildo) and arrested almost everyone involved.[12]

Buenos Aires had indeed suffered a series of military setbacks: the porteño army had been defeated by royalist troops in Alto Peru; Portuguese troops had occupied parts of the Banda Oriental; and Viceroy Elío, in Montevideo, had used the Spanish navy to impose a successful blockade of the Río de la Plata. Under these circumstances the Buenos Aires government, now more than ever in need of an alliance with Paraguay, accepted all of the conditions detailed in the July 20 note—with the exception of the ratification clause—for Paraguayan participation in the confederation of Platine states.[13] Attempting to achieve by diplomacy what the porteño army had failed to accomplish militarily, General Belgrano and Dr. Vicente Anastasio de Echevarría came to Asunción to formalize the accord.

Serving as chief negotiator, Francia succeeded in frustrating the porteño emissaries' instructions "that the province of Paraguay remain subject to the Buenos Aires government."[14] But while settling upon the Treaty of October 12, 1811, in which the porteños accepted all Paraguayan demands—even the ratification provision—the remaining members of the junta agreed, over Francia's objections, to a vaguely worded reciprocal military pact between the two provinces.[15] Nevertheless, the October treaty clearly represented a diplomatic victory for the Paraguayans. Its implicit recognition of Paraguayan independence could leave little doubt that continued efforts to reassert porteño authority, even in the name of the *"causa común,"* were little more than a pretext to resubjugate the province.

Following this brief period of relative cooperation, Francia again raised the question of military interference in governmental affairs. The immediate source of the conflict was the release of several prisoners, who had been jailed under Francia's direct orders, by the military members of the junta.[16] Denouncing "the bitterness of extortion and violence by some few prevailing by arms," on December 15, 1811, Francia once again retired from the government.[17] In his lengthy letter to the cabildo, he called for the convention of a new congress. Reasoning that only frequent congresses could protect the provincial government from domination by a small group of ambitious men, Francia implied that this was in fact already the case by pointing out that "the celebration of a congress which has as its base the free and general will of the province is inevitable, and no one should complain, because only those who fear being judged fear a congress."[18]

The following day the three remaining members of the junta answered Francia's charges, accusing him of creating a "public clamor" by use of such "novelties and divisions" as his demand for a new congress. "You will understand," the junta warned Francia, "that from this moment you become especially responsible for all the damages and injuries which follow. . . . "[19]

Francia, still pressing his demand for a new congress, wrote back, "Now I am answered that this is to introduce novelties and divisions, [and by] threats fulminated on this pretext, without noting that the free communication of ideas is a natural right of man. . . ." Discarding gentlemanly pleasantries, he bluntly demanded to know if the junta was afraid of what the decisions of a new congress might be.[20] Evidently it was, for rather than consent to a new congress, the junta accepted Francia's resignation and appointed Gregorio de la Cerda, an unprincipled and opportunistic administrator, to replace him.[21]

Francia's polemical battle, although it won him some backing in the cabildo and among the public, failed to rally sufficient support to arrest the power of the military or the Paraguayan junta that it dominated.[22] Upon leaving the government, Francia took up residence at his chacra, where he conducted a campaign to expand his popular base and personal authority. For nearly a year (from December 15, 1811, to November 12, 1812) he continued building a power base among the Paraguayan people. During this time, large numbers of farmers, small ranchers, peasants, peons, minor clergy, and townspeople of the interior were invited to Ibaray to discuss the course and nature of the new government. The people's constant visits and lengthy discussions led eventually to the mass assemblies of 1813, 1814, and 1816, and served to shift the center of political gravity from the capital to the countryside.[23] The message from Ibaray these people brought back was truly a subversive one: in the clearest terms, Francia had told them that the people of Paraguay had been betrayed by their revolution; that the only change had been the replacement of the Spanish elite by the creole elite; that, in short, only the masters had changed. In the cynical words of John Parish Robertson,

> he was all meekness and condescension to the *lower*, all hauteur to the *higher* classes of society. His plan was to imbue the country people with a feeling that they were misgoverned by a few ignorant men devoid of merit; and to insinuate if *he* should once come back to power how different it would be. He represented to them that the object of the revolution had been to overthrow the aristocratic pretensions of Old Spain; whereas it was now apparent that these pretensions were only superseded by others more

odious, because they were set up by men whom they knew to be no more than their equals, some of them their inferiors.[24]

Activated in large part by Francia's political education campaign, the people of Paraguay would soon exercise their "natural rights" in the political affairs of the society. And, necessarily, such effective popular participation would mean the beginning of the end of elitist creole rule in Paraguay.

By late 1812, internal and external developments had once again placed Paraguay in a crisis situation that demanded Francia's return to the government. The creole elites were rapidly becoming polarized along the lines of the *unitario-federal* conflict, which was coming to a head in the great Río de la Plata. Twice the cabildo had intervened to prevent the junta from deviating from Paraguay's policy of nonintervention, a policy strongly identified with Francia.[25] To complicate matters, Paraguayan porteñistas and porteño agents, such as Días de Bedoya in Asunción and Ramón Duarte in Concepción, had stepped up their agitation for union with the port.[26] By mid 1812, porteño activity had reached the point where the junta felt it necessary to expel the malcontents from the province.[27] Yet even the junta itself was divided over these issues: the military representatives, Yegros and Caballero, leaned toward the autonomist, or *federal*, position while the two civilians, de la Mora and de la Cerda, generally regarded as porteñistas, actually prepared a plan to establish closer relations with Buenos Aires.[28]

Externally, the province was still surrounded by hostile forces. In the north, the Portuguese and their native allies, constantly raiding Paraguayan settlements and outposts, threatened to overrun the northern frontier. In the south, in addition to the continued harassment of river traffic by the Spanish fleet, Portuguese armies continued to occupy the Banda Oriental and send detachments into the Missions district, occasionally clashing with Paraguayan forces.

Further, in what would become a perpetual demand, the Buenos Aires triumvirate in early 1812 had pressed for a 1,000-man contingent for its army in the Banda Oriental, which was beginning a campaign against the Portuguese. "In return," the porteños promised, "this government will help you with money and munitions and anything else that you may need, and in case the Portuguese threaten your province our divisions will be there to defend you."[29] The Paraguayan junta refused to comply with the request, pointing to the impending threat from the Portuguese who had just occupied the Paraguayan fort of Borbón on the northern frontier. In a clear demonstration of its ineffectuality in the conduct of foreign relations, the junta had unnecessarily irritated the porteños by casting further doubt upon their commitment to the liberation struggle. The junta opportunistically dispatched an emissary to the captain of the Spanish fleet stationed in the Paraná River in a futile attempt to negotiate the lifting of the Asunción blockade, which had crippled the province's commerce.[30]

These events reflect several fundamental aspects of the early conflict in the Río de la Plata. Buenos Aires, desperately in need of troops for its diverse Spanish and Portuguese fronts, wielded control over the international arms traffic to force unity and participation in the *"causa común."* Buenos Aires hoped that by controlling the flow of arms and munitions to the provinces, it could keep them so weak that they would be unable to defend themselves against porteño centralist designs; in this weakened position, the porteños reasoned, the provinces' continued fear of the royalists would force them to remain tied to Buenos Aires. But the provinces were not so easily coerced. They sought independence not only from Spain but from porteño dominance as well. Paraguay, faced with the additional danger of a Portuguese invasion, refused to weaken itself even further by deploying troops outside its borders. When Buenos Aires learned of Paraguay's latest refusal to supply aid, it accused the province of indifference to the struggle against the royalists and began applying punitive measures. The Paraguayan junta pleaded in vain for the return of several Paraguayan ships which the porteños had recaptured from the Spanish in Montevideo.[31] A related incident contributing to the deterioration of relations occurred when the Paraguayan junta sold a shipload of Paraguayan products in Santa Fe. On its return voyage the Paraguayan vessel fell prey to the Spanish, only to be retaken by a porteño gunboat that captured the Spanish craft several days later. But when Paraguay demanded the return of its ship and the 53,000 pesos it was carrying, Buenos Aires flatly refused.[32]

Finally, the Buenos Aires triumvirate abandoned its policy of negotiations with the provinces and returned to a policy of sanctions. It doubled the tax on "foreign tobacco, or [tobacco] from provinces who have separated from this Superior Government."[33] This return to coercive measures touched off civil war in the Río de la Plata, which resulted in the fall of the conservative porteño triumvirate. But for Paraguayan commerce this change of porteño government resulted in little, if any, relief because the caudillos and governors of the other river provinces intermittently imposed import, export, registration, port-of-call, transit, stamp, and license taxes whenever they had the power to do so. For example, Santa Fe alone levied a tax of 4,465 pesos on a Paraguayan government shipment valued at 36,687 pesos, collecting nearly one-eighth of the shipment's total value.[34]

Complicating the already deteriorating situation, the new porteño government nullified all previous agreements and called for a general congress of the former provinces to establish a central government in the Río de la Plata; furthermore, it announced that before the assembly convened, it would send a special envoy to Asunción to discuss Paraguay's future.[35] While recognizing the advantages of cooperation in matters concerning foreign relations, defense, and commerce, the provinces were well aware of the danger that such a general congress would be dominated by the porteños, who would attempt to impose a centralist government under their control. These fears proved to be well founded. All porteño governments, *unitario* or *federal*, insisted upon maintaining the port's political and economic supremacy. In the coming decades, the provinces consistently rejected the centralist governments for which their representatives had voted at the various constitutional assemblies.

In a surprisingly realistic appraisal of their own incapacity to conduct the forthcoming negotiations with the porteños, and under growing public pressure, the military and its representatives in the junta once again called upon Francia for leadership. On November 12, 1812, Yegros and Caballero wrote Francia: "With the current variations of circumstances and urgencies [we] imperatively require your rapid reunion and incorporation" into the junta.[36] Francia again agreed to return to the government, but this time, because of the insecurity of the creole elite, the strength of his popular support, and the urgent need for his proven abilities, the conditions that he was now able to impose amounted to a coup against both the porteños and the military.

The agreement, formalized by the accord of November 16, was signed only by Francia, Yegros, and Caballero. It stipulated that all future government orders must be signed by the three of them, thus giving them veto power over the entire junta and thereby effectively prohibiting the two remaining porteñista civilian members from taking any independent action. Of greater significance, Francia, obviously having gained experience in Paraguayan power politics from the previous year's confrontation with the military, forced the creation of a second army battalion which, along with half of the province's munitions, was placed under his direct and sole command. The accord specified,

> Dr. Francia will be the commander of this new corps, and from now on will be in charge of its organization, discipline, and regimen; without his consent and conformity, said second battalion will not be deployed, given tasks, or dissolved. . . . The duties of those employed in the second battalion will also be freed from the junta, proposed and elected by its cited commander to whom will be delivered, for his custody, one-half of all armaments, as well as one-half of the existing munitions in the ammunition dumps and warehouses.[37]

Not given to repeating the same mistake, Francia, now commanding one-half of the province's armed forces, not only had secured his own political position, but had taken a major step in eliminating the military from Paraguayan politics.

The Paraguayan junta, now under the virtual direction of Francia, was finally ready to respond to the porteño invitation to attend the 1813 consititutional congress of the United Provinces of the Río de la Plata. After a lengthy review of Paraguay's complaints against Buenos Aires, the junta's missive concluded rhetorically: "If in your opinion the treaties are no longer valid, if there no longer is a union, alliance, or confederation, then why, or with what intention or idea, is Paraguay invited to this congress?"[38]

In an attempt to calm Paraguayan suspicions and promote the advantages of annexation, the porteños sent the secretary of the

Buenos Aires government to Asunción. Arriving in mid 1813, Nicolás de Herrera met unexpectedly strong opposition to his proposals. Not only did the *enviado extraordinario* fail to gain support for annexation, but his attempt to convince the junta to send delegates to the constitutional congress provided the occasion for Paraguay formally to declare its independence. The junta, clearly reflecting the wishes of Francia, told Herrera that it did not possess the authority to send Paraguayan deputies to the congress. A decision of such magnitude, they declared, could only be resolved by a general congress of the Paraguayan people, the preparation for which would take several months. In the meantime, the junta lodged Herrera in the old customshouse and placed him under close surveillance.

During the ensuing months, Herrera, frustrated by Paraguay's independent stance and finding his threats and arguments unpersuasive, turned to more extreme measures. In July he advised the porteño government that "perhaps in such circumstances it would be advantageous for Your Excellency to prohibit absolutely the commerce of this province, and the importation of our cattle, by which it subsists. . . ."[39] Next, the *enviado extraordinario* resorted to bribing sympathetic government officials. In August he reported to his superiors "that some of the 100 coins . . . have been distributed among the individuals of that government, and were received with demonstrations of the greatest pleasure," and that he was "reserving the rest to divide among the most important persons of the congress, and others. . . ."[40]

While the porteño envoy was busily engaged in his extraordinary diplomacy, Francia intensified his campaign against Buenos Aires. Taking direct action against the porteñista faction in Paraguay's government, Francia forced the retirement of both de la Mora and de la Cerda.[41] A month later, formally charging the two with intrigue and subversion, the junta expelled them from Paraguay, thereby depriving the porteñista faction of its principal advocates.[42] Only a few weeks before the popular congress convened, Herrera, with no opportunity to bribe "the most important persons of the congress," as he was forbidden even to circulate among the arriving delegates, frantically set to work preparing a written presentation of the porteño position which he intended to deliver to the assembly. But his efforts would prove futile, for at this same, as John Parish Robertson observed, Buenos Aires "began to be considered not only as a foreign power, but as one of which their policy was at direct variance with the best interests of Paraguay."[43]

Unlike the previous assemblies, which had been dominated by Asunción "notables," the 1813 congress, as would the 1814 and 1816 congresses, proportionately represented the geographic distribution of Paraguay's population. In late August the junta sent detailed instructions to the local cabildos throughout the province explaining election procedures. With suffrage defined as the "free use and exercise of the free and natural rights inherent to all citizens regardless of their estate, class, or condition," the upcoming congress was to consist of "1,000 deputies from the villages, towns, districts, and departments in proportion to the number of their inhabitants."[44] Small villages such as Pilar were allotted fifteen delegates, while larger towns like San Isidro de Curuguaty and Villarrica were allowed forty-five and fifty-five representatives, respectively.[45] The junta's instructions emphasized that the deputies were to be chosen by "free and popular elections which will be held in each of the named places, by all, or the majority, of their respective inhabitants."[46] Further, all married men, as well as all single men over the age of twenty-three, without distinction of property or literacy qualifications, were required to vote in the local elections.*

In early September the delegates began arriving in Asunción for what would be Latin America's first popular congress. During these weeks preceding the congress, the representatives—small farmers, shepherds, cattle graziers, yerba collectors, boatmen, village shopkeepers, traders, woodcutters, Indian alcaldes, as well as "the more wealthy merchant, and the substantial hacendado"—had ample opportunity to converse at length with the man about whom they had heard so much. Francia, already Paraguay's most renowned and respected political figure, "made himself personally and familiarly acquainted with the humblest deputy that came into town."[47]

In his discussions with the deputies, Francia, as John Parish

---

*Reflecting the dominant political and social norms of the period, just as with slaves, no mention was made of women; they were neither elected as delegates to the congress nor permitted to participate in the elections.

Robertson clearly explained, emphasized the antiimperialist nature of Paraguayan nationalism: "[He] imbued the lower classes (of which seven-eighths of the deputies to congress were to be composed) with a suspicion, deep and strong, that the only object of Buenos Aires in sending an ambassador to Paraguay was that of subjecting it to her own ambitious views, and of embroiling it in her own revolutionary principles, for the promotion of her own treacherous ends."[48]

On September 30, 1813, the junta (now a triumvirate) convened the more than 1,100 delegates in the Templo de Nuestra Señora de la Merced.[49] Although Pedro Juan Caballero officially presided over the assembly, the effective leadership came from Francia, who "had formulated the policies, set the agenda, prepared the material and proselytized the masses."[50] With the Spanish disenfranchised and the porteñistas effectively eliminated from the political process, the nationalistic political consensus overwhelmingly favored Francia's antiimperialist foreign policy, which was adopted in its entirety. On the opening day the delegates took up Paraguay's relationship with Buenos Aires. They refused even to entertain the motion that Herrera be permitted to attend the congress,[51] and by nearly unanimous vote decided that Buenos Aires had in bad faith violated the treaty of October 1811. The treaty, together with its implied military alliance, was declared null and void.[52] In a second vote, the deputies totally rejected the porteños' centralist plan by refusing to send delegates to the constitutional congress of the Río de la Plata.[53]

In the following days the popular assembly addressed the other major issues and divided into committees to draft its decisions. In a general meeting on its final day, October 12, the congress officially ratified "the governmental plan proposed by Dr. Francia."[54] As published in the *bando* of October 21, 1813, the first authentically popular assembly in Latin America empowered to establish its own form of government proudly announced the creation of the first autonomist nation in Latin America—the Republic of Paraguay.[55]

The seventeen articles of the *bando*, Paraguay's first "constitution," were a masterpiece, reflecting and balancing the dominant power factions within the new nation. The first two articles reaffirmed the decision not to participate in the upcoming congress of the Río de la Plata and, emphatically proclaiming Paraguay's sovereignty and independence from its metropolises, annulled provincial status by proclaiming Paraguay a republic. Careful not to provoke a reaction from the military, the popular assembly did not insist upon installing Francia as sole head of state at this time. Rather it decided upon a consular executive to direct the new nation. Never intended as the final form of government—for the *bando* explicitly called for another popular congress to be held in one year—the consular form of government served as a way temporarily to unite Paraguay's two predominant antiimperialist factions—the creole military elite, represented by Fulgencio Yegros, and the nationalistically politicized masses of Paraguayans, represented by Francia. The consuls, formally sharing equal authority and each commanding one-half of the nation's troops and armaments, were assigned alternate four-month periods of active rule. Within this arrangement, however, the assembly chose Francia to serve as head of state during the first and last periods. Thus it would be Francia who would occupy the prominent post for eight months of the coming year. In addition, articles 12 and 13 provided for a superior tribunal of appeals, which would serve as the final interpreter of the laws.[56]

Immediately following the conclusion of the congress, Herrera, while being careful not to commit Buenos Aires to recognition of Paraguayan independence, resumed his attempts to obtain troops and money. Hoping to salvage same sort of union, he proposed in a meeting with Francia that Paraguay and Buenos Aires publicly demonstrate their fraternity in the independence struggle by means of an alliance and commercial treaty. Francia, comfortably resting upon the nationalistic mandate of the Paraguayan people, replied, "Paraguay does not need treaties in order to maintain fraternity and defend the common liberty." Diplomatically hinting that future reconciliation was still possible, Francia suggested "that at the best opportunity this province will unite with the general system of the others," and concluded by assuring the porteño envoy "that in any event, and in all circumstances, Paraguay will sustain at all costs its proclaimed independence, without ever entering, in any case, in conciliation and accord with the oppressors of our liberty."[57] Several days later, at a second meeting with both consuls, Herrera found his proposals referred to the cabildo, which unhesitatingly rejected the idea of any alliance that would commit Paraguayan troops or aid to the porteños.[58] Explaining that an alliance with Buenos Aires at that time would not be in the national interest, the consuls suggested that the chances for a future agreement would be greatly improved if the porteños would commit themselves to alleviating the new taxes imposed by Santa Fe on Paraguayan shipping.[59]

After further discussions with the principal consul, Herrera finally concluded that "Francia's propositions do not have any other objective than to gain time and to enjoy, without a dispute, the advantages of independence. . . . He has persuaded the Paraguayans that the province is an empire without equal, that Buenos Aires is flattering and praising it because it needs it; that under the pretext of union [Buenos Aires] is trying to enslave the continent."[60] The porteño envoy, realizing that this last insistence on Paraguayan nationalism signaled the complete failure of his efforts, returned to the south in early December, the month during which Buenos Aires once again imposed heavy duties on Paraguayan yerba and tobacco.[61] With the single exception of the emissary sent in 1830 by Juan Manuel de Rosas shortly after he first assumed power, Nicolás de Herrera was the last porteño envoy to enter Paraguay until after Francia's death more than a quarter of a century later.

5 | THE ESTABLISHMENT OF THE POPULAR DICTATORSHIP

The creation of the Paraguayan consulship reflects a phenomenon widespread throughout Latin America during the early independence period. Following the overthrow of the centralized administrative structure of the Spanish colonial empire, provinces typically attempted to broaden the distribution of political authority by forming large executive juntas made up of representatives from the prominent creole factions. Personal rivalries and conflicts among the contending interest groups, however, made such "representative juntas" cumbersome and inefficient.

With the solidification of powerful political coalitions, these initial attempts at "creole democracy" reversed themselves, giving way to a concentration of power in the hands of those most able to impose their will. Buenos Aires exemplifies this trend within the emerging creole governments: beginning with the thirty-member Junta Grande, the porteños soon established a triumvirate, which was shortly replaced by the Poder Executivo, a virtual dictatorship. A similar process occurred in Paraguay, where the original five-man creole junta had been pared down to a truimvirate by the time the 1813 congress created the consulship, which, in turn, lasted only a year before yielding to a single head of state.

Yet the Paraguayan consulship was not simply a step in the path toward Francia's absolute rule, but, rather, the beginning of it. Yegros, early resigning himself to a subordinate role in the new government, continually deferred to Francia's wishes. Even during his own term, Yegros remained little more than a figurehead; he delegated all the most important functions to his co-consul.[1] In partial recognition of this reality, the cabildo, in June 1814, after each consul had served one term, set Francia's annual salary at 3,500 pesos, while assigning to Yegros a salary of only 3,000 pesos.[2]

Immediately upon his election as consul, Francia began building an efficient, honest, and loyal government administration. For the important position of the governmental secretary, Francia overrode Yegros's preference for Mario Larios Galván, the former secretary of the junta, and appointed instead the candidate of his choice, Sebastían Martínez Sáenz.[3] Extending the authority of the national government into the interior of the nation, Francia appointed new regional officials and judges, who, although empowered with broad authority, were required to refer all important matters directly to the consuls.[4] Rather than continuing to impose "notables" as governmental administrators, Francia, consistent with his popular philosophy, selected these new officials directly from the Paraguayan people. As Rengger observed: "Under the government of the Spaniards, the judges were chosen from the rich landed proprietors and merchants . . . [whereas] . . . under the present government, the judges are taken from the lower classes of society. . . ."[5] In fact, during Francia's entire tenure, not only judges but military officers and high administrative officials also were drawn directly from the populace.

Even before the creation of the consulship, a concerted effort to destroy the socioeconomic foundations of the Spanish elite in Paraguay was under way. Although the Spanish, like many Paraguayan creoles, were ardent opponents of porteño centralist ambitions—for union with the porteños would have been a major obstacle to Spanish intentions of reestablishing royal authority in Paraguay—this commonality of interests did not overshadow the traditional creole-Spanish antagonisms. Nurtured by centuries of imperial rule, creole enmity toward their former masters equaled, if it did not surpass, the Spaniards' "deeply rooted hatred of the creoles."[6] As one of his first acts following the overthrow of the Spanish administration, the then commander of the barracks, Pedro Juan Caballero, levied an enormous "contribution" of 60,000 pesos upon the twenty-eight wealthiest Spanish merchants of Asunción.[7] Less than a year later, the junta enacted the Inheritance Law of April 1812, which established the state as heir of all foreign residents who died without "legitimate heirs" (i.e., children born in Paraguay). Although Francia had already withdrawn from the junta when it promulgated the inheritance edict, he certainly must have approved of the measure, for his methodical attacks against the power of the old Spanish upper class bear out John Parish Robertson's declaration that "he, in his turn, not only hated but despised them (the Spaniards); and on their ultimate ruin and annihilation, *as a body*, he had, at an early stage of his career, no doubt determined."[8]

Among the first acts of the consuls was the removal of all Spaniards from public office.[9] Next they attempted to deport the growing number of Spanish refugees who were fleeing to Paraguay. "The multitude of resident European Spaniards, and those who have fled from other Provinces and daily arrive in this city," the government announced, posed a serious threat because of their "insulting airs . . . seditious meetings . . . and their prognostications of the reestablishment, with our extermination, of the Province's slavery."[10] To control the influence of these foreigners, the consuls ordered all Spaniards who did not have legal Paraguayan citizenship to present themselves immediately in the public plaza, for a census. Hoping to send the transients to Corrientes, the consuls wrote to the lieutenant governor, José Leon Domínguez, inquiring if he would admit a group of several hundred into his territory.[11] After conferring with his superiors in Buenos Aires, the governor agreed to accept the unwanted Spaniards, but before the deportation could take place the porteños reversed the decision, reasoning that the Spanish would only add to the growing threat to Corrientes presented by Artigas's *federal* forces.[12]

Having failed to deport the Spaniards, and therefore forced to accept them as permanent residents of Paraguay, the government began enacting measures to ensure that their former masters would never again regain their dominant position. The consuls utilized the census list to levy another round of heavy taxes upon these relatively affluent Europeans,[13] and shortly thereafter issued a decree aimed at the "civil death" of the Spaniards as a class. In order "to cut off and to guard against the pernicious influence . . . the connections and relations, that the European Spanish have contracted, and incessantly contract, with the citizens of the Republic," on July 1, 1814, the government forbade the Spanish to marry any but indigenous, mulatto, or black women. They further prohibited Spaniards from acting as godfathers, or serving as witnesses at the weddings of Paraguayans.[14]

In the following years these measures, together with the state inheritance law and the systematic waves of forced "contributions," succeeded in completely destroying the traditional Spanish upper class. Although this relatively short-term goal seems to have been of primary concern to the consuls, there are strong indications that the long-range effects of miscegenation were also considered, such as Yegros's boast that he signed the law "to establish the crossbreeding of the race."[15]

Threatened by the internal subversion of the Spaniards and the pro-*federal* elements in the army, and surrounded by the hostile Portuguese, *federal*, and porteño forces, the Paraguayan government was faced with the immediate task of strengthening and reorganizing the nation's armed forces. Together with establishing tighter control over the local militias[16] and building a more efficient regular army, this meant eliminating the old elites from the military and filling its ranks with loyal supporters who could be relied upon to defend their government. Being careful "not to select those young men who belong to families of any note,"[17] Francia attempted to enlist only unmarried volunteers between the ages of eighteen and thirty. But in the case of volunteers, just as with conscripts, the commander in charge of recruitment was to "be especially careful not to accept any that are of bad reputation in their public conduct, but only those from whom honor, proper subordination, and the fulfillment of their obligation in the service to which they are destined can be expected."[18] The government's new policies gave nationalistic significance to military service. Reflecting the growing nationalism of the Paraguayan people, the indigenous town of Belén for example, offered, "entirely of our own will, twenty-five armed Indians" complete with their own horses and supplies.[19]

Faced with the continuous Portuguese-Indian raids on the

northern frontier and the ravage of the missions by both porteño and Artiqueño armies, the consuls established a series of new forts along the nation's borders. In an almost frantic effort to acquire the necessary arms and munitions for these garrisons, the government drew upon all possible sources. After dispatching John Parish Robertson to Buenos Aires to secure a shipment of arms, it requisitioned, with indemnification, all available firearms and two private frigates, which were fitted with light cannon and deployed to patrol the rivers.[20]

As the *unitario-federal* struggle intensified in the Río de la Plata, Francia unwaveringly adhered to his policy of nonintervention in the affairs of the neighboring states. By 1814 José Artigas, owing to his growing victories against porteño centralism, had become the champion of the *federal* cause throughout the Río de la Plata. In search of allies, he attempted to convince Francia that Paraguay should join him in the armed struggle against their common enemy. Failing to persuade the principal consul, Artigas then tried to convince Yegros, who, in the past, had openly displayed his sympathy with the *federales*.[21] Although neither consul responded affirmatively to these communications, they left the issue open because they were aware that Artigas commanded widespread sympathy among the pro-*federal* elements of the Paraguayan army.[22] In fact, the commander of the Asunción barracks, Antonio Tomás Yegros, had spent time during the previous year canvassing southern Paraguay "indoctrinating the people in favor of Artigas."[23]

Undeterred by the consuls' rejection of his overtures, Artigas wrote directly to the pro-*federal* Paraguayan subdelegate of the Missions, Vicente Antonio Matiauda, proposing that he attack a small porteño army as it was fleeing across the Missions territory, thus leaving the Oriental armies free to march against the Spanish in Montevideo.[24] Matiauda, seeing a unique opportunity to secure the Missions for Paraguayan commerce and communications, as well as to capture the arms of the porteño army, began the offensive without waiting for consular authorization.[25]

When the consuls learned of Matiauda's intent, they emphatically forbade their subordinate to take any action, and ordered him absolutely to "abstain from alarming or mobilizing the population . . . or from committing hostile acts; but rather always maintain a defensive position and observe a judicious neutrality, without taking part in the present dissensions and conflicts between the Government of Buenos Aires and the Orientales commanded by General Artigas." Explaining the reasoning behind Paraguay's policy of neutrality, they concluded by warning the subdelegate that "we should limit ourselves to the keeping of peace and tranquillity in the interior and the exterior, avoiding, as far as possible, a civil war, which should be considered the worst of all possible evils, especially in this period of revolution. For indeed, nothing do our enemies wish so much as that our cause, as well as that of those free peoples, be weakened and mutually destroyed in order to plant once again the banner of their despotism on our ruins."[26]

Thus rebuffed, Matiauda renounced his commission as a Paraguayan officer, defeated the porteño army on his own authority, and joined the ranks of Artigas's followers. Reiterating their neutrality in the civil war, the consuls again criticized the action of their subordinate and in a communication to the governor of Corrientes even offered their mediation and good offices to bring about a conciliation.[27] During the coming decades, Paraguay's inflexible policy of defensive neutrality and absolute nonintervention became the hallmark of Francia's administration. Indeed, regardless of the numerous crises, not once did Paraguayan troops cross their national boundaries.

As a means of dispersing the pro-*federal* elements within the army and thereby consolidating his own forces in the capital, Francia dispatched an expedition formed exclusively of Yegros's troops to the northern frontier[28] and pointedly commissioned many prominent military officers to command these distant posts.[29] These moves, along with the "voluntary" retirements of other principal military figures, such as Vicente Ignacio Iturbe and Antonio Tomás Yegros,[30] left the strategically critical Asunción barracks under the control of officers and soldiers loyal to Francia. To consolidate his military strength further, Francia filled his own battalion to the maximum and created a special unit of well-armed, experienced, and loyal grenadiers. By late 1814 he held a clear superiority of military strength.[31]

As the date of the 1814 mass congress approached, the government once again sent election instructions to the local authorities. Reiterating the principles of the previous year's instructions, the consuls further facilitated the elections in the sparsely populated districts by assigning the task of organizing the electoral assemblies to the local judges, who were to serve as the presidents. Expressly limiting the functions of the presidents, many of whom had been appointed to their posts by Asunción during the previous year, the instructions warned the judges to "leave all of those gathered in the fullest and absolute liberty to deliberate, and elect the people that they want as representatives; thus the presidency will be limited to maintaining and guarding order."[32]

As the representatives began arriving in Asunción, the Francistas began an active campaign to abolish the consulship in favor of a single magistrate to govern the nation.[33] Francia himself held frequent meetings at which he emphasized that it was he, not Yegros, who had effectively governed during the past year. These gatherings also provided Francia the opportunity to explain in detail his nationalistic ideas to the numerous clergy, military officers, governmental officials, merchants, and estancieros who came to discuss the political future of the nation.[34] But it was among the rural representatives that Francia continued to draw his greatest support; the capital was the center of resistance to his campaign.[35] Francisco Wisner, summarizing the political thrust of the Francista campaign, explained that it was the great majority of the rural deputies who supported "Francia's aims, which were the most patriotic, as he would maintain the independence of the country at all costs."[36]

At the same time a group of Asunción "notables" led by Pedro Juan Caballero, Juan Manuel Gamarra, and José Teodoro Fernández began forming an opposition to the Francista bid for exclusive power. While openly proposing that the consulship be continued for another two years, the military leaders covertly began preparations for a coup d'etat. Perhaps in recognition of Francia's military superiority, Yegros, who had been informed of the opposition's plans, refused to support his old comrades.[37] On the contrary, he supported Francia in frustrating the coup; the consuls exiled the three leaders from the capital on September 26, only a week before the congress convened.[38] Yet the danger of military intervention was not so easily eliminated, for immediately after the congress had adjourned, a movement among the disaffected officers directed against the new Francista civilian government grew to the point where plans for a coup were openly discussed. Recalled by Francia from exile at his ranch, Caballero, whose sympathy with the conspirators proved less than his fear of civil war—a civil war that the Francistas, given their clear superiority of military strength and massive popular support, certainly would have won—utilized his great prestige to dissuade the dissidents from taking action against the government.[39]

Amid the intrigue of the conspiring army officers, the congress convened October 30, 1814. Like the previous congress, it comprised over a thousand delegates chosen in proportion to the overwhelmingly rural distribution of the nation's population. Furthermore, even though many of Francia's political enemies were included among the Asunción delegates, overall "three-fourths of them [the delegates] were poor men."[40] With nearly 90 percent of the rural votes,[41] Francia was immediately elected president of the congress.[42] In his opening address, Francia, characterizing the consulship as cumbersome and inefficient, called for the establishment of a one-leader government capable of responding rapidly to the numerous foreign aggressions and the raging civil war in the Río de la Plata, as well as to the social, political, and economic problems within Paraguay. In the three hours of debate that followed, the opposition moved that the consular government be extended for three more years.[43] But the Francista congress easily overrode this motion and overwhelmingly voted to create the single-magistrate form of government.

In an incredible bid to avoid defeat, Deputy La Guardia, a leader of the opposition, actually proposed that Francia and Yegros draw lots to determine which consul would govern the nation. Denouncing the motion as a ploy, the Francistas insisted that such an important decision could not be left to chance, but had to be decided by the conscience of each delegate.[44] Sustaining the objection, the congress voted Francia their future leader. Following a lengthy discussion over the title their new head of state should bear, it was

> resolved by public acclamation of the majority of the Congress, with the exception of a few individual dissidents, that the authority and Government of the Republic which until

now has been in the two Consuls, will become united and concentrated in the Citizen José Gaspar de Francia, with the title of Supreme Dictator of the Republic, [and] with the same form of address as the previous Government, for the period of five years.[45]

Before adjourning, the congress, in another effort to establish a judicial power, decided to create a superior tribunal of justice which would rule upon any litigation not resolved by the government.[46]

In a politically prudent move Francia had ordered an armed honor guard and military band to assemble at the meeting hall, even though all arms were to have been deposited in a safe place at the disposition of the congress.[47] While the troops certainly had been summoned to render honors, their presence also assured that the disaffected army officers would not interfere with the electoral process. And, in fact, all did proceed smoothly. As its last act, the assembly appointed twenty members to finish the work of the congress in the name of the majority.

The following morning this committee convened. As its first order of business it resolved that, as the nation's harvesting season fell during October, future congresses would be held in May; but, as May was only six months away, the next congress was scheduled for May 1816. It was further resolved that, because so many delegates had to spend several weeks away from their agricultural work traveling to and from the capital, future congresses would comprise only 250 members, elected by their local communities "in proportion to the respective population of each territory."[48]

After Francia's swearing-in ceremony the convention adjourned to join the festivities that had begun the night before when the news of Francia's election had spread rapidly throughout Asunción. According to John Parish Robertson's firsthand description, "the insensate populace celebrated, with mirth and music, and festive meetings that night, the decision of the congress."[49] It took two days for the line of people wishing to congratulate El Dictador to pass through the reception held in his honor. Needless to say, not all of the well-wishers were Asunción "notables"; as Robertson, in a characteristic example of class arrogance, noted, "many belonging to the classes of a lower grade were admitted to these levees. . . ."*

With his election as dictator, Francia, having been granted an absolute mandate by the Paraguayan people, expanded the attack upon the old European Spanish ruling class to include the Catholic Church. There was another group in the republic, Robertson reported, "that Francia hated and condemned as heartily as he did the old Spanish, and that was the clergy, — secular and regular,—but more especially the latter. He hated the friars for the influence which they exercised over the people and for the open profligacy of their lives."**

According to contemporary accounts, the Paraguayan Church differed little from its ecclesiastical counterparts throughout Latin America. Supported by threats of divine retribution from a jealous and vengeful God, as well as the more mundane sanction of corporal punishment administered directly by His self-proclaimed representatives, the church confirmed its privileged status through the tyrannical promotion of superstitious beliefs

---

*Robertson and Robertson, *Francia's Reign of Terror*, p. 16. Robertson's class arrogance typifies the attitudes of the chauvinistic Europeans who arrived in Latin America at the onset of the neocolonial era. Although these Europeans were acutely aware of class distinctions, and reserved their greatest displays of contempt for the "lower classes," their disdain for all creoles was nothing less than undisguised racism. Robertson, apologetically excusing himself from further creole characterizations, explained to his readers, "I have already sufficiently remarked, wherever the subject came legitimately before me, on the ignorance and immorality which I found to pervade all classes of Paraguay" (*Francia's Reign of Terror*, p. 158).

Similarly, Rengger, while commenting upon the Marriage Bandos of 1814 and 1823, which forbade all foreigners to marry among themselves or into the creole elite, felt it "necessary to observe, that those measures which were directed against foreigners, fell with equal severity on the women of Paraguay, who naturally preferred any other American, or a Spaniard, to their own countrymen" (*The Reign*, p. 98).

In a classic example of contemporary chauvinism, Charles Darwin, while bemoaning how the Latin Americans had "willfully thrown away" the great potential of the Río de la Plata, speculated for his reading audience "How different would have been the aspect of this river if English colonists had by good fortune first sailed up the Plata! What noble towns would now have occupied its shores!" (*The Voyage of the Beagle*, p. 119).

**Robertson and Robertson, *Francia's Reign of Terror*, p. 27. Even more vitriolic was Rengger's observation: "The clergy, both regular and secular, were, with few exceptions, bigoted to excess, and plunged in all the irregularities that generally accompany superstition. The curates and the monks lived publicly in a state of concubinage, and so far from being ashamed of so doing, they were known to boast of it. The prior of the Dominicans, amongst others, told me, that he was the father of twenty-two children by different mothers" (*The Reign*, p. 182).

among the Paraguayan people. Apart from any authentic spiritual service it may have provided the people, and despite the courageously progressive acts of individual clerics, the church's propagation of the Divine Right of Kings doctrine had distinguished it as the principal, and most efficient, ideological weapon of the Spanish colonial empire. Its pseudomystical rituals and theatrically staged processions, complete with ostentatious displays of precious ornamentation, saintly images, and awe-inspiring music, all combined to inculcate the masses with a fatalistic resignation to their oppressed social condition. While perhaps overstating the case, John Parish Robertson provided insight into the enormous influence exercised by the clergy when he observed that "Paraguayans reverenced a pai (or father), as the immediate representative of God; they blindly and implicitly followed the instructions given to them, and did whatever was required at their hands."[50] It was precisely through such means that the church fulfilled its reactionary historical role of maintaining the status quo by granting legitimacy to the Spanish empire and the class privilege of the Spanish-American elites.

The tone of El Dictador's attacks against the church was set by a Francista representative in an enthusiastic speech delivered at the 1814 congress in support of the consul's actions against the Europeans. The delegate, insisting that the former ruling class should not be permitted to leave Paraguay with its fortunes,[51] declared, "All Europeans undecided at the beginning of our glorious Revolution should consider themselves civilly dead." Drawing the obvious link between the European Spanish and the Paraguayan church, he demanded that "Europeanism, which has been tolerated until now in the regular and secular clergy, must necessarily be destroyed at its roots," and promised that in the future

> the ecclesiastical state will be precisely arranged and modified, in all of its aspects, to the system of the Liberty of the Fatherland, so that any Priest who has not decided in favor of the system of Liberty of the Fatherland, or who is not useful to the public cause, will not be able to preach, hear confession, receive offerings, nor direct or minister . . . because any other thought is alien to the pious intention of the Catholic Church.[52]

In the coming years this same anticlerical, although not antireligious, orientation characterized the government campaign against the power and abuses of the Paraguayan church.

The bishop of Paraguay, Pedro García de Panés, had arrived in Asunción during the last years of the colonial era. At first he had cooperated with the creole junta and had even given the new government his blessings; but with Francia's return in November 1812, Panés claimed the traditional position of the *patronato real*, under which the Paraguayan church was subject only to its own hierarchy and ultimately to Spanish royal authority.[53] Before his election as dictator, Francia had not occupied a position of sufficient strength to challenge the established ecclesiastical hierarchy. But in mid 1815, empowered with a dictatorial mandate, he moved to bring the Paraguayan church under national jurisdiction.

Taking the first step in the nationalization of the church, El Dictador forbade "all interference, or exercise of jurisdiction of foreign authorities or prelates from other countries," leaving the Paraguayan religious communities "free and absolved of all obedience, and entirely independent of the authority of Provinciales, Capitulos, and general visitors from other states, provinces, or governments." Further forbidding the nation's clerics from accepting "titles, appointments to ecclesiastical offices, faculty appointments, dismissory letters, degrees of graduation, degrees of competence, guidance, discipline, or of any other religious policy," the edict concluded by retaining Bishop Panés as the religious community's highest authority.[54] As the first application of the decree's intent, Francia proceeded to abolish the Holy Office of the Inquisition in Paraguay.[55]

Six months later Francia took the next step in nationalizing the church. He removed the second and third highest Spanish church officals, Archdeacon Antonio Miguel de Arcos y Matas and the vice-general of the diocese, José Baltasar de Casafús, reasoning that it was only fair that Paraguayans, rather than foreigners, hold these positions. "The general security, the public welfare, the consolidation of the liberty and independence of the Republic," Francia declared, required the dismissal of the Spaniards, as "the influence that these employees have upon public opinion in all parts is well known. It is easy to calculate the damages that will result to society if by opposition, or indifference, these employees debilitate the adopted system or oppose the newly established order."[56] Three days later, El Dictador consolidated both positions and assigned them to Roque Antonio Cespedes, a native Paraguayan and loyal supporter of the popular regime.[57]

Francia might have continued more rapidly in nationalizing the church at this date if he had not been forced to deal with pressing foreign affairs. By 1815 José Artigas, the caudillo of the Banda Oriental, reached the height of his power as standard-bearer of the *federal* cause throughout the Río de la Plata. His grand plan was to create a confederation of Paraguay, the Banda Oriental, Corrientes, Entre Rios, and the Portuguese province of Rio Grande do Sul to counter the power of the porteños.[58] Expounding upon his recent victories in Santa Fe and Córdoba, the Oriental caudillo, again attempting to appeal directly to Francia, proposed an alliance to solidify the *federal* gains.[59]

Perhaps realizing that Francia would reject any offer of a military alliance, Artigas had written earlier in the same year to Manuel Cavañas, the caudillo of the Cordilleras and hero of Tacuarí, urging him and Fulgencio Yegros to mobilize their followers and take control of the government. According to Artigas's emissary, Cavañas felt that such a plan held little hope of success, but intended to explore the possibility with Yegros.[60] Not surprisingly, as the countryside was the base of Francia's power, the conspiracy never gained a foothold, although it remained undetected until 1822 when it was finally uncovered in the lengthy investigation that followed the 1820 Great Conspiracy.[61]

Frustrated by this latest example of Francia's inflexible policy of neutrality and nonintervention, Artigas ordered his troops to occupy the Missions' capital of Candelaria. In late July 1815, at the height of his power—having recently taken control of La Bajada (the port of Entre Ríos) and Corrientes—the *federal* caudillo closed the river to Paraguayan and porteño traffic.[62]

Until its occupation and alliance with Artigas, Corrientes had enjoyed friendly relations with Paraguay, although Francia had always recognized that "our common enemies will try by all means that are within their reach to disturb our tranquillity."[63] By interrupting Paraguayan commerce, raiding the Paraguayan Mission yerbales, and occupying Candelaria, Artigas's hostile forces converted Paraguay's cordial neighbor into its most active enemy. Francia, now fearing an invasion, mobilized troops in Asunción, Paraguarí, and Villarrica, and deployed both land and naval forces to the southern frontier to watch *federal* troop movements. The crisis reached such serious proportions that Francia even considered taking the offensive. In a communique of October 2, 1815, he informed the commander of Pilar "I am taking measures with the idea of preparing an expedition of at least 4,000 men."[64] But, as would be the case five years later when another *federal* invasion army was poised on the southern bank of the Paraná River, external events intervened to eliminate the immediate threat to Paraguay. Renewed Portuguese aggression in the Río de la Plata forced Artigas to withdraw his army to defend the Banda Oriental.

Earlier that year, Artigas's forces had captured John Parish Robertson on his return voyage to Paraguay with a cargo largely composed of arms and munitions consigned to the government. Among his personal effects the *federales* found a letter from the *porteño* government naming Robertson as its authorized representative,[65] and offering twenty-five rifles for every one hundred recruits that Francia would commit to the port.[66] In an attempt to cause further dissension, Artigas capitalized upon this discovery by sending copies to his sympathizers in Paraguay to demonstrate that "Francia was selling Paraguayans like dogs for muskets."[67] But, bowing to British military might, the Oriental caudillo, after confiscating the armaments, permitted Robertson to continued on to Asunción with the remainder of his cargo.*

Upon his arrival in the capital, the merchant adventurer informed Francia that, as arms and munitions were considered articles of war, there would be no official protest of the confiscations by the British authorities. Based upon England's enthusiastic support of the independence movements in Latin America, the various Paraguayan governments had been particularly sympathetic to the Robertsons, who for the past several years had

---

*Robertson and Robertson, *Francia's Reign of Terror*, p.99. Robertson's immediate release after Artigas received a letter from the commander of the British fleet demonstrates the power of English gunboats in the Río de la Plata, even at this early date. As Robertson proudly pointed out; "Captain Percy's conduct was above all praise, showing that, where the British flag waves over floating artillery, not a hair of the head of a British subject can be unjustly touched with impunity."

been operating in Asunción. Taking British claims of free navigation at face value, and hoping to utilize British prestige and naval strength to open the river, Francia had even attempted to establish commercial and political relations with England the previous year.[68] But it now became clear that the British would not extend themselves to ensure the safe passage of the most critical of all imports—the arms that were essential to maintaining independence. Claiming not to understand "such fooleries," and outraged at Robertson's part in the porteños' "odious proposal," Francia ordered the Scottish merchant to conclude his business and leave the country within two months.[69]

Buenos Aires, in other attempts to reestablish relations with Paraguay in 1815, sent a series of communications to the new republic. Without offering any recognition of its independent status, and neglecting to mention the growing *federal* power, the porteños insisted that Paraguay attend the scheduled consititutional assembly, emphasizing that unity was more important than ever since Napoleon had been driven out of the Iberian Peninsula and Ferdinand VII, back on the Spanish throne, had assembled a powerful army destined for the reconquest of the Río de la Plata. Pointing out "that Chile and Lima are occupied by the enemy . . . and that Buenos Aires has exhausted all of its resources," the supreme director of Buenos Aires continued to offer arms and munitions in exchange for "3,000 men who will be received in this Capital with applause and recognition."[70] Francia, unmoved by the porteños' alarm, rhetoric, or control of the war matériel traffic, analyzed relations with the port in a letter to the delegate of Pilar:

> In reality there is little use in replying to those official notes, for they do no more than to bring up old matters which have oft been discussed, and are now antiquated and all but forgotten. These messages also attempt to give the appearance of favoring the protection of the commerce of our Republic . . . which they [Buenos Aires] have sought only to ruin with exorbitant and indeed barbarous taxes, violating the good faith of the treaties. If they were not acting with disguised intentions, with clear deception, and with frivolous tricks, they would have done better to send us our seven good cannons which are still in Buenos

Aires. . . . there is no need now to send us all this useless mass of letters, gazettes, and new regulations of theirs with which they only wish to make a show of force.[71]

In attempting to persuade the local caudillos to mobilize their followers against the government, Artigas had completely misread the political situation. The porteños and disenchanted upper-class Paraguayans, in contrast, held no illusions of organizing a popular uprising; indeed, Francia's identification with the masses became a central issue in the elite's propaganda campaign against El Dictador and Paraguay's popular government. The following excerpt from a pamphlet written by a Paraguayan priest and published by the official Buenos Aires government press in 1815 serves to illustrate the class orientation of both Francia's administration and its opposition.

> You who have his extravagances in front of you know better than I the differences between his behavior toward the country people and toward the noble citizens of the capital. You have been shown by experience that when a *guacarnaco* or *espolón* campesino arrives at his door, immediately he grants him his most familiar treatment and a free passport to embrace him. He is overwhelmed to see this caped, taciturn man, overflowing with joy. With such affection does he receive his great guest! He takes him by the hand, he introduces him to his study, he treats him with great affection, he flatters him, he slaps him on the back, and having filled him with satisfaction he seats him at his side. In this way he prepares him better to impress in his soul his suggestions, in this way he makes him swallow without repugnance the poison of his Machiavellianism; like the serpent, entwined among the flowers giving its poison to the unwary ones who come close to it, or like the Sphinx that attracts unwitting people in order to devour them. On the contrary, if a cultured and noble citizen asks for an audience, he is seen transformed into another very different figure, ferocious as his character. After making him wait for a long time at his door, he admits him into his majestic presence with a quixotic gesture, with an affected severity, with an insufferable haughtiness. And after hearing him with impatience, with a few words he dryly dismisses him.[72]

Indeed, the people of Paraguay enjoyed unrestricted access to El Dictador. "Dr. Francia, the caraí-guazú of the people, was always available to them, holding nightly audience with the helpless Indian, the tired campesino and the aggrieved boatman."* Far from being a haughty despot arbitrarily ruling over an intimidated people, Francia maintained permanent and direct contact with the previously dispossessed masses.

With extreme confidence in the popular regime he had been so instrumental in establishing, Francia was able to attribute the constant factional fighting in other Latin American nations to their lack of popularly based governments. In a succinct statement of his political philosophy, Francia, upon receiving the news that José Rondeau had assumed the office of supreme director in Buenos Aires, analyzed the port's continuous turmoil in a letter to the comandante of Pilar:

> I have in my possession the gazette that you sent me containing the news of the new revolution in Buenos Aires. These convulsions are the consequence of a nation which still vacillates in its true aim and destiny because it still is not unified, *because it does not have a truly popular form.* For this very reason, at the time of the institution of the independent Republic here, I established the great Congresses at periodic intervals to make certain that the nation would join together in the same sentiments and so that we would all advance under a solidly based system. This does not occur in Buenos Aires, and it is for this reason that each faction which prevails perhaps has different ideas that provoke another commotion. The present faction shall probably not be the last, for everything has happened in this same manner since the beginning.[73]

It is essential to understand, however, that Francia did not equate a popular form of government with a "representative democratic" form of government. An important point of historical clarification is that, regardless of the multitude of "democratic" constitutions promulgated during the nineteenth century,

---

*Williams, "Dr. Francia," p. 316. The Guaraní term *caraí-guazú*, or "Great Señor," was the unofficial title by which Francia was respectfully referred to among the people of Paraguay.

what was known as democracy in Latin America was profoundly antidemocratic. If democracy prevailed as an ideal, it existed in name only. Only the elite participated in the political process; the vast majority of the people were excluded by voting requirements based upon sex, income, property, or literacy. "A generous estimate of the political participation of the male population in all Latin American nations would probably approach 2 to 4 per cent during most of the nineteenth century."[74] By selectively eliminating all but the elite, such "democratic" governments provided a facade of popular participation over what was often a political mechanism for the exchange of power among the various elite groups. More important, however, the myth of representative democracy served as a modern and effective ideology to aid in perpetuating the elite's domination over the other 95 percent of Latin Americans.

To Francia, democratic form was not an end in itself, but a means through which the masses of Paraguayans could express their true interests. With the national consciousness formed and institutionalized in the popular dictatorship, the huge democratic assemblies had served their purpose; the task now was to implement the people's will to end the centuries-old injustices of Paraguayan class society. As is generally true of successful anticolonial social revolutions, after the initial phase of unified "nationalistic" opposition against the common enemy, the popular demands of the Paraguayan Revolution for fundamental restructuring of society assumed priority. Class cooperation, in other words, gave way to class confrontation.

Realizing that the accomplishment of the goals of the revolution would mean the end of their privileged status, the rich and powerful virtually stopped political squabbling—the government was no longer theirs to fight over. If at this relatively early date some sectors of the creole oligarchy still did not comprehend this fundamental change, the election of Francia as perpetual dictator soon dissolved any remaining illusions. In the coming years Paraguay's popular regime would render obsolete the vestiges of traditional political ideology. No longer would the elite be permitted to define their own self-interests as the interests of society at large; no longer would the state be available to administer the "interests of society" to benefit the few at the expense of the many.

As the 1816 general congress approached, the Francistas launched a month-long propaganda campaign to expand the purpose of the upcoming assembly. Pointing to Francia's unquestionable honesty, diplomatic abilities, tireless energy, and ardent patriotism, they emphasized El Dictador's successes in maintaining Paraguay's independence while avoiding involvement in the civil war exploding throughout the Río de la Plata. But of greatest importance was Francia's early revolutionary action of establishing social justice and order: the appointment of new officials and judges drawn from the masses, the clean-up campaign against corruption in public office, the assault upon the socioeconomic foundation of the former Spanish ruling class, the reorganization of the armed forces, the establishment of new fortifications along the northern frontier to protect the inhabitants from the increasing Indian and Portuguese forays, the containment of the porteñista and pro-*federal* factions, and the beginning of national regulation of the church. By early 1816, under Paraguay's popular dictatorship, "thieves, murderers, and beggars had disappeared. Working men enjoyed full security. The tranquillity made economic development possible."[75] When one considers Governor Lázaro de Rivera's estimate, less than two decades earlier, that nearly one-half of the Paraguayan population lived "in total poverty . . . suffering with patience the terrible effects of nakedness, misery, and oppression,"[76] the fundamental reason for El Dictador's massive popular support becomes obvious.

Perhaps because of the strength of his position, Francia did not wait for the expiration of his mandate before further consolidating the power of the popular dictatorship by extending his term from its original five years to the duration of his life. Led by a prominent Francista delegate from the northern river town of Concepción, José Miguel Ibáñez, "the idea to confer power *for life* came from the rural class, from the countryside."[77]

Whereas the military had played an important part in the 1814 congress, they were not a significant element in the 1816 assembly, for by this time not a single officer who had defeated General Belgrano or overthrown Governor Velasco remained in the army.[78] Furthermore, only token opposition to the new regime was permitted, as Francia informed the delegates shortly before the congress convened: "The government certainly will not admit to the General Congress those that have been observed or shown themselves in opposition to the Cause of Liberty, or those that are partisans of its enemies; and although they will be tolerated, when by their sinister or depraved influence they do deliberate, their voice will be worthless and void."[79]

Using the fraternal title of "Citizen," adopted from the French Revolution, the first resolution of the congress declared that

> in view of the complete confidence that the Citizen José Gaspar de Francia has justly merited from the people, he is declared and established Perpetual Dictator of the Republic during his life, with the condition of being exceptional.*

The second article, noting that Francia had refused to accept the 12,000-peso annual salary that the congress had initially voted him, established El Dictador's salary at 7,000 pesos annually. The third article officially abandoned the idea of yearly congresses and resolved that "the Republic will have a General congress each time, and when, El Dictador feels it necessary." The last article, including an ecclesiastical oath to "love and respect the orders of our Supreme Government," took the next step in the nationalization of the Paraguayan church by ordering that the prayer formerly said for the king during mass would in the future be dedicated to "our Dictator and his committed people and army."[80]

There would not be another general congress until after El Dictador's death a quarter of a century later, and the concept of an autonomous judicial authority received no further mention. Nevertheless, the resolutions of the 1816 congress and the election of Francia as "perpetual" dictator must not be misunderstood as merely another Latin American usurpation of power. On the contrary, "it was not the imposition of one man, but of a people. What then triumphed was not Francia's will, but that of the nation."[81] The establishment of the popular dictatorship was neither spontaneous nor arbitrary; it was the direct consequence of the historical struggle within Paraguayan society.

---

*ANA, SH, leg. 226, Acta del Congreso, June 5, 1816. The last qualifying phrase was a deliberate attempt to avoid establishing a precedent of lifelong dictatorships.

6 | THE CONSOLIDATION OF LATIN AMERICA'S FIRST POPULAR REGIME

While the elite's dissatisfaction with Francia began even before he assumed absolute power, his actions after election as dictator served only to heighten their discontent. Two weeks after he was elected perpetual dictator, Francia placed further restrictions upon the regime's opponents.

In mid June 1816, he banned all public gatherings which did not have the express permission of the government and all religious processions except those that fell "on the same days fixed by the calendar and in accordance with those already known by local custom."[1] This measure was directed specifically at denying a public forum for the growing elite opposition, but at the same time it struck a devastating blow at one of the church's most effective mechanisms for maintaining the superstitious awe of the people. It is important to note that, in addition to achieving a security measure and an attack against the mystical authority of the church, by abolishing the frequent and costly processions Francia also eliminated one of the major expenditures of the church.[2]

During these early years, the oligarchy, unable to overthrow the popular regime, expressed its frustration through verbal opposition and petty harassment. Francia's irritated response to these limited but systematic attempts to undermine the government's authority was to levy heavy fines against the dissidents. For example, in 1817 the Spaniard Francisco Riera received a 2,000-peso fine for his "obstinate rebelliousness in not respecting the constituted authorities of the native American government."³ Such fines must have been widespread, for treasury records show that by 1818—the first year for which documentation is available—a total of 86,614 pesos had been confiscated from individuals (see table 2).

Although such repressive measures certainly played a role in the 1820 Great Conspiracy, in which the Spanish and creole elites joined together in a disastrous attempt to destroy the popular regime, the real roots of the class conflict lay in Francia's refusal to compromise the nation's independence. As early as 1815, anti-Francia propaganda warned that continued resistance to porteño hegemony would result in the closing of regional ports to Parguayan products, which would effectively mean the permanent loss of much of the yerba market, as the consumers of yerba would substitute coffee, chocolate, and other beverages.⁴ Indeed, the policies adopted by the porteños following the 1816 constitutional assembly at Tucumán struck at the heart of the nation's monocultural economy, devastating the socioeconomic foundations of the Paraguayan oligarchy.

The election of Juan Martín de Pueyrredón as supreme director of the United Provinces of the Río de la Plata at that assembly marked the resurgence of porteño centralism, touching off a new round of civil war between the provinces and Buenos Aires. Intended to build a massive army by drafting recruits from each province as it was subdued, Pueyrredón's *Plan to Pacify Santa Fe, Dominate Entre Ríos and Corrientes, and Subjugate Paraguay* called for the establishment of porteño authority by force of arms. In a clause recalling General Belgrano's tactics six years earlier, the porteño officers were advised that "before making use of any arms, much paper, in proclamations and manifestos, should be employed . . . [for] . . . those people still believe when they see something written, and if it is printed, they grant it a blind faith."⁵ As the first step in preparation for the invasion of the "rebellious province," Buenos Aires prohibited the importation of Paraguayan cigars or rolled tobacco of any sort "until the incorporation of Paraguay."⁶ Pueyrredón next ordered a blockade of all trade and communications, and the confiscation of property belonging to residents of Paraguay.⁷

Shortly after imposing the blockade in 1817, Pueyrredón dispatched Colonel Juan Baltazar Vargas, a native Paraguayan, "to try to effect a revolution in favour of Buenos Aires, by availing himself of the discontent which was known to prevail among the principal families of Paraguay."[8] Upon his arrival in Asunción, Vargas secretly enlisted the aid of a number of upper-class Paraguayans. But he set to work with such ill-concealed enthusiasm that within a year he and several accomplices were apprehended and publicly executed. However, most of the conspirators, like those of the aborted 1815 conspiracy, escaped detection until the early 1820s, when the investigations surrounding the Great Conspiracy revealed the full extent of the oligarchy's sedition.

In July 1817, the leader of the *federal* struggle against the porteño *unitarios*, José Artigas, once again attempted to reach an accord with Francia.[9] But again Francia elected to suffer the consequences of the hostilities of both factions rather than participate in "the worst of all possible evils," thereby jeopardizing Paraguayan independence; he insisted upon maintaining an inflexible policy of neutrality and nonintervention in the civil war. The consequences for Paraguay's economy can be seen in figures 1 and 2.

The combined *federal* and *unitario* assaults devastated the nation's commerce. Exports fell from 391,233 pesos in 1816 to 291,564 pesos in 1818, to 191,852 pesos in 1819, to a mere 57,498 pesos in 1820. Likewise imports, as reflected in import taxes, fell from 83,640 pesos in 1816 to 58,480 pesos in 1818, to 42,643 pesos in 1819. They rose to 69,647 pesos in 1820 owing to the developments of the civil war,* only to resume their decline to 44,346 pesos in 1821, finally reaching their low point of 4,824 pesos in 1822 (see Appendixes C and G).

In inverse proportion to the decline in commerce, the oligarchy increased its opposition to Francia and the popular regime. Commerce was, after all, the lifeblood of the elite. As John Parish Robertson observed:

---

*In 1820 three major developments brought temporary relief for Paraguayan commerce. The provinces, reacting once again to porteño attempts to dominate them, overwhelmingly rejected the 1817 centralist constitution, finally causing the collapse of *unitario* authority in Buenos Aires. Also in 1820, a successful insurrection within the *federal* ranks saw the powerful caudillo from Entre Ríos, Francisco Ramírez, defeat Artigas, thereby shattering the *federal* pact. As part of Ramírez's attempts to reorganize the opposition against the porteños, he lifted the blockade on Paraguayan commerce for several months. Crowning these events, Brazil, capitalizing upon the confusion and disunity in the Río de la Plata, annexed the Banda Oriental.

Figure 1. Paraguayan Exports, 1816–1820

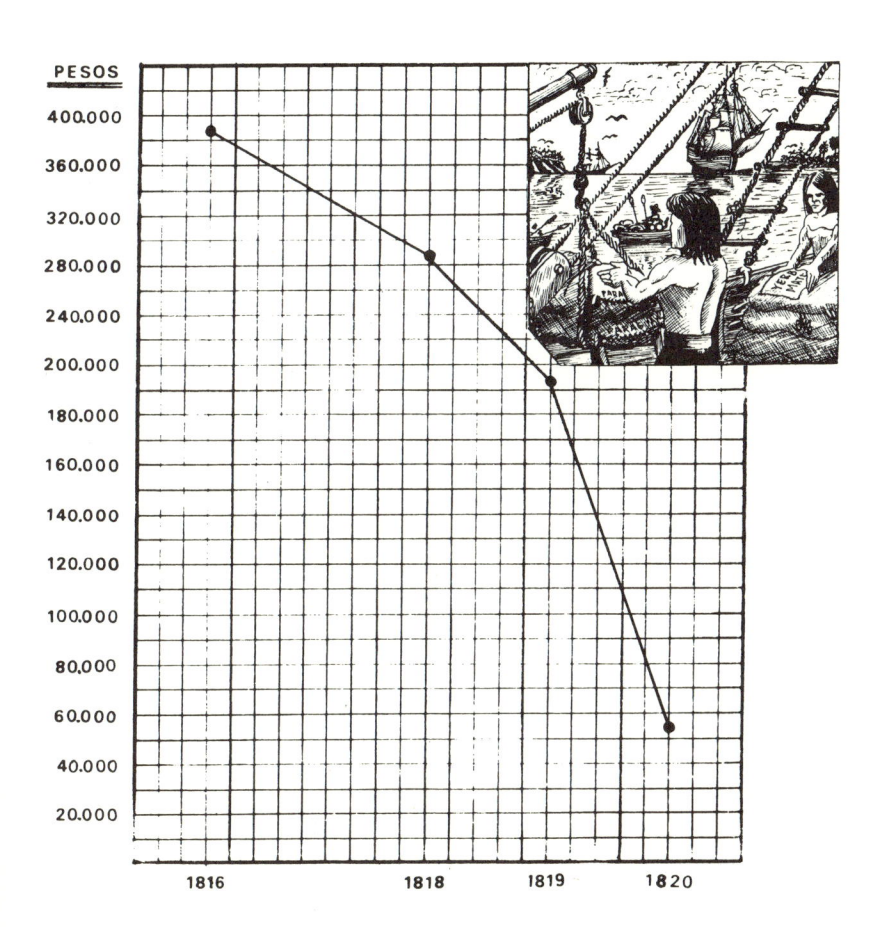

Compiled from Appendix "C", Paraguayan Exports

Figure 2. Paraguayan Import Taxes, 1816–1824

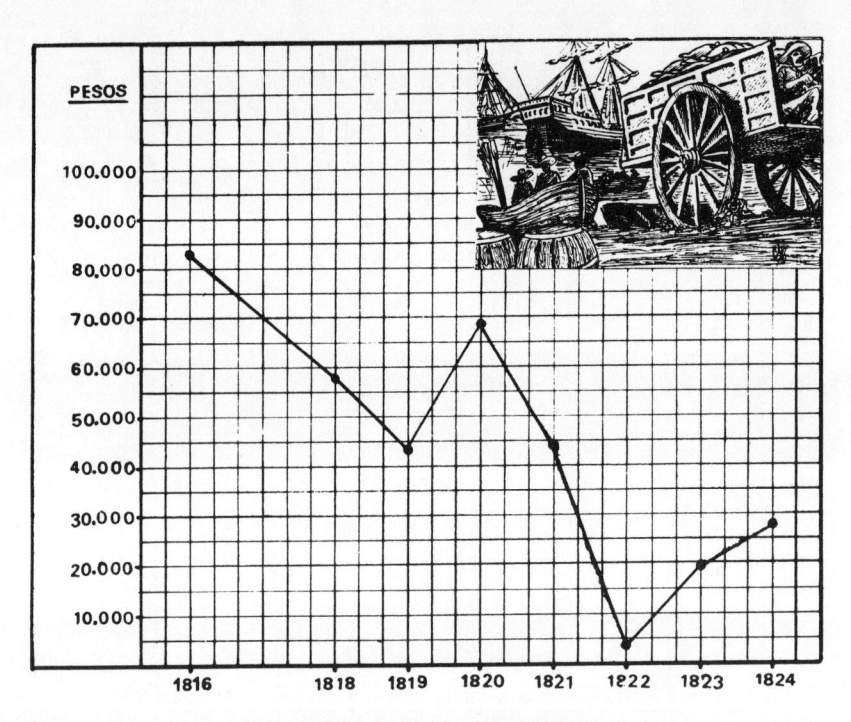

Compiled from Appendix "A",
Paraguayan National Budgets

> Paraguay then had, though not her Dukes and Marquises, yet her comparatively wealthy classes; and they were those who received and divided among them the annual returns for the produce they had shipped, with its profits, to the amount already stated of about 360,000 £ [pounds]. There were about 500 families participating in this return. . . .*

The annihilation of "their commerce," the Scottish merchant concluded, wreaked havoc "among the aristocracy of Paraguay."

Noting that by 1820 the prices of exports had fallen "so much that the proprietors were on the point of ruin," Rengger explained, "The merchants whose warehouses were glutted with the herb of Paraguay [yerba] and tobacco, saw their capital not only unproductive but every day sensibly decreasing, in consequence of the deterioration which their property was daily undergoing, and the expenses of keep."[10] The consequence of these conditions was, according to Robertson, that "at length, a solemn league and covenant was entered into by a number of the most respectable citizens of Paraguay" to overthrow the government.[11]

The frequent meetings at Fulgencio Yegros's estancia aroused Francia's concern to the point where, in January 1820, he ordered the former consul to take up residence in the capital.[12] Apparently undaunted by the government's scrutiny, a number of the conspirators continued their clandestine meetings at the Asunción home of Dr. Marcos Baldovinos, where they decided that the coup should commence on Good Friday. On that day Francia was to be assassinated during his customary afternoon walk. At the same time a number of other assassinations were to be carried out; the intended victims included the governmental secretaries and the commanders and officers of the Asunción barracks.[13] Indeed, as Francia revealed shortly after learning of the plan, "every person in office, was to be destroyed."[14] Following the purge, Yegros was to assume control of the government; Pedro Juan Caballero and Captain Miguel Antonio Montiel would take charge of the army, supported by several other officers already involved in the plot.[15]

---

*Robertson and Robertson, *Francia's Reign of Terror*, p. 218. Typically, Robertson greatly exaggerated both the profits and the size of the oligarchy. Chaves, in perhaps a more realistic estimate, identified the oligarchy as the "cien familias" (*El Supremo Dictador*, p. 272). Also see Chaves, *El Supremo Dictador*, p. 144.

But on March 28, only three days before the planned assassinations, the police arrested 4 of the conspirators as they left Baldovino's home. A fifth member of the cell, Juan Bogarín, managed to escape. However, being a highly religious person, the following day Bogarín confessed the details of the plan to Fray Anastasio Gutiérrez, who, as part of the penance, instructed him to reveal the entire plot to El Dictador. Within hours of receiving this information, Francia arrested 35 of the principals, including his former co-consul, Fulgencio Yegros. By the end of the following month the number of prisoners apprehended in Asunción and in several interior towns had grown to 178.[16] Those arrested, according to a fellow oligarch, came "from the country's most prominent families."[17] Francia, taking a surprisingly lenient attitude toward his would-be assassins, "contented himself with sending them to prison, and confiscating their property."[18]

Six months later, the imminent threat of an invasion linked with the conspiracy elevated the situation to a national crisis. In mid 1820 Francisco Ramírez overthrew José Artigas in a bloody revolt and assumed leadership of the *federal* forces. In September, Artigas and a small band of followers fled to Paraguay, seeking refuge. Francia grated them asylum, believing it to be an inherent right of national sovereignty.[19] Artigas then informed Francia that the Entrerriano caudillo planned to invade Paraguay and requested material support to return and engage his former ally. Maintaining his policy of neutrality, Francia not only refused to supply the arms, but also denied Artigas's request for residence in the Missions. El Dictador dispersed the *federal* troops throughout Paraguay and, assigning the Oriental caudillo a pension, he confined Artigas to the rural town of San Isidro de Curuguaty, eighty leagues from Asunción.

Arriving in Corrientes the following month, Ramírez, who had lifted the *federal* blockade several months previously, now offered guarantees of Paraguayan commerce and even armaments in exchange for Artigas.[20] But, holding to his policy of giving protection to all deserters, fugitives, and refugees who sought political asylum, Francia ignored Ramírez's offers.*

---

*Indeed, the granting of asylum to Artigas caused other problems for Francia, as the Portuguese feared an alliance against their empire. Although Francia had formally closed the

Infuriated by Francia's silence, Ramírez began preparations for an invasion. He conscripted the Guaraní inhabitants of the Missions and started to correspond with the malcontents within Paraguay, using Paraguayans returning home from Corrientes as couriers.[21] Indeed, the invasion force was well prepared, for as Ramón de Cáceres, second in command of the *federal* forces, later recalled, "Ramírez planned to invade Paraguay with 3,000 combat-hardened men, and, led by his best squadron, undoubtedly would have destroyed Francia, and Paraguay would today be a province of the Argentine Republic."[22]

As a precaution against the belligerent forces rampaging throughout the Río de la Plata, the government had steadily increased the budget of the Paraguayan armed forces from 133,123 pesos in 1816 to 150,947 pesos in 1818, to 175,200 pesos in 1820 (see Appendix A), which, not including the naval forces, increased the size of the army from 842 soldiers in 1816 to 1,413 soldiers in 1818, to its maximum size during the reign of Francia of 1,793 soldiers in 1820 (see fig. 4 and Appendix H).

Informed that Ramírez was now in league with the Paraguayan conspirators, Francia mobilized another five to ten thousand militiamen and reinforced the defenses along the Paraná River.[23] In addition, he enacted a number of measures designed to maintain internal security; along with confining all Correntinos to the northern town of Concepción, "as soon as he was apprised of the preparations begun by Ramírez, he resolved to give no more passports for going out of Paraguay" because, as Rengger reported, "he dreaded lest some of those allowed to quit the country, might serve as guides to the enemy, and facilitate an invasion by them."[24] During this period, anyone attempting

---

northern frontier in 1819 due to increased Portuguese-Indian raids, he had used this channel to calm Portuguese fears in mid 1820 by explaining to the Paraguayan commander of Concepción, so that he in turn would inform the Portuguese commanders of Miranda and Coimbra, that "due to my pacifist spirit, and desiring to live in peace with everyone, I have not wanted to help the caudillo Artigas against them, hoping that our moderate behavior will be a new motive to conserve the good harmony . . . with our neighbors" (ANA, SH, leg. 232, Francia al Comandante de Concepción, May 7, 1820). In mid 1821, after actually granting asylum to Artigas, Francia once again addressed the continuing fears of a union by assuring his commander at the fort of Borbón that he had given "Artigas a refuge out of pure humanity and charity" (ANA, SH, leg. 235, Francia al Comandante de Borbón, May 12, 1821).

clandestinely to leave Paraguay did so at the risk of execution.*

Fortunately for Paraguay, the turns of Platine politics alleviated the invasion threat. The revolt and subsequent alliance with the porteños of Estanislao López of Santa Fe forced Ramírez in November 1820 to return to the south in an attempt to crush the rebellion of his former ally. He did leave, however, a sizable force in the Missions with orders to give all possible aid to the Paraguayan rebels.[25] Although consumed by efforts to reassert dominance over the Plata's complex realignments, the *federal* caudillo never lost sight of his dreams to conquer Paraguay. Indeed, the "criminality" of the Paraguayan expedition became a major propaganda issue used against Ramírez and his allies by the progressive porteño government of Martín Rodríguez who, faced with the Brazilian occupation of the Banda Oriental, called for the unity of all the provinces against the Portuguese empire's pretensions.** But in spite of porteño rhetoric, the Ramirista forces remained poised at the Paraguayan border. Not until the defeat and death of the Entrerriano caudillo at the battle of Córdoba on July 10, 1821, did the specter of invasion fade.

Meanwhile, in an attempt to discover the extent of the conspiracy, Francia continued to interrogate prisoners and began a concerted campaign to discover other enemies of the regime. Information was supplied not only by investigating government officials, but "the people also . . . [for when they] saw that, if a revolution were effected in favor of the upper ranks, they must necessarily lose their eligibility to place, [they] took part with the Dictator."[26] Obviously such an atmosphere presented opportunities not only to denounce political subversives, but also to settle personal vendettas and vent long-suppressed class antagonisms. Yet Francia hardly encouraged such excesses. As Rengger observed, "The Dictator . . . was never known to reward either a spy or informer."[27]

---

*After the immediate crisis had passed, Francia relaxed the severity of this measure. Exit from the country without prior authorization was still forbidden by the government, but when clandestine attempts were "unconnected with political objectives"—as in the case of the French merchant, Louis Escoffier, who in mid 1823 engineered a daring and nearly successful escape—the captives were sentenced to prison (Rengger, *The Reign*, p. 89).

**See the official government press, the *GBA*, May 7, 1821, in which the "criminal designs" of Manuel de Sarratea, who had "offered Ramírez 800,000 pesos, 2,000 blacks, cannons and as many rifles as he wanted for the Paraguayan expedition," are denounced.

Actually, the most damaging information was not uncovered by Francia's "espionage system," which consisted primarily of the masses reporting upon the activities of the oligarchy, but resulted from the vigilance of the border security. In early June 1821, a Paraguayan military detachment captured Juan Alfaro while he was attempting to sneak across the Paraná River. In his possession they found a letter, addressed to the chief of the Ramirista forces, in which Alfaro urged Commander Cáceres to expedite the aid that had been promised the conspirators. The letter assured Cáceres not only that many insurgents were still at large, but also that the entire Spanish element would actively help the movement.* The next morning Francia ordered the Spaniards to assemble in the plaza of Asunción, and, after announcing the contents of Alfaro's letter, arrested all three hundred. Those considered the least dangerous, "such as were of the humblest condition," were shortly released, while "the more distinguished persons remained in prison nearly nineteen months."[28]

Francia used this occasion to break the economic power of the old Spanish ruling class. The Spaniards were released only after making an enormous "contribution" of 150,000 pesos to finance a Paraguayan expedition to alleviate the near-total blockade of the nation's commerce.[29] Although such an expedition proved unnecessary, the Spaniards' generous "contribution" certainly served El Dictador's purposes. Not only did it bring a considerable sum into the state treasury, but, as Rengger noted, while at the time of their arrest the Spanish "still formed the leading class, if not of the country, at least of the capital," after their imprisonment and "contribution," "the greater part of the Spaniards . . . were reduced to absolute poverty."[30]

On July 3, 1821, one month after the capture of Alfaro's letter to the Ramirista caudillo, another Paraguayan border patrol in-

---

*Wisner, El Dictador, p. 107. As the initial unity among the Spanish and creoles in 1810–11 against the porteños reflected the commonality of their class interests, so the realliance of the elites in the early 1820s demonstrated the degree the Paraguayan class conflict had reached. In the intervening period of the upper class's heightened conflict within itself, during which the government levied repressive measures against the old Spanish ruling class, the creole elite sanctioned such government actions. As Mario Antonio Molas noted: "Then the Spaniards were thought to be our enemies and these arbitrary procedures, without warning that the process to which one was becoming accustomed would in time be turned upon ourselves, did not attract our attention" (Clamor," p. 242).

tercepted an even more incriminating and alarming missive, this time from Cáceres to Pedro Juan Caballero. Instructing Caballero to inform Yegros that help would be coming very soon, the commander of the Ramírista forces unwittingly served the Paraguayan conspirators their death warrant.* The confirmation of the continued connivance between the internal and external enemies elicited Francia's severest measures. El Dictador demanded that the prisoners give a full written confession within twelve hours, and in cases "when he could extract nothing from the latter [the prisoners], he directed that they should be put to the torture."[31] According to Rengger's description, the torture used by Francia reached the following extremes:

> The Dictator gave a set of written questions each day to his first secretary. The latter put them to the prisoner in the presence of an officer and registrar, and brought back the answers to the Dictator, who, when they were insufficient, sent the prisoner to the "Chamber of Truth," the name of the place where the torture was applied. There he received from one to two hundred blows of a leather whip on the back, when the examination recommenced. This operation was repeated sometimes every two or three days, on the same individual, until his answers were such as to satisfy the Dictator. The prisoner then signed the examination. Some of these unfortunate persons received thus, at different times, as many as five hundred lashes, and yet no confession could be wrung from them; and a servant, from

---

*There is some confusion concerning the chronology of this last communication from the Ramírez forces to the Paraguayan conspirators. The available primary documentation indicates that there was only one letter rather than the two that are commonly referred to (e.g., see Chaves, *El Supremo Dictador*, pp. 279, 280, 282, 283). Rengger refers to only one letter (*The Reign*, pp. 63, 64), which he claims was sent from Ramírez to Yegros. He continues his narration by explaining that, in order to find out more details, Francia began torturing the prisoners, after which they were immediately executed. Wisner also mentions only one letter (*El Dictador* pp. 106-10) dated July 3, 1821, which was not from Ramírez himself, but rather from his chieftain, Commander Cáceres, to Juan Pedro Caballero with instructions for Yegros. He also states that torture to obtain more information began in response to the letter, followed immediately by the executions beginning July 17, 1821, the actual date of the first executions. Consequently, as both authors follow a chronology of (a) letter, (b) torture, (c) executions, a logical interpretation—and the one which this work accepts—would be that Rengger, for the sake of journalistic simplicity, synthesized events, thus blurring the precise date, author, and addressee of the letter; therefore the two letters mentioned by him and Wisner are actually one and the same.

whom they thought of extorting some information relative to his master, fell victim to this severity sooner than utter a word.[32]

Finally, Francia obtained the identities of other conspirators, who, surprisingly, made little effort to avoid apprehension. Faced with the alternative of attempting a perilous escape through the Gran Chaco—the domain of Paraguayan military patrols and fierce indigenous nations—the subversives "remained perfectly inactive, and allowed themselves to be apprehended without the least resistance. This absence of energy, among men who were in general remarkable for their courage, proceeded from the expectation they entertained of every moment hearing of an invasion by Ramírez."[33] But, unbeknownst to either the conspirators or Francia, the invasion would never come, for at this very moment Ramírez was fighting the battle of Córdoba, where he lost his life.

During these weeks, the government's ruthless investigation forced Dr. Baldovinos to give a full confession, and Pedro Juan Caballero to commit suicide in his prison cell. Two weeks after the interception of Cáceres's letter, Francia ordered the execution of the principal conspirators. On the morning of July 17, 1821, the execution began with Fulgencio Yegros, Captain Miguel Antonio Montiel, and Dr. Juan Arístegui;[34] during the following days, as many as twenty more conspirators faced the firing squad.* With few exceptions, during the remainder of

---

*As is the case with many other facts concerning Francia, the number of executions following the Great Conspiracy has been greatly exaggerated. Rengger (*The Reign*, p. 67) claimed that forty took place. Mario Antonio Molas, in the vehement 1828 anti-Francia diatribe he sent Colonel Manuel Dorrego, the governor of Buenos Aires, in an attempt to convince him to invade Paraguay, claimed sixty-eight executions ("Clamor," p. 251). Wisner (*El Dictador*, p. 116) accepted this larger figure, as did Guillermo Cabanellas (*El Dictador del Paraguay, El Doctor Francia*, p. 269).

The work of Cabanellas contains the most complete list of those allegedly executed, including all of the people mentioned in the other works, as well as several others for which this author could not locate the original sources. In alphabetical order (followed by Cabanellas's reference and the original sources when available), these twenty-one people are: the brothers Isidoro and Jesus Acosta (p. 269; Molas, p. 253); Dr. Juan Aristegui (p. 267; Wisner, p. 115); José Joaquín Baldovinos (p. 342, Molas; p. 251), his son José Baldovinos (p. 342), and Dr. Marcos Baldovinos, the brother of José Joaquín Baldovinos (p. 269; Molas, p. 251); Señor Centurion, the brother-in-law of the Acostas (p. 266; Molas, pp. 249, 253); Señor Escobar (p. 269; Ramón Gil Navarro, *Viente años en un calabozo*, p. 44, claimed that the two brothers, Angel and Miguel Escobar, were executed by Francia, but offered neither a date nor a reason); Señor Godoy, another brother-in-law of the Acostas (p. 266; Molas, pp. 249,

Francia's tenure Paraguay witnessed no other political executions.*

Francia's methods were indeed cruel and harsh, but in order to understand such measures within their historical context it is essential to realize that they were not extraordinary. For centuries the whipping and execution of common people had been accepted as an everyday practice. In his ten years in office (1796—1805) Governor Lázaro de Rivera executed 260 people as part of the routine maintenance of traditional Paraguayan class society.[35] What is actually extraordinary is the remarkably limited violence and death that accompanied the profound structural changes wrought by Paraguay's popular social revolution.

Although Francia released a great number of state prisoners in 1824, of the approximately five hundred that remained—including members of virtually all of the nation's "notable" families—most languished in prison until El Dictador's death. Manuel Pedro de Peña said, "We were six hundred prisoners in that jail in 1840, and scarcely a third were murderers and thieves. Four hundred or more men belonged to the most decent and cultured class of the country."[36]

Mass imprisonment and executions crushed the elite's potential as an immediate threat. The popular regime, furthermore, assured the destruction of the elite as the dominant social class by denying them the institutions they had traditionally employed in maintaining their privileged position, and by systematically confiscating their wealth. Paraguay had supported two elite classes, each with distinct yet related socioeconomic foundations. At the very top of the social pyramid, above the creole elite, rested

---

253); Manuel Iturbe (p. 269; Cabanellas claimed that Capitán Ignacio Vicente Iturbe was also executed at this time, but on the next page contradicts himself by reproducing an undated letter from the son of Juan José Machaín to Manuel Gondra which stated that his father and Iturbe were executed on May 27, 1836); Lieutenant Sergio Latoree (p. 269; Molas, p. 251); Capitán Miguel Montiel (p. 267, Wisner; p. 115) and the other brothers Montiel (p. 269; actually, Cabanellas did not specify how many brothers were executed and, just as with all the others, neither did he give his source, but Molas, p. 244, claimed that the nine brothers Montiel were arrested by Francia, although there is no mention of their execution); and Fulgencio Yegros (p. 267; Molas, p. 251).

*Rengger, *The Reign*, p. 107, and Chaves, *El Supremo Dictador*, pp. 438, 439. A realistic approximation based upon a review of the primary source documentation would place the total number of political executions during Francia's entire tenure at no more than forty.

the old Spanish ruling class and its supporting institutions, among the most important of which was the Catholic Church.

Even before the sweeping reforms that followed the Great Conspiracy, Bishop Panés, evidently unable to adapt to the changes wrought by the new regime, found his mental faculties steadily deteriorating; he finally resigned in 1819.[37] Under the custody of his alcoholic nephew, Frey Pedro de la Rosa Panés, the bishop retired to his mansion where he lived lavishly on contributions collected by the clergy.* Under his replacement, the loyal vicar-general, Roque Antonio Cespedes, the coming years saw the enactment of a series of measures which stripped the church of its enormous social, political, and economic power.

Several months after discovering the 1820 Great Conspiracy, the government banned all religious brotherhoods** and required the clergy to swear a loyalty oath.[38] Further tightening state control, the government abolished the *fuero eclesiástico*—the traditional ecclesiastical exemption from civil courts—thus

---

*ANA, SH, leg. 237, Presentación al Dictador de Alejandro García Diez y Juan Perez Bernal, undated, but on Papel Sellado for 1824 and 1825. Also see Rengger, *The Reign* p. 178. In 1829 Panés found himself the object of Francia's scathing criticism. "For the last ten years," Francia admonished, Panés "has not wanted to comply with his obligation, and has entirely ceased to exercise his ministry. . . . In such circumstances it does not seem just to obligate the poor priests to continue contributing [funds] for the sumptuousness and squandering of a man who is not only useless, but furthermore, an enemy of the sacred cause of the nation." The Doctor of Theology recalled "the prejudice and superstition by which, abusing the sacred name of God and the veneration and worship owed to the Supreme Being, he had maliciously imbued the People, through their ignorance and gullibility, to remain subjugated to Spain. . . ." More than Panés's political intransigence, the contradiction between "the Christian spirit which is professed" and the fact that "this Spanish Bishop has never felt obligated to give a sermon to the poor Paraguayan people from whom, through his pretended Divine Authority, he has already extracted and consumed close to 100,000 pesos. . . ." particularly outraged El Dictador (BNRJ, CRB, Auto de Francia de 23 de julio de 1829, as cited by Chaves, *El Supremo Dictador*, pp. 326, 327).

Regardless of such verbal assaults, Francia, perhaps for political reasons, took no punitive action against the retired bishop. Panés not only escaped arrest during the 1821 general encarceration of the Spanish, but in 1838, after partially regaining his mental health, he was reinstated at the age of ninety, with only a few months to live, to his former position as Bishop of Paraguay (Wisner, *El Dictador*, p. 159).

**During the early independence period, such religious brotherhoods habitually served as bastions of Spanish conspiracy to restore royal authority in America. Although documentation is not available for early republican Paraguay, a remarkably complete account of such intrigue can be seen in the series of letters sent to the king of Spain in the late 1820s from a similar club in Buenos Aires, whose expressed purpose was "to reestablish the authority of the metropolis in this colony (BNRJ, CDA, 1-28, 36, leg. 32, pp. 1–38).

bringing the Paraguayan clergy directly under civil jurisdiction.[39] Three years later, Francia closed the Church's Royal Seminary of San Carlos and confiscated its lands.* And it seems hardly coincidental that in 1824—the year Pope Leo XII issued his encyclical ordering the archbishops and bishops of America to support the efforts of Ferdinand VII to reestablish royal authority in the Western Hemisphere—Francia accelerated his attack upon the economic foundations of the Paraguayan Church by secularizing the monasteries and expropriating their vast properties.[40] Some of this property was put to military use, such as the pasturage of the convent of Merced, which was converted into an artillery park, and the buildings of the Recoletos, which became army barracks.[41] But, as part of the extensive land reform enacted by the government, most of the land was either distributed among landless Paraguayans and immigrant refugees as homesteads, or designated as state estancias.

In addition to confiscating its land, by 1824 the state had also assumed financial control of the church. Regulating the expenses of the local parishes through their respective municipal governments, the national government assigned relatively large clerical salaries,[42] and until the mid 1820s continued paying the traditional annual annuity to the Asunción cathedral.[43] But in 1828 the state began confiscating the excess wealth of the churches throughout Paraguay; by 1840 the government had appropriated, in cash alone, 37,580 pesos from thirty-nine churches and two religious funds (see table 2). In 1828, as part of the overall shift of priorities to provide more funds for public works, the government, which had already ceased providing the cathedral its annuity, retired its three aging canons.[44] For the remainder of Francia's tenure, with the exception of the weekly masses for the armed forces, the salaries of the cathedral's proprietary priest and its sexton,[45] were the national government's only Church related expenses.**

---

*ANA, SH, leg. 441, Auto de Francia de 23 de marzo de 1823. For an idea of the amount of land owned by the church and its related institutions, it should be noted that 876 families received homesteads from the lands of the Royal Seminary of San Carlos alone. See chapter 7 for further details.

**It should be noted that Bishop Panés continued collecting money from contributions given to priests until his death in 1838. See ANA, NE, leg. 3114, Comprobantes de la inversión del dinero perteniciente al Cuartas de Curas en pago de aquileres de la casa, en alimientos y mantención del Obispo, November 3, 1829–December 1, 1838.

Table 2. State Appropriations, 1816–1840*

	State Inheritance	Confiscations from Church	Collection of Debts	Fines and Confiscations	Forced Contributions	Peso Totals
1816	4,220 + 896 [a]	2,796	107	1,068 [b] + 527	5,772 [c]	15,386
1817				3,644 [d]	7,352 [c]	10,996
1818	15,417 [f] + 49 [f, a]	3,157 [l] + 2,992 [f]	284 [f]	86,614 [l] + 399 [f]	6,045 [c]	114,957
1819	1,386 + 464 [a]	3,284 [e] + 2,000 [l]	13,179 [e] + 1,052 [l]	6,289 + 2,266 [l]	5,729 [c]	35,649
1820	1,515	539 [l]	1,576	871 [l]	6,286 [c]	10,787
1821	4,123	2,478	267	1,353 [l] + 1,221	6,000 [c]	15,442
1822	12,797 + 7,345 [a]		2,885	12,123	6,000 [c]	41,150
1823	10,824		5,651	404	5,494 [c]	22,373
1824	7,194 [g]	653 [g]	2,344 [g]	2,070 [g]	138,932 [g, h] + 5,145 [c]	156,338
1825	2,637 [i]		6,716 [i]	12,343 [i]	5,273 [c]	26,969
1826	6,382 [j]	273	8,039 + 1,491 [i]	22,930	6,000 [c]	45,115
1827	6,163		8,619 749 [i]	43,260 [k] 1,597	6,920 [c]	67,308
1828	4,542	1,648 [l]	3,202	925		10,317
1829	7,838	6,121 [l] + 4,978 [m] + 241	403	8,652 [l, n] 1,080 [k]		29,313
1830	7,866 [l]	3,346 [l]		5,415 [l,n]		16,627
1831	2,964	850 [l]	163			3,977
1832	165	4,840 [l]	300			5,305
1833	735	2,574 [l]	67	200		3,576
1834	1,993	421 [l]	3,356	5,109 [l]	27,295 [p] + 283 [q]	38,457
1835	2,552 + 1,856 [l]	6,282 [l]	615	1,696 [l]	1,407 [p] + 214 [q]	14,622
1836		1,479 [l]		771 [l]	133 [q]	2,383
1837	323	690 [l]	613	39,601 [l]	48 [q]	41,275
1838	1,113 [l] + 412	2,304 [l]	6,822	10,186 [r] + 998 [l]	1,236	23,071
1839	1,302 + 933 [l]	4,591 [l]	429	3,947 [l] + 966	3,000	15,168
1840	35,618 [l,t] + 5,008	2,434 [l]	8	8,240 [s] 4,064 3,861 [l]		59,233
Totals	156,632 (18.97%)	60,971 (7.38%)	68,937 (8.35%)	294,690 (35.69%)	244,564 (29.62%)	825,794

*Archival references are found in note 46.

As there were no formal banking institutions, the Spaniards—particularly the church, which possessed large sums of cash—also functioned as the nation's creditors. Of course, credit was not extended out of benevolence, but rather out of necessity, for, given the extreme poverty and chronic shortage of hard currency in Paraguay, Spanish credit served as the oil which lubricated Paraguayan commerce.*

Intervening directly in the Spanish credit system, the state confiscated even wealth "hidden" in the form of debts, primarily incurred by less affluent Spaniards and creoles. The state collected all debts owed to individuals who had died without legitimate heirs, debts owed to prisoners whose property was confiscated, and debts owed to the secularized religious corporations and brotherhoods.** From this source alone, the government appropriated the considerable sum of 68,937 pesos.

As detailed in table 2, Paraguay's popular regime appropriated enormous cash sums from the oligarchy.[46] During its tenure of the more than a quarter-century, the state "inherited" at least 156,632 pesos, mainly from the Spaniards, who, dominating the relatively lucrative commercial sector of the economy, held a

---

*The following partial list of one of Asunción's principal moneylenders, Bishop Panés, will give an example of Paraguay's credit system. All documents are found in ANA, NE, leg. 1168. November 5, 1810—300 pesos to the Spanish merchant Pedro Josef de Molas for one year; as collateral, Molas offered his slave Simón. November 14, 1811—30 pesos to the merchant Bernado Granze for four months. December 19, 1811—500 pesos to the creole merchant from Yaguarón, Manuel Granze; Granze was one of the porteño conspirators jailed by Governor Velasco in February of this same year. July 25, 1812—30 pesos to Bernardo Antonio Veron. October 27, 1813—125 pesos to Mariano Ferreyra for two months. April 16, 1814—50 pesos to Doña Maria Antonia Benítez for six months; as collateral Doña Maria offered her person and property. July 20, 1814—100 pesos to the creole merchant Manuel Antonio Reinoso for four months. September 1814—200 pesos to the creole merchant and estanciero José Antonio Pereira for one year; as collateral Pereira offered his person and property. June 3, 1815—50 pesos to the Spanish merchant Olegario Rozas for three months. July 29, 1815—100 pesos to the Spanish merchant Pedro Regalado Betancur for seven months. August 1, 1815—50 pesos to Fernando Patiño for one month. November 8, 1815—100 pesos to Dr. Marcos Baldovinos for four months; as collateral Baldovinos offered his person and property. August 25, 1816—87 pesos to the creole merchant Manuel Antonio Reinsoso. March 10, 1818—100 pesos to Fulgencio Yegros. July 2, 1818—300 pesos to Fulgencio Yegros.

**As an example of the collection of such debts, see ANA, LC, leg. 17, entry for November 23, 1820, which registers the payment of 1,125 pesos to the Treasury by Juan Pedro Caballero, an amount which he originally had borrowed from Frey Maciel, who at this date was a prisoner due to his participation in the Great Conspiracy. Caballero himself was taken prisoner in May 1821 (Molas, "Clamor," p. 248).

large portion of their wealth either in actual capital or in easily liquidated assets such as merchandise. Another 60,971 pesos were taken from the church, while fines and confiscations from individuals amounted to 294,690 pesos. In addition, the state's forced "contributions" brought in 244,564 pesos, for a grand total of not less than 825,794 pesos. (It should be noted that these figures represent minimal sums as they include only data for which specific documentation was available.) The magnitude of the appropriated wealth can be gauged by the fact that it was a sufficient amount to have financed the entire national government apparatus, including the army, for a period of six or seven years.

Of course, not all of the oligarchy's wealth lay in actual cash. The creole elite—the other class constituting the oligarchy—held the bulk of its wealth in the form of means of production, principally in land, estancias, and livestock.[47] Consequently, much of the government's socioeconomic attack upon the creole conspirators took the form of property expropriation. Although it is impossible to place a monetary value upon the confiscated property, several mid-1820 estimates establish the national domain as including more than half of Paraguay's rich central region.[48]

One example of Francia's attack on the native oligarchy, although exceptional in its vitriolic approach to the cult of personalism, can be seen in El Dictador's actions against Manuel Atanasio Cavañas, the most powerful caudillo of the Cordilleras and the hero of Tacuarí. Years after the (natural) death of Cavañas, who left no heirs, Francia raised the issue of his complicity in Artigas's 1815 attempt to overthrow the government. Ordering Cavañas's wealth confiscated and applied to the expenses of the public works, El Dictador also revoked his title of colonel and decreed that it be expunged from all official documents.[49] Six years later, upon the death of Cavañas's widow, Francia confiscated the family property, turning the houses over to the schoolteacher at Piribebuy; the religious statues to the mayordomo of the town church; the clothes to the servants; the steel, salt, and tobacco to the state estancia of Gazarí; the cotton to the army for the troops' clothing; and the books to the new public library of Asunción. All remaining articles were sold to the neighboring populace at reasonable prices.[50]

In late 1824 the government dismantled the last of the oligarchy's institutions by abolishing the Asunción cabildo—the capital's municipal council—which, during the colonial period, had served as the local governing body of the province's "notables." After a decade of promoting this so-called bastion of "creole democracy," even to the extent of spending public works funds for the construction of a new meeting hall, Francia found that the cabildo continued to exercise its traditional antidemocratic function. Noting that the Asunción cabildo, "having continued in this city only according to its old usage . . . [was therefore] not a popular institution, but only an arbitrary establishment of the extinguished Spanish regime," Francia abolished the institution, declaring, "Neither does it have, nor can it have, or exercise, legitimate representation of the Public."*

With the counterrevolution crushed, the elite, prohibited from exercising their traditional privileges, reluctantly retreated from the center of the national stage. As Rengger observed:

> The families of greatest consideration amongst the Creoles—those who had the greatest reason to fear the Dictator, retired to their country houses or farms, and sought security in a solitary and obscure life. The Spaniards, for the most part merchants, after having been ruined by contributions and fines, devoted themselves, though unwillingly, to agricultural pursuits.[51]

Unlike the traditional Latin American coup d'etat, in which one section of the elite seizes power from another, the Great Conspiracy was not an intraclass conflict, but rather a class confrontation that pitted the interests of the elite 5 percent of the population against the well-being of the remaining 95 percent of Paraguayans. And while the historical development of Paraguayan class conflict is itself remarkable, its conclusion is even more striking. The oligarchy lost.

---

*ANA, SH, leg. 237, Decreto Supremo de 30 de diciembre de 1824. It should be noted that the cabildos of the interior towns, with the exception of the Villarrica cabildo (closed by the Decreto Supremo de 31 de diciembre de 1824, ANA, SH, leg. 237), continued to function throughout Francia's administration.

7
POPULAR PARAGUAY

Beyond the dismantling of the nation's class society, the full significance of the Paraguayan Revolution can be appreciated only through an understanding of the extraordinary constructive achievements of Francia's administration. It is important to realize in understanding this process that El Dictador applied the same high standards that he set for himself to his entire government.

Following his election as consul in 1813, Francia embarked upon a vigorous, and successful, clean-up campaign, removing numerous officials whose corruption had permeated previous administrations.[1] With the establishment of the state prison system,[2] the government's relentless enforcement of civil responsibility not only checked the abuses of the old functionaries, but, with equal severity, was applied to the new officials of popular origin. Rengger's observations point to the stringent standards and the class composition of Francia's new administration:

> He broke several officers, who, having been raised from the dregs of the people, had signalised themselves by their insolence towards their fellow citizens. Several commanders of the circles (departments) were dismissed for a similar cause; and some were punished for their extortions. These he replaced, if not by individuals of the first class among the people of Paraguay, at least by farmers, who might be supposed to attach some importance to their own reputation and the public good.[3]

Francia's maintenance of strict administrative morality was facilitated by the extreme simplicity of the governmental apparatus he had established. The central government consisted of only the chief of police, the minister of the treasury, the governmental secretary (whose functions included those of attorney general and minister of the interior), the "defender of the poor and minors," and a small staff. For administrative purposes Paraguay was divided into twenty regional departments, which themselves were subdivided into several smaller units. At the head of each department were three officials—a commander or delegate, a tax collector, and a judge—all commissioned by Asunción. On the local level, the populace elected its own municipal officials. All government functions and functionaries were subject to Francia's close supervision.

Throughout his reign, El Dictador personally audited the books of government tax collectors. Testifying to Francia's meticulousness are the numerous entries in the national budgets which show that tax and rent collectors reimbursed the state treasury for even the smallest underpayments, sometimes for less than a single peso.[4] Other examples of Francia's careful adherence to procedure abound. When his brother Pedro, who was serving as the administrator of Ytá, proved incompetent, Francia promptly removed him from office; when he found that the foreman of the state estancia of Tacutí had pilfered the money from the sale of twelve hides, El Dictador immediately confined him to the prison colony of Tevegó where he was assigned to the public works program.[5] Nor were government officials the only citizens subject to such vigorous supervision. Notified that an English merchant had advanced 1,100 pesos in merchandise to a Paraguayan merchant who later went bankrupt, Francia ordered the debt collected by the state and instructed the delegate of Itapúa to pay the Englishman in full when he returned.[6]

But Francia's involvement in diverse governmental affairs was not simply the result of a penchant for detail. Traditionally, the elite had a monopoly on education and administrative experience; the vast majority of Paraguayans remained conditioned by a culture forged over three centuries of forced subservience—a culture which punished initiative as insubordination, imposed superstition and fatalism as religion, and encouraged resignation and docility as civic responsibility. Consequently, when the popular regime removed the elite from their traditional offices, it was faced, like all revolutionary governments, with an acute shortage of trained, competent personnel. The problem was so severe that even as late as 1830, Francia, in a rare expression of frustration, complained to the delegate of Itapúa: "[I find myself] strangled here [in Asunción] without being able to breathe under the immense number of duties and occupations which fall on me alone. Since the government is without the workers and aides it ought to have on all sides, by necessity, I am making up for and carrying the weight of positions which ought to be filled by competent employees."[7]

Despite such formidable obstacles, the popular government succeeded in maintaining fiscal stability, constructing a strong national defense industry, reducing taxes to a minimum, enacting a sweeping land reform that covered scores of state estancias, producing a wide variety of consumer goods which it sold to the public, coordinating an extensive public works program, establishing Paraguay's first public education system, and creating a balanced economy based upon diversified animal and agricultural production.

Outlining the principles which guided this radical transformation of Paraguayan society are the following excerpts from the "Political Catechism" prepared by Francia for use in the primary schools.

Question: What is your country's government?
Answer: The reformed fatherland.
Question: What do you mean by reformed fatherland?
Answer: Its regulation by known and just principles founded in nature, in man's necessities, and the conditions of society.
Question: Who is it that declaims against this system?
Answer: The old Spanish government officials that proposed that we surrender to Bonaparte, and those ambitious for authority.
Question: How can one prove that our system is good?
Answer: By positive deeds.
Question: What are these positive deeds?
Answer: The abolition of slavery without affecting the owners, and to esteem public works as the common burden, with the total suppression of taxes.

Question: Can a state exist without income?
Answer: No, but taxes can be reduced so that nobody is pained by paying them.
Question: How can this be done in Paraguay?
Answer: By working in community, cultivating the municipal possessions which are destined for the public good, and reducing our needs, according to the law of our divine teacher Jesus Christ.
Question: What will be the results of this system?
Answer: To be happy, which we will bring about by remaining vigilant against the undertakings of the bad people.[8]

To a remarkable extent Francia fulfilled the catechism that he promulgated. An examination of the national budgets reveals the remarkable fiscal stability that the government was able to maintain—unique in an age in which corruption-ridden Latin American governments found it necessary to float enormous quantities of freshly minted currency, increase taxation, solicit "generous" foreign concessions, and incur ballooning national debts in their frantic attempts to stave off challenges from popular movements and rival elite groups. As demonstrated in figure 3, Francia maintained consistently balanced and self-sustaining budgets throughout the entire period of his tenure.

In terms of both government programs and expenditures, national defense received the highest priority. Even during his term as consul, Francia began requisitioning and importing war matériel,[9] while at the same time initiating a major effort to increase state production of arms and munitions. Embarking upon a national campaign to gather scarce yellow metals used for rifle fixtures, even from "individuals who want to get rid of any furniture of this type," the state established armories in Asunción and Pilar.[10] Under the personal direction of the master craftsman Miguel Tiragalo and Francia himself, state-employed gunsmiths, blacksmiths, and carpenters not only repaired weapons, but by 1816 were manufacturing firearms.[11] Similarly, the government established several factories which employed hundreds of workers to manufacture cloth and tailor it into uniforms for the Paraguayan army. The magnitude of these state-owned and operated industries is reflected in the fact that the employees' salaries averaged nearly 8 percent of all government expenditures throughout the years of Francia's tenure (see Appendix A).

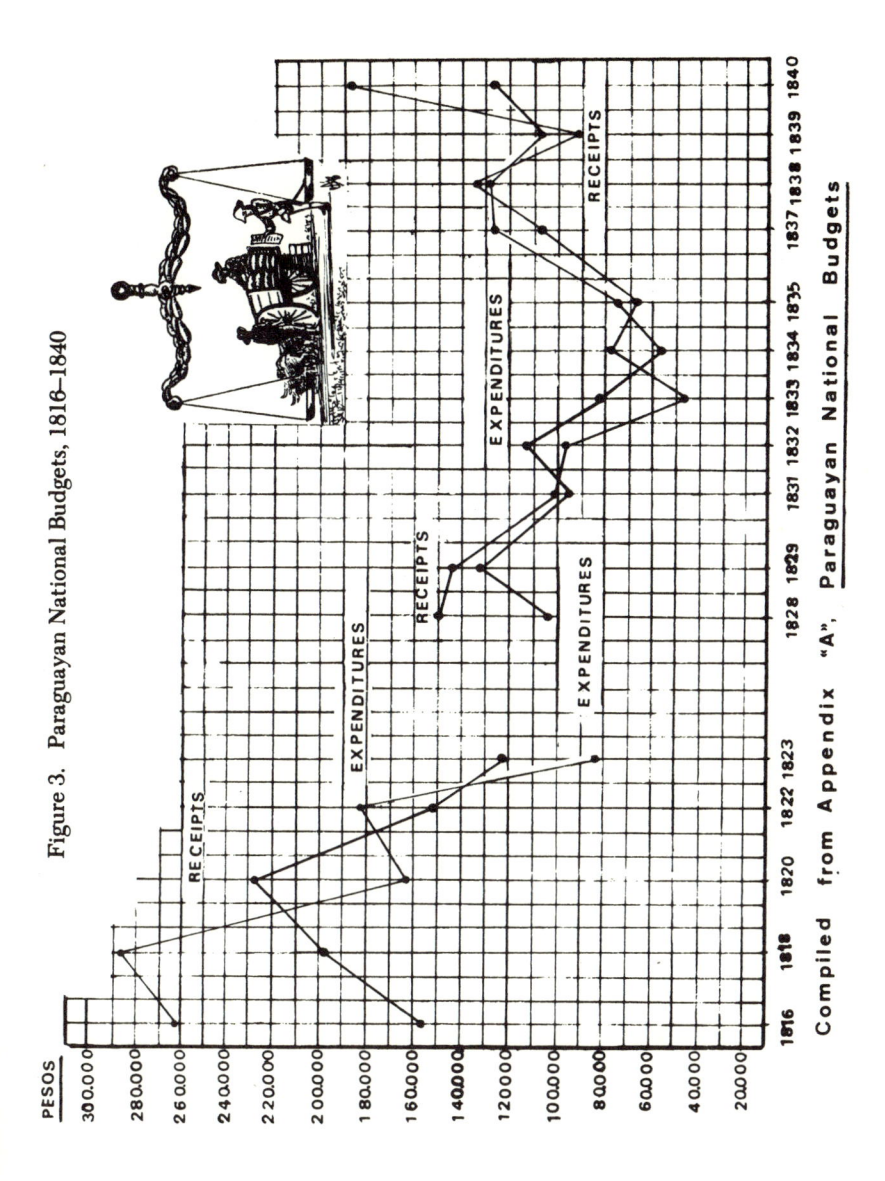

Figure 3. Paraguayan National Budgets, 1816–1840

Compiled from Appendix "A", Paraguayan National Budgets

The construction of war vessels was another major area of emphasis. While the Paraguayan shipbuilding industry was still in its infancy, the consuls expropriated, with indemnification, privately owned ships, which state employees then converted for military use.[12] By 1815, however, the state industry had grown to the point where it could launch its own vessels. In the ensuing years the government constructed approximately one hundred river craft, including sloops, flatboats, and enormous canoes, completing construction of the national navy by the mid 1820s.[13] During these years shipbuilding costs amounted to five percent of government expenses (see Appendix A).

In addition to the industries mentioned above, several thousand men and women found employment working on state estancias and in their own homes molding rifle balls; collecting saltpeter (which permitted the manufacture of gunpowder); curing hides and working leather into saddles, straps, and bags; fitting artillery and marine cannon mounts; and raising livestock to mount and feed the nation's armed forces.[14] It is important to note that these state industries did more than simply produce war materials and provide employment for Paraguayans; perhaps even more significant, much like any "war effort," the constant reminder of the crisis at hand and the intense psychological involvement of direct participation through daily activity must have served as a consolidating element, mobilizing the young nation behind its popular government.

The armed forces themselves constituted by far the most important, and expensive, part of the nation's defense, averaging 64 percent of government expenditures throughout the years of Francia's administration.* Consequently, as illustrated by a comparison of figure 4 and figure 3, the four periods of rising national expenditures closely correlate with increases in the size of the army. The first three buildups directly correspond to national crises: the 1816–20 increase reflects the government's response to the threats posed by the growing elite opposition which culminated in the Great Conspiracy; to the heightened

---

*See Appendix A, Paraguayan National Budgets. Annual percentages are calculated by dividing annual military expenditures by the total annual government expenditures, after subtracting the annual sale of state products to the troops. Although military expenses averaged 64 percent of the national budgets, it should be noted that the actual social cost of the Paraguayan military was considerably less because during periods when the army was not mobilized, many soldiers were employed in the public works.

Figure 4. Paraguayan Army, 1816-1840

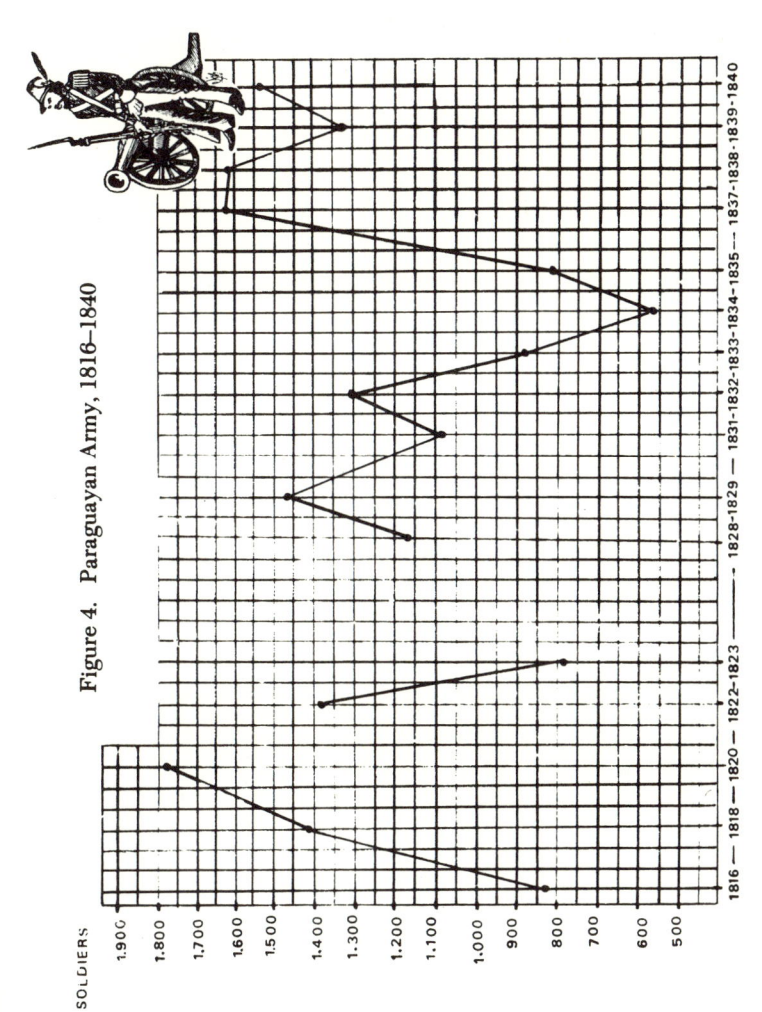

1816 — 1818 — 1820 — 1822-1823 —————— 1828-1829 — 1831-1832-1833-1834-1835 — 1837-1838-1839-1840

Figures for the years 1828, 1834, 1837 and 1839 are compiled from Appendix H, *Paraguayan Army*. All other years are calculated upon yearly military salaries found in Appendix A, *Paraguayan National Budgets*.

tensions with the porteños brought about by their imperial designs and attempts to provoke an uprising in Paraguay; and to the combined porteño and *federal* assaults against Paraguayan commerce, as well as Francisco Ramírez's planned invasion. The 1828–29 increase reflects the well-founded fear that with the end of the Cisplatine War (1825–28), Brazil and Argentina would form an alliance and jointly wage war against Paraguay (see chapter 9); and the 1831–32 increase reflects the armed conflict with Corrientes during the early years of the decade. The increase beginning in 1835 seems to represent a response to the Farroupilho Revolt (1835–45) in the neighboring Brazilian state of Rio Grande do Sul and the general chaos generated by another round of the Argentine civil wars which began in 1836, sweeping the entire Río de la Plata by the end of the decade.[15] This last buildup may quite possibly also represent an attempt by the aging dictator to assure the continuation of the popular regime.*

---

*If indeed the strengthening of the army during this last period did include an attempt by El Dictador to assure the continuation of Paraguay's popular government, his intentions proved successful. Although four governments separated Francia's death in 1840 from the establishment of the presidency of Carlos Antonio López in 1844 (see the chronology for specific dates), the oligarchy was unable to reestablish its dominance. The continuity between Francia's popular regime and the governments of Carlos Antonio López (1844–62) and Francisco Solano López (1862–70) is apparent not only in the similarity of their basic policies, but even in the fact that many of the functionaries of Francia's government continued to serve in the subsequent governments.

Perhaps the most obvious example of this continuity is Juan Manuel Alvarez, who served as the government's minister of the treasury from 1827, throughout the four interim regimes, and into the administration of Carlos Antonio López (ANA, LC, legs. 27–50). In addition, Alvarez also held the position of temporary secretary of the consular government during March and April 1841 (ANA, SH, legs. 246, 247, Comprobantes de la Tesorería General, April 1–May 1). Finally, in 1844, due to his advanced age and ill health, Alvarez retired from the government (ANA, SH, legs. 246, 247, Decreto del Presidente Carlos A. López, August 31, 1844) and continued living upon his government pension until his death in 1857 (ANA, NE, leg. 2753, Comprobantes de la Tesorería General, 1844–57).

Another example of a functionary of Francia's administration who continued his service in the following governments is Domingo Francisco Sánchez. As a young man in 1826, Sánchez began public service as the scribe of Policarpo Patiño, the Secretary of Francia's government. From 1832 he worked as the secretary of the Alcalde de Primer Voto, José Manuel Ortiz. After serving as the secretary of the General Congress of March 1841, Sánchez filled the post of secretary of the consular government until its dissolution in March 1844. In the first year of Carlos Antonio López's administration, Sánchez began service as secretary of the government, a position he continued to hold until 1860 when he was named minister of foreign relations. With the establishment of Francisco Solano López's administration in October 1862, Sánchez became minister of the interior and president of the cabinet. On May 25, 1865, he became vice-president of Paraguay (Olinda, Massare de

Several important insights can be derived from the statistical data on the military. First of all, the generally accepted figure of a standing army of from four to five thousand men is greatly exaggerated.[16] At its height in 1820, the army's total composition did not quite reach eighteen hundred regular soldiers;* and, based upon reliable statistics, an average for Francia's entire tenure would be just above twelve hundred soldiers.** Promoted by Francia's "inexplicable" policy of secrecy, the exaggeration of the size of the Paraguayan military served to deter the numerous invasions that Paraguay's belligerent neighbors periodically planned throughout the years of his government.

Furthermore, it seems clear that the primary function of the Paraguayan army was not aggressive, but simply to defend national sovereignty. Amounts of military expenditures corresponded directly to real threats to Paraguayan independence. Thus, during crisis periods its ranks tended to increase, while during normal circumstances statistics reveal a marked trend toward decreasing the size of the armed forces.

Perhaps most revealing is this facility to expand and contract the military establishment. Consistent with Francia's early antimilitaristic actions, statistics establish a minimum ratio of privates and noncommissioned officers to commissioned officers at an incredible 42 to 1 (see Appendix H). With no generals, colonels, or majors, the army's handful of captains and lieutenants were periodically rotated and were never permitted to spend

---

Kostianovsky, *El Vice Presidente Sánchez*, pp. 14, 15, 24, 42, 43, 47). Sánchez continued as his nation's vice-president throughout the War of the Triple Alliance (1864–70) until March 1, 1870, when he, along with President López (and the Paraguayan Revolution), was killed at Cerro Corá by the Allied Forces (Justo Pastor Benítez, *Carlos Antonio López*, p. 243).

*This figure is derived by dividing the 1820 monthly military salaries by the average military salary for 1828 (see Appendix H. Paraguayan Army), the closest year for which data on specific military salaries were available. Although statistics are not availble for 1821, the period of greatest danger from Ramírez's invasion forces, it is reasonable to conclude that the army was further increased during this year. It should be realized that during military mobilizations the armed forces were swelled by calling up as many as 5,000 to 10,000 local militia soldiers. In the event of an actual invasion, as during the War of the Triple Alliance (1864–70), all citizens, both men and women, could be relied upon to defend the nation.

**In the thousands of archival documents reviewed in the preparation of this work, there is not a single mention of the overall size of the army. Evidently, only Francia and the treasurer, from whose records these statistics have been compiled, actually knew the total size of the Paraguayan military establishment. Indeed, even these records rarely specify the deployment of all of the companies, and therefore it is possible that they do not include all of the troops stationed in the frontier garrisons.

long periods of time together. In this manner, the popular government made sure that not even the ranking officers knew the overall size of the armed forces; therefore, uncertain of the actual strength of their commands in relation to the entire army, they were discouraged from taking either unified or individual action against the state. Unlike the military castes of traditional Latin American countries, Paraguayan military officers did not make up an autonomous force in themselves; rather, they remained truly servants of the nation.

In spite of the enormous military expenditures, to an extraordinary extent Francia was able to fulfill the objective of his Political Catechism that "taxes can be reduced so that nobody is pained by paying them." As demonstrated in figure 5, during his administration Paraguay experienced a radical reduction in taxes; they declined from 222,131 pesos, or 84 percent of total government revenue for 1816 (the first year for which documentation is available), to 31,084 pesos, or 16.5 percent of the 1840 revenue receipts (see Appendix A). It should be noted, however, that the dramatic decline in tax revenue between 1816 and 1830 was not the result of government tax policy, but reflects the loss of import, export, and sales tax revenues caused by the drastic decline in international trade. Yet it is significant that, despite the decrease in revenue, with the exception of the creation of a small tax on tanneries (1826—28)[17] and the *derecho de ventage* (1823–32)[18]—a modest tax on livestock and agricultural products brought to Asunción for public sale—the state neither increased existing taxes nor levied new ones during this critical period.

In 1830 the government did decree a major reduction in those taxes most burdensome to the masses. Most notably, it reduced by one-half the *alcabala*—a 4 percent sales tax levied on all commercial transactions—and it also abolished the *diezmo*—a 10 percent tithe on all agricultural production collected by the state on the church's behalf—replacing it with the *contribución fructuaria del verano y invierno*—a 5 percent tax on both summer and winter crops.[19] Five years later the state lowered these two principal taxes even further; the *alcabala* from 2 to 1 percent, and the *contribución fructuaria* from 5 to 4 percent.[20] In 1837 the latter was once again reduced, this time by the elimination of the taxes on the winter crop.[21] The effect these tax reductions must have had on the Paraguayan people can be gathered from

Figure 5. Paraguayan Taxes, 1816-1840

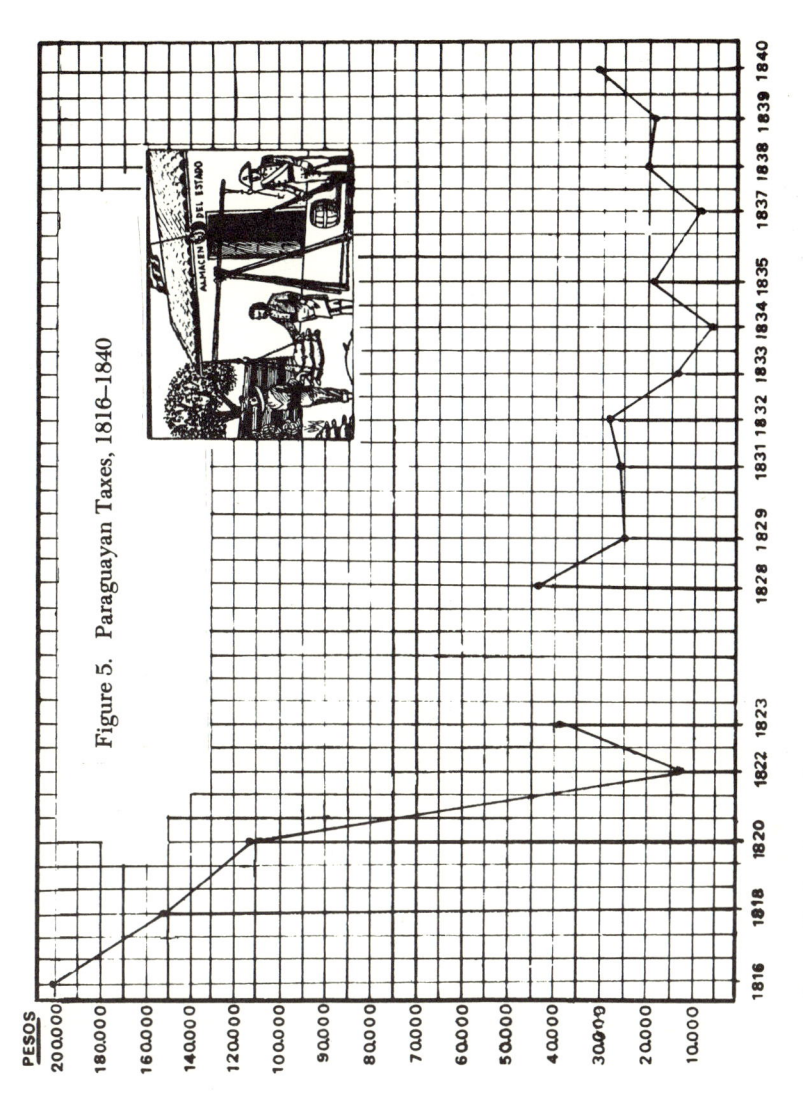

Compiled from Appendix "A", Paraguayan National Budgets

the fact that government income from these two major taxes amounted to 23,290 pesos in 1829 (93 percent of all tax revenues for that year), whereas the national budgets register them as only 6,902 pesos for the last year of Francia's tenure (22 percent of all tax revenues for 1840)—an impressive tax reduction of 71 percent (see Appendix A).

Even while enacting such enormous reductions in the people's tax burden, the government did not lack adequate funds, because it was also developing new sources of state revenue. Already in possession of the lands formerly held by the Spanish crown and the property confiscated from the oligarchy,[22] Francia in the early 1820s moved further to increase the national domain by confiscating several large former Jesuit estancias and other church lands, such as the Seminary of San Carlos and those lands held by monasteries and brotherhoods.[23] Of equal importance, in September 1825 the government annulled the royal land grants—which, because they had been granted as political favors, were most often held simply for speculative purposes and had therefore remained virtually unused[24]—and ordered all landowners to present legitimate titles to their properties under penalty of confiscation by the state.[25] As a result of these measures, the national domain by early 1826 included the entire Mission and Chaco territories as well as more than one-half of the rich central region of Paraguay.[26] Francia distributed much of this land in a radical agrarian reform, while converting the remainder into numerous state-owned and -operated estancias, which became a major source of national production and revenue for the government.

The first estancias were founded with livestock acquired through the collection of the *diezmo*[27] and confiscations from the creole and Spanish oligarchy[28] for the purpose of providing food, mounts, equipment, and clothing for the armed forces.[29] But under the watchful eye of El Dictador, who required all administrators to submit monthly reports,[30] the function of the estancias grew beyond its original bounds. By the late 1820s both the number of estancias and their herds of livestock—which included cattle, oxen, horses, mules, sheep, and milk cows—had proliferated far beyond the needs of the army. Spanning the entire republic, the more than seventy-five state estancias (see Appendix I) produced an excess of livestock and related products, which the government either distributed among the needy[31] or sold in the local markets at moderate prices.[32]

The government also sold agricultural products* and the goods produced by its textile and iron industries. These products became increasingly available because the temporary disruption and subsequent reorientation of the economy forced the development of not only private but also nationalized light industry in Paraguay.[33] Along with considerable quantities of imported goods, the state offered for sale to both the troops and the public at the state store in Asunción a variety of products including various types of axes, hatchets, machetes, adzes, knives, door locks, scissors, harmonicas,[34] candles, soap, ponchos, sheets, hammocks,[35] and hats.[36]

Initially, the army consumed most of the state production and imported goods. Although between 1816 and 1823 gross income from state sales averaged 12.4 percent of government revenues, only 1.3 percent came from sales to the public, while 11.1 percent came from the military.[37] Actually, during this period the state's industrial and commercial activities were not primarily a means of government revenue, but served instead to provide essential materials for the armed forces; when the expenses of the state industries are deducted, profits from sales averaged only 3 percent of the government's income.[38]

During the later period of Francia's tenure (1828–40), as indicated in figure 6, the sales of state products came to represent the single most important source of the government's income.[39] While average sales to the military rose 24 percent,[40] as can be seen in figure 7, it was sales to the public—with an average increase of more than 1,000 percent[41]—that accounted for this dramatic increase. The bulk of the sales to the public were of Paraguayan manufactured goods, imported merchandise, and—to a lesser, although still considerable, degree—agricultural products and animals; by the late 1830s, the government also sold increasing quantities of metals, glassware, and crockery (see Appendix A). As an extension of the government's early policy of

---

*The state acquired large quantities of agricultural products, which included not only the traditional yerba and tobacco, but also such products as hams, honey, bacon, and guava, through the collection of the *diezmo*, and after 1830, in decreasing amounts, through the *contribución fructuria*. This decrease largely accounts for the decline in the sales of agricultural products to the public during the 1830s. See Appendix A.

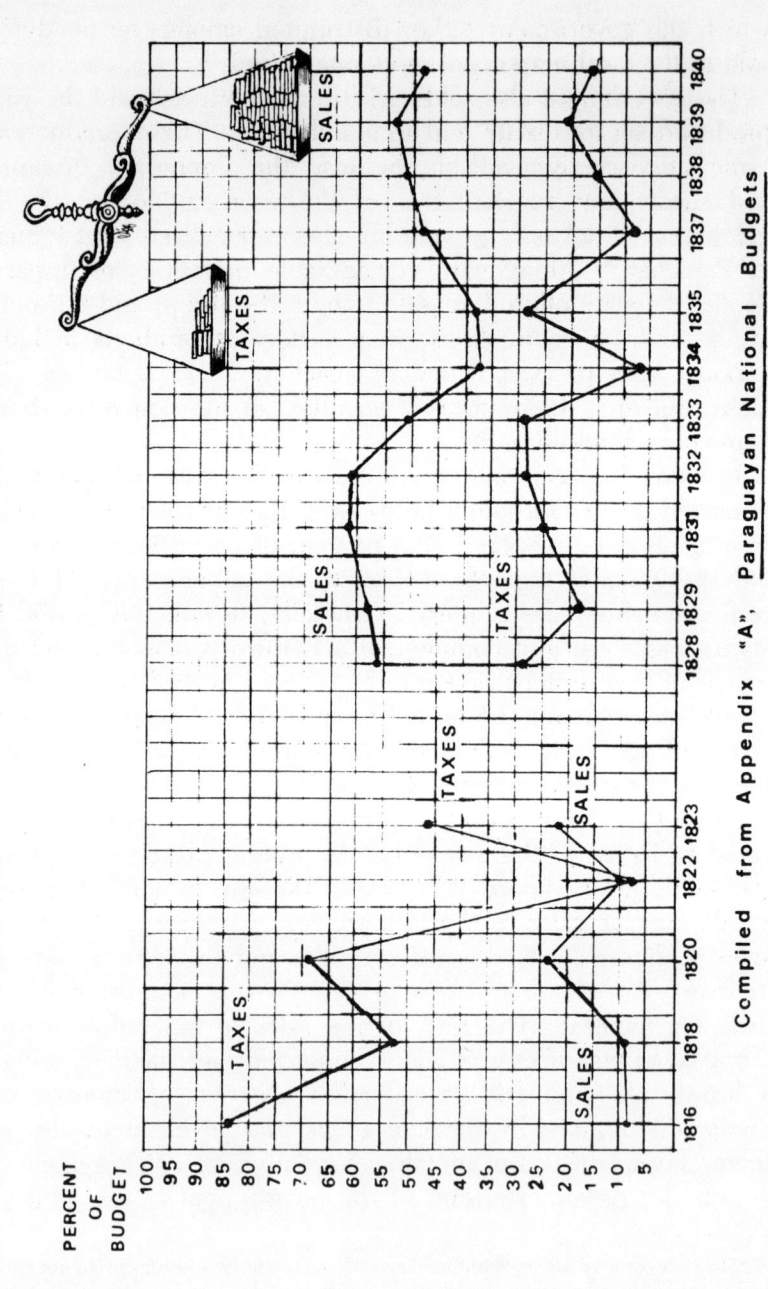

Figure 6. Paraguayan Taxes and Sales, 1816–1840

Compiled from Appendix "A", Paraguayan National Budgets

Figure 7. Paraguayan State Sales, 1816–1840

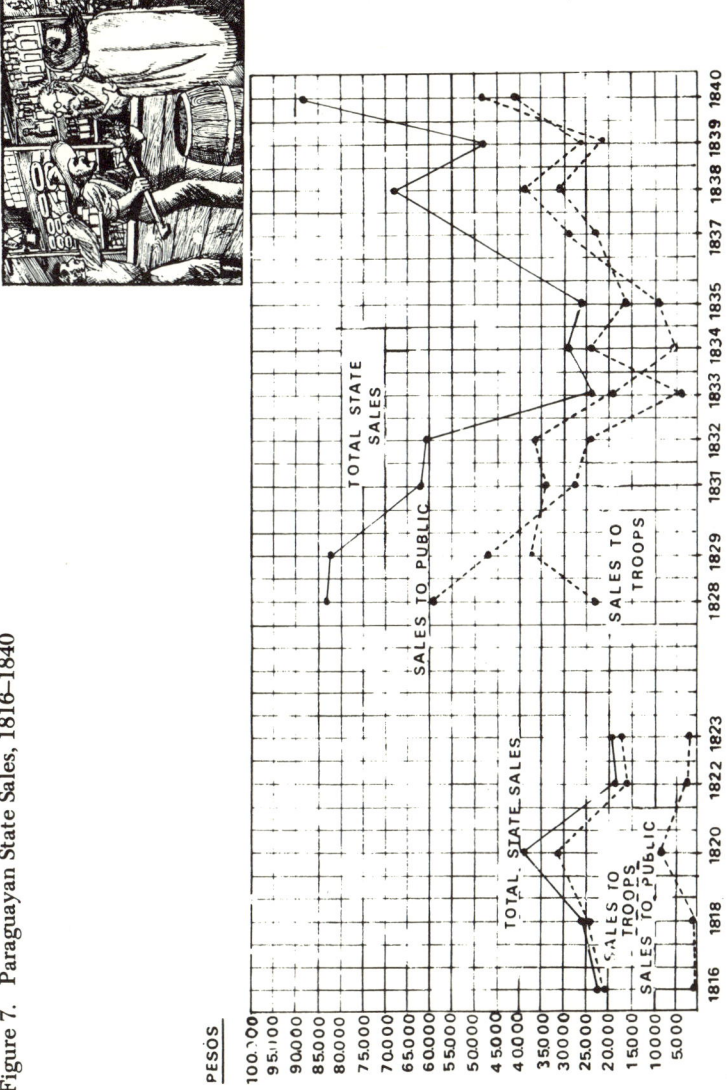

Compiled from Appendix "A", Paraguayan National Budgets

regulating the price and quality of medical care,* during the last years of his administration El Dictador established a number of state pharmacies which, from 1835 onward, sold increasingly large quantities of medicines to the public (see Appendix A).

As demonstrated in Figure 6, the two primary sources of state revenue—taxation and the sale of state products—actually reversed their initial importance as government income. During the early period (1816–23), taxes averaged 54.9 percent, while sales amounted to only 12.4 percent;[42] but by later in Francia's administration (1828–40), taxes averaged only 19.4 percent, while state sales had grown to provide 50.2 percent of all government revenue.[43]

Among its other accomplishments, the state enacted an extensive public works program. The manner of financing and conducting these programs exemplifies several aspects of the Political Catechism's principle of considering public works "the common burden." Although coordinated and directed by the national government, the various public works programs fell under the administration of the municipalities, which received their revenue from the sale of agricultural products grown on municipal lands as well as from several local taxes.[44] To meet extraordinary expenses of the public works program, El Dictador levied special taxes on the wealthy citizens in the form of "contributions."** Labor was provided through the assignment of army troops and

---

*In response to numerous complaints received from the countryside denouncing the so-called medical doctors who had been "administering unknown drugs to the patients and demanding excessive fees, and what is worse, with fatal results, [and] without any degrees, licenses nor authorization," beginning as early as the consularship the government forbade any person from practicing medicine without a state license of competence and ordered the local judges to immediately submit the names, nationality, reputation, degree or license, as well as the fee schedules, of all medicos and *curanderos* in their districts. (ANA, SH, leg. 223, Decreto de los Consules, no date).

**Unfortunately, the scattered and incomplete municipal documentation makes it impossible to determine the precise cost of the public works programs. But Rengger (*The Reign*, p. 167) reported that throughout Paraguay a monthly tax was levied on all businesses, and in Asunción an additional, considerably larger tax was levied on commercial warehouses. For partial documentation, see Category C of the Forced Contributions found in table 2. Also see ANA, LC, leg. 22, 1823, entry 16, which begins registering a monthly "contribution" for public works levied upon "the wealthy citizens and property owners of this city [Asunción]." In addition, partial documentation of public works expenditures is included in the State Operating Expenses category of Appendix A, and can be found in the appropriate Libros de Caja.

the employment of local workers.⁴⁵ In addition, Francia, in abolishing the practice of whipping criminals as a means of punishment, directed that they be assigned to periods of labor on the public works programs.*

Another aspect of the public works program can be seen in the 1816 complaint of the Asunción cabildo against don Juan Vicente Lagle y Rey. In order to procure necessary construction materials, the government required a minimum quota of bricks from all large factories. All manufacturers complied except Lagle, the wealthiest brick manufacturer. After being threatened with a monthly fine of 50 pesos until he provided 5,000 bricks, Lagle ridiculed the order by delivering "only 4,000 unserviceable bricks when his factory had more than 9,000 according to his own declaration." Even after the mayor spoke to him, Lagle still refused to provide usable bricks or to sell them at a reasonable price. Finally the municipal authorities tried to convince Lagle that "for the Social Contract he [should] abdicate his natural liberty and subdue his ambitious intentions." Failing in their attempts to impress the obstinate Lagle, the frustrated city officials referred the matter to El Dictador. Consistent with the priorities of popular Paraguay, Francia, subordinating private ownership of the means of production to the public welfare, admonished Lagle into fulfilling his "Social Contract."⁴⁶

Among the first of the public works projects the government undertook in Asunción was the paving of streets⁴⁷ and the introduction of public lighting for the first time in Paraguayan history.** The following decades saw the construction of approximately forty state buildings, offices, and houses in the capital.⁴⁸

By far the most energetic—and controversial—program was Francia's improvement of the city streets, whose condition was a shameful legacy of the Spanish governors. In violation of imperial

---

*As an example, see ANA, SH, leg. 393, Gill a Francia, September 28, 1825, in which the Commander of Pilar complained that although he was assigning the cattle rustlers sent him by the local judges of the district to the public works, he did not consider this adequate punishment, especially since the local judges no longer had Francia's authorization to punish them first by whipping. Also see Jośe Antonio Vázquez, *El doctor Francia*, pp. 622 and 623, for an 1827 case in which Francia prohibited a priest from beating a parishioner.

**ANA, NE, leg. 1232, Cuenta . . . Mayordomo de proprios . . . Asunción, año 1818. Jośe Antonio Vázquez notes that although, even for the era, the lighting was modest, Asuncíon consumed more than 500,000 candles annually, which provided work for numerous people (*El Dr. Francia*, p. 34).

law, Asunción was one of the few Spanish settlements not laid out in the familiar gridiron pattern characteristic of the Spanish-American world. It looked more like a Portuguese town, with narrow, winding streets that during the rainy season became virtual rivers, carrying a mixture of mud and debris, as well as animal and human excrement, from the upper, wealthy section of the city down through the lower, poorer areas. In 1821, to correct these conditions, the government began to straighten, widen, and cobblestone the major streets of the capital. As a result of this ambitious effort—which was not entirely successful, for even upon completion of the project many of the streets were still nearly unusable during the heavy rains*—many homes had to be either moved or destroyed.[49] Since the less affluent owners of houses and property expropriated by the project received indemnities,[50] the uncompensated wealthy Spaniards were understandably quite irate over their treatment. They were further distressed, as Rengger observed, because it was Francia's intent "that in the future the capital should be peopled by the natives of Paraguay, not the Spaniards, to whom had hitherto belonged all the best houses."[51]

Throughout Paraguay, not only in the capital but in the interior towns as well, the government continued to build the nation's infrastructure. Between 1822 and 1827 the village of Pilar, for example, was virtually reconstructed; streets were improved, the central plaza renovated, and several public buildings constructed, along with new bridges and even a new church. In 1829 the state built two new public meat markets, complete with corrals and sheds, in Villarrica.[52]

In an effort at total integration of the nation—economic and political, that is, as well as social integration—the government coordinated a far-reaching program of road and bridge construction. Francia initiated this program shortly after his election as dictator and continued it throughout his years in office. Existing roads were repaired and widened, while new ones were opened through the backlands to connect the outlying towns and districts with the capital.[53] Local judges were given the tasks of

---

*To this day, in order to cross many streets in downtown Asunción during the heavy rains, one must either wade through gushing water or pay a one-guaraní toll to use the plank "bridges" attended by barefoot shoeshine boys.

road inspection and ensuring that the thoroughfares remained in excellent condition and open to public traffic, even if it was necessary to employ force, such as in cases where the roads passed through private tracts of property.[54] Such an extensive road system undoubtedly contributed to Paraguay's growing internal commerce and general prosperity.*

Francia not only initiated Paraguay's first massive program of public works but also fathered the nation's first public education system. Although public primary schooling theoretically existed during the colonial period, in reality what schooling there was benefited only the elite because—except in the capital, where the schoolteacher was paid from the municipal treasury—parents were required to pay the teachers for each child who received instruction.[55] Needless to say, the impoverished masses could ill afford the luxury of providing their children with a primary education. In recognition of this problem, Francia shifted the burden of paying teachers to the respective municipal authorities, and specifically assigned the task of establishing new schools to the local judges commissioned by the national government.[56]

By the mid 1820s these measures had evidently begun to take effect, for virtually all accounts agree upon the astonishingly high literacy rate among the Paraguayan people. Confirming Rengger's report that nearly all Paraguayans were literate, the naturalist Jean Etienne Richard de Grandsire, who spent a brief period in the southeastern border town of Itapúa in 1825, observed that "almost all of the inhabitants know how to read and write" and noted further that "the people can request the Dictator to educate their children at the expense of the State."[57] In 1828 primary education was made mandatory,[58] and three years later, at least in some areas, the national government began to provide part of the schoolteachers' compensation in the form of clothes and cattle delivered from the nearest state estancia.[59] Finally, in 1834, Francia formally established standardized

---

*Although incomplete and scattered documentation makes it difficult to reconstruct the precise volume of internal trade, the sales tax receipts of products brought to the small northern town of San Pedro in 1835 (ANA, NE, leg. 1286, Comprobantes de la Receptoría de San Pedro, 1835) indicate a vigorous commercial activity. Among these products were large quantities of salt, tobacco, corn, cotton, rice, wine, aguardiente, hides, rosaries, crockery, axes, machetes, knives, scissors, iron, steel, shirts, hats, ponchos, handkerchiefs, and various types of cloth, including imported English linen.

salaries for Paraguay's 140 rural schoolteachers, who were in charge of the nation's 5,000 pupils.*

The kernel of truth behind traditional history's charge that El Dictador "suppressed education" is found in looking beyond primary schooling, for in 1823 Francia did close the virtually defunct Royal Seminary of San Carlos.** But in the mid 1820s, as Rengger noted, several private seminaries were established in the capital, "in which youth of both sexes receive a tolerably regular education."[60] Considering the technical limitations of an early nineteenth-century agricultural society, it is understandable that the state did not place the highest priority on secondary schooling. The necessity of directing the nation's resources toward production—the basis of Paraguay's autonomy—may very well account for the government's failure to establish a secondary public school system.

Yet in 1836 Francia did inaugurate Paraguay's first public library. Located in Asunción, it contained an estimated 5,000 volumes,[61] most of which had been either "inherited" by the state or confiscated from the private collections of the oligarchy.[62] It should be noted, as a reflection of Francia's priorities, that throughout the years of his tenure no import tax was ever established on either munitions or books.

The good reputation Paraguay enjoyed throughout the Río de la Plata region at this time can be seen in the contemporary work of César Famín. Although he never actually entered the country, Famín reported, "Everyone is working, Francia has abolished beggary, he has encouraged new means of production

---

*ANA, SH, leg. 242, Resolución de Francia, August 30, 1834. During the preceding years Francia had solicited lists of students from the rural schoolteachers. See Jośe Antonio Vázquez, *El doctor Francia*, p. 39, for such an example. Although the salary of Asunción's school teacher, José Gabriel Tellez, was reduced by this same decree, he still received approximately twice the salary of a rural schoolteacher (see Appendix A), which was set at six pesos per month, the same as for a rural skilled worker. For an example of rural wages, see ANA, NE, leg. 739, Casimiro Rojas á Francia, September 30, 1838.

**By early 1823 the Seminary of San Carlos had nearly ceased to function. It had no students studying grammar and only thirteen part-time students studying Latin. This decline was due to the lack of qualified professors and to the fact that no priests could be ordained since Bishop Panés had retired. See the series of documents leading to the closure of the Seminary in ANA, SH, leg. 441, Solicitud del Rector Mariano Agustín Goyburú, January 7, 1823; Francia a Goyburú, March 21, 1823; Goyburú a Francia, March 22, 1823; and Auto de Francia de 23 de marzo de 1823.

and has built fast roads, safe and economical ... and all the inhabitants of Paraguay ... know how to read, write and count."[63] The social progress and tranquillity of Paraguay attracted many deserters and other refugees from the Argentine and Brazilian civil wars.[64] As Rengger observed, "very large numbers of strangers" came to the borders seeking entry into the country; while Spaniards were generally not admitted, for all others "ingress remained free."[65]

Just as it had done with José Artigas and his five hundred followers, the Paraguayan government, after screening the immigrants, dispersed them throughout the nation, resettling many in the sparsely populated northern region.[66] The large numbers of people seeking refuge from the death and destruction of the raging civil wars help account for the rapid growth of Paraguay's population; in four decades it swelled from some 100,000 people in 1798[67] to approximately 375,000 people by the late 1830s.*

El Dictador also insisted upon granting asylum to runaway slaves.[68] He also created the office of *defensor de pobres*,** whose functions included representing slaves in their grievances against their masters.[69]

Regardless, however, of the progressive measures he took concerning slavery, and in spite of the fact that he manumitted his own two personal domestic slaves,*** Francia never attempted to abolish slavery as an institution. Although slavery was never a

---

*Wisner, *El Dictador*, p. 140. Wisner reported that Francia conducted a census in 1831, arriving at a total population of 375,000. Although archival research failed to uncover any trace of an 1831 census, partial records of an 1838 census are found in ANA, NE, legs. 3281, 3283, 3284, 3286, and 3287. Yet Wisner's figure seems a plausible one; since there were no major wars, epidemics, or famines during this period, a 3 percent growth rate of the 1798 population of 100,000 would result in 326,000 people in 1838. The remaining 49,000 people could very well be accounted for by immigration.

**From 1814 to 1825 the *defensor de pobres* was an Asunción municipal office, although it also handled cases referred to the capital from the interior. In 1822 Francia created the office of the *defensor de indios* (ANA, SH, leg. 235, Supremo Orden de 10 de julio de 1822), and shortly thereafter the office of the Defensor de Minores (Rengger, *The Reign* p. 111). These offices remained under Asunción municipal jurisdiction until the abolition of the cabildo in 1824, when the consolidated office became a national government position.

***ANA, LC, leg. 37, entry 366, August 11, 1834, in which Francia paid the state treasury 550 pesos for the liberty of his two slaves, who technically were the property of the state. But one of them, José Maria, lost his freedom within several months as punishment for stealing money from the treasury.

major labor system in Paraguay,* it continued to exist throughout this period.

If Paraguay's popular government failed to eliminate the institution of slavery, it did destroy the colonial institution of latifundia. Attacking the traditional land tenure system, the state leased land to both landless Paraguayans and immigrants at very moderate rents for indefinite periods, under the sole condition that it be cultivated or turned into pasturage.[70] Homesteads varied in size and rent. The smallest homesteads, called ejidos, averaged a little more than two pesos rent per year; the larger ones, such as those distributed from the former lands of the Seminary of San Carlos, averaged nearly four pesos per year; while the largest homesteads, leased from other state lands and parts of the state estancias, averaged twenty pesos per year.[71] Although complete documentation is not available for the actual number of homesteads leased by the state, a sound statistical sampling establishes the total number by the end of Francia's tenure at well over 6,000.[72] These lands supported at least 49,000 people, or 13 percent of the nation's population; in other words, one out of every eight Paraguayans lived on a farm or on an estancia leased from the government.[73]

To complement this radical land reform, the government aided the homesteaders and other needy Paraguayans with frequent remissions of clothes[74] and tools,[75] as well as cattle from the prospering state estancias.** Such measures did not amount simply to a policy of sustained welfare. Designed to provide initial assistance and temporary relief they served as yet another

---

Judging from partial census data (see p. 119n for archival references), no more than 2 percent of Paraguay's population were slaves. It should be noted that at least those slaves employed by the state received a salary equivalent to that of a free person performing the same labor. For examples, see ANA, NE, leg. 1298, Comprobantes de la Tesorería General, nos. 322 and 503, 1838.

**For examples, see ANA, SH, leg. 240, Francia al Comandante de Villarrica, April 27, 1829, in which the government sent 800 cattle to be distributed among the needy people of the vicinity, just as it had done in San Isidro and Concepción; and ANA, SH, leg. 240, Francia á Ramírez, September 3, 1830, in which the government distributed cattle among the needy people of the district of Itapúa and Curuguatí. Also see ANA, SH, leg. 412, Estancia de Surubí . . . año 1832, and ANA, SH, leg. 378, Francia al subdelegado de Santiago, January 2, 1840; and ANA, SH, leg. 244, Francia al Comandante de la Villa de Labrador, April 9, 1840, in which the government sent 48 axes, 6 adzes, 20 machetes, 100 steel wedges, and 700 cattle to be distributed among the needy settlers of Terecañí.

element in the overall effort to change the monocultural nature of Paraguay's economy.

As explained in the previous chapters, under Paraguay's colonial export economy, human, natural, and capital resources were concentrated in the maximum production of the cash crop of yerba, and to a lesser extent in tobacco. Thus, while providing prosperity for the national and international elites, the traditional export economy left the great majority of Paraguayans in dire poverty. But the postindependence government, forced by the temporary paralyses of the economy to diversify national production, embarked upon a major campaign to develop a balanced economy which would produce a variety of products to meet the needs of the Paraguayan people.

The case of cattle raising serves as a clear example of the nation's new economic orientation. Because of its monocultural economy and latifundia land-tenure system, Paraguay, in spite of ample natural resources of its own, depended heavily upon the import of cattle from other provinces of the Viceroyalty of La Plata. Nicolás de Herrera did not exaggerate the extent of Paraguayan dependence when he advised his porteño superiors that as a punitive measure it would be advantageous "to prohibit absolutely the commerce of this province, and the introduction of our cattle, by which it subsists."[76] As early as 1815, the disruption of the regional economy by the *federal* forces severely restricted the purchase of Argentine cattle, thus causing further shortages of meat in Paraguay. Not until the next decade did the scarcity of meat cease to be a major national problem.[78]

By the mid 1820s, however, the Paraguayan cattle industry had grown to such an extent that rather than importing Argentine livestock, Paraguay actually began exporting beef.[79] Further, by the late 1820s and early 1830s, the proliferation of Paraguayan cattle, and the exceptional demand caused by epidemics which devastated southern Brazil's livestock industry, set market forces of supply and demand into motion, resulting in a thriving export commerce through the southeastern trading town of Itapúa.[80] By 1829, livestock—which included beef cattle calves, oxen, and bulls[81] amounted to more than 20 percent of all Paraguayan exports (see Appendix C).

Yet within this economic bonanza lay the classic contradiction of export economies. Many of the nation's landowners concentrated on raising cattle and neglected the cultivation of their fields. Agricultural production also suffered from the increasing herds of uncontrolled animals that habitually roamed though neighboring farms detroying crops. Consequently, the concentration of Paraguay's resources in the cattle industry not only limited and damaged agricultural production, but because of the large number of cattle that were exported, it kept the price of beef artificially high in Paraguay.

To compound these problems, by 1830 Paraguay's rich central region had reached its carrying capacity; that is, the pasturage could no longer support an increase in the number of cattle without severely depleting the vegetation upon which the livestock grew and fattened. As Francia explained to the Delegate of Itapúa: "The various state estancias are overflowing and I do not know what to do with so many cattle, and the worst of it all is that because of this, now they do not even fatten."*

The situation can be clearly summarized. The forces of an export economy, responding to the laws of supply and demand, functioned to distort the economy by an overconcentration of human, natural, and capital resources for the maximum production of the most profitable product, thus leading to the classic symptoms of dependent economies: prosperity for the few, scarcity and high prices for the many.

To counter such distortions, Francia enacted a series of measures to assure that the economy developed in the best interest of the entire nation. As early as 1825 the government required all landowners to cultivate at least a portion of their lands.[82] Those who did not work their lands were subject to rather severe penalties. For example, thirty-two farmers in the district of Pilar who had abandoned their agricultural pursuits in favor of raising cattle exclusively were fined one cow each for their refusal to comply with the government order.[83] In the most densely populated areas, the state, in 1827, began regulating the amount of livestock each property owner could maintain; and under penalty of moderate fines required them to erect fences or otherwise control their livestock in order to prevent damage to nearby

---

*ANA, SH, leg. 240, Francia a Ramírez, September 3, 1830. Francia solved this problem of excess cattle by limiting their numbers and increasing their distribution among the needy. See p. 120n** for archival references.

crops.[84] Finally, in 1831, since these measures by themselves proved inadequate, the government adopted the radical and unprecedented policy of prohibiting the export of livestock.*

Such rational control of the livestock industry clearly demonstrates the priorities of the popular administration. Not only did Francia's policies protect Paraguay's pasturage from destruction by excessive herds of animals, thus conserving a natural resource, but they also, by further ensuring that the cattle remained within the nation to provide food for the people rather than riches for the elite, led to a 40 percent decrease in the price of beef within a few years. In 1829 the price of beef cattle averaged five pesos each; by 1832 the average price had declined to four and one-half pesos; and by the following year, 1833, the average price had fallen to three pesos, the level at which it remained for the remainder of the decade.[85]

As part of its campaign to develop a balanced economy, the government, also began a concerted campaign to diversify and increase agricultural production. Another legacy of the imbalance of the colonial economy further limited Paraguay's agricultural potential. With emphasis upon maximum production of yerba—which was collected in its wild state—and tobacco— which readily grew during the mild semitropical winter—the province had adopted the Spanish schedule of planting a single crop in May (the European spring, but the Paraguayan fall), even though such staples as rice, corn, peanuts, and vegetables thrive during the hot summer months. Thus Paraguay had forgotten the ancient Guaraní practice of planting two crops per year.[86]

In October 1819 a locust invasion swept into the nation from the Chaco. Despite the general mobilization to fight the menace, the insects succeeded in destroying the entire harvest. Thereupon Francia ordered all farmers—under penalty of heavy

---

*Unfortunately, the original decree of May 19, 1831, could not be located through archival research, but it is referred to by Francia the following month in his correspondence with the Delegate of Itapúa (ANA, SH. leg. 241, Francia á Ramírez, June 4, 1831). Also see ANA, NE, leg. 1273, Ramírez á Francia, June 13, 1831, in which the delegate explains that he had advised the estancieros that they would be fined if they violated the prohibition. The continued exportation of cattle until 1832 was due to the time needed to fatten the large numbers of cattle purchased prior to the May 1831 decree (BNRJ, CRB, 1-30, 2, leg. 6, Ramíez á Francia, August 30, 1831, and ANA, SH, leg. 241, Ramírez á Francia, December 30, 1831).

fines—to replant immediately. To their general surprise this second crop proved even more abundant than what had been expected from the original harvest.[87] Ever since this return to ancient practice, Paraguay has grown both summer and winter crops, which has proven to be by far the most varied and productive method of agriculture.[88]

In addition to requiring all property holders to work their lands, in certain areas the government even designated that particular crops, such as wheat and cotton, be cultivated.[89] Further, local officials were empowered to assign vagrants to help with the planting and harvesting; those who refused found themselves laboring at public works as state prisoners. As Wisner pointed out in his example of the one hundred or so vagrants thus assigned to the public works, "All the people, men and women alike, dedicated themselves to useful works in such a manner that life in Paraguay . . . developed in a tranquil atmosphere of comfort and order."[90] Indeed, confirming Wisner's report, and in striking contrast to the other areas of the Río de la Plata through which he had traveled, the naturalist Grandsire informed Baron von Humboldt that "one travels through Paraguay without arms. One does not see beggars: everyone works."[91]

Testifying to the destruction of Paraguay's monocultural economy, trade statistics record that in 1800—an average year during the late colonial period—the province exported 2,739 tons of yerba; in 1816—the first year for which documentation is available in the national period—yerba exports had grown to 3,624 tons; but during the last decade of Francia's tenure (1829–39), annual yerba exports averaged only 237 tons (see Appendix C). With its newly balanced economy, Paraguay's land easily provided ample rice, corn, manioc, potatoes, sweet potatoes, peanuts, wheat, cotton, and numerous varieties of vegetables to meet the needs of the people.[92]

Domestic production became so abundant that during the 1830s Paraguay actually began exporting small, but increasingly larger, quantities of corn, rice, dried manioc, and onions, as well as honey, sweets, cheese, and hams (see Appendix C). Indeed, during the bumper-crop years of 1833 and 1837, not all the agricultural production could be consumed internally, which created growing pressure among the larger producers to export greater quantities to the Argentine provinces.[93]

The government's refusal to yield to these economic pressures once again revealed the distinction between Paraguay's popular regime and its elite-dominated, dependent neighbors. Clearly it was in the interest of the agricultural elite to force the opening of greater markets for their products, but no longer did any elite command the power to define their own interests as the interests of the entire nation. There was no reason to risk being drawn into Argentina's civil wars, especially since the nation's independence had been secured, and "above all," as Francia pointed out, "since Paraguay does not need them because it is self-sustaining."[94]

Consequently Francia continued uncompromisingly to apply the axiom, often reiterated yet rarely practiced, that served as the basic governing principle of popular Paraguay; as El Dictador explicitly stated shortly before his death, "Private interest should be subordinated to the common and general welfare."[95]

PART 3
The Struggle for Autonomy

THE COMMERCIAL ESCAPE VALVE | 8

Regardless of its declaration of political independence, and in spite of the internal consolidation of the popular regime, Paraguay still had not achieved total independence; it had yet to overcome its colonial heritage of economic dependence. Paraguay's only commercial water route, the Río de la Plata, was still controlled by Buenos Aires. In full recognition that a nation, to be truly sovereign, must possess economic independence as well as political independence, Francia sought to escape the dependency which continued to subordinate Paraguay to the regional and world metropolises. Consequently, Paraguayan foreign policy centered upon developing a new overland trade route across the Missions district to Brazil, thereby releasing the powerful political and economic pressures within the nation caused by the blockade of its international commerce.

The year 1811 saw the overthrow of Governor Bernardo Velasco, who since 1806 had simultaneously governed Paraguay and the Missions. The strategic region between the Paraná and Uruguay rivers (see map 4) became a disputed area, claimed by both Paraguay and Argentina. In fact, the region's capital, Candelaria, located directly across the Paraná from Itapúa—southern Paraguay's major political, military, commercial, and population center—was designated as the alternative capital of both the Asunción and Buenos Aires governments in the event of a crisis.[1]

Despite Paraguay's strong claim to the Missions—based not

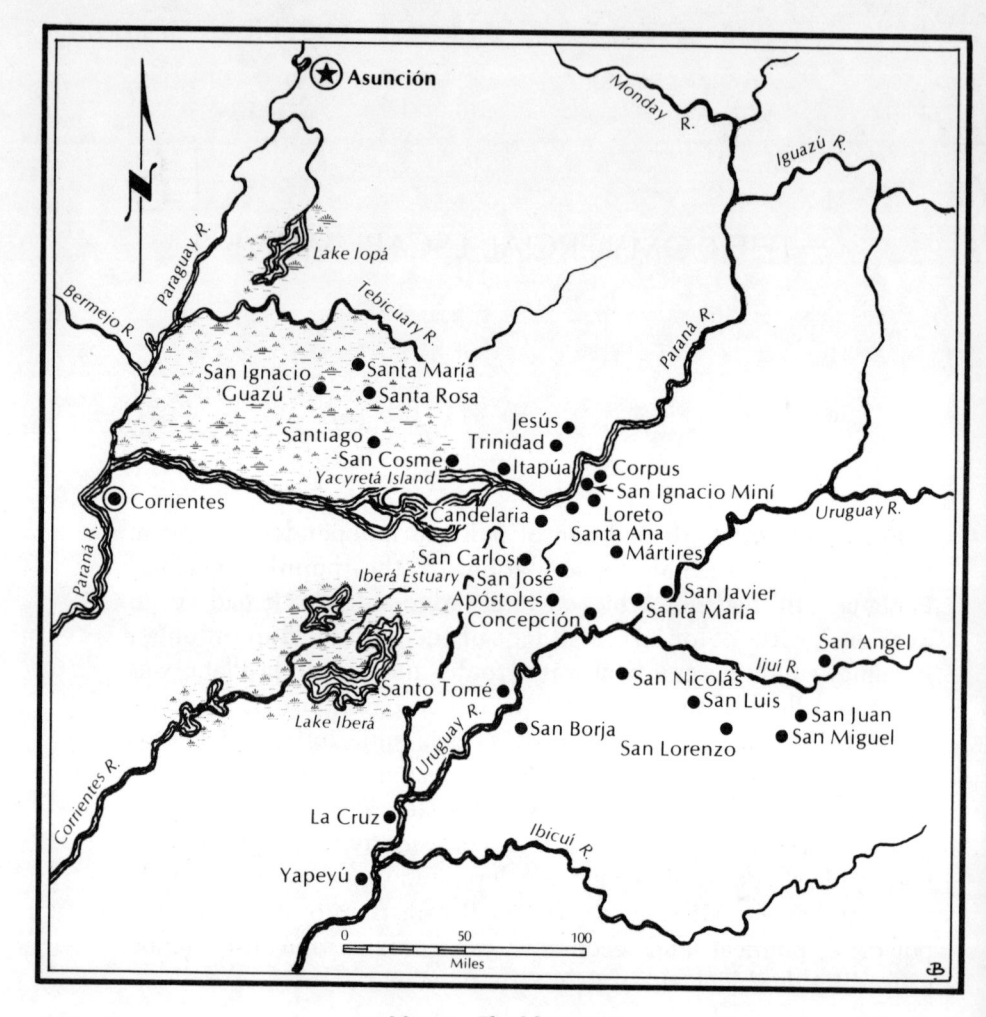

Map 4. The Missions

only upon their common political, economic, and military history, but, even more important, upon their common Guaraní heritage and culture—Francia was unable to control the area. During the early independence period, the Missions district, because of its strategic location, was the home base of José Artigas; it was at the mercy of invading porteño and Brazilian armies, and of marauding bands of armed deserters and local bandits.[2] The combined effects that these groups had upon the district can be gathered from John Parish Robertson's report after a brief visit to the Missions in 1814:

> The population has dwindled down to eight thousand; the public buildings are now not only dilapidated, but ruined; and the scattered Indians are almost as much at a loss for subsistence, as when they wandered in the woods. Their towns have been repeatedly burnt and sacked during the revolution; and their cattle, horses, sheep, and bullocks have all been destroyed or carried away. The natives of Misiones themselves have been pressed into the armies of the revolutionary chiefs, and the wives and children often left to perish.[3]

Only in the early 1820s, with the dissolution of the *federal* forces and the Brazilian occupation of the Banda Oriental, could Paraguay once again begin to exercise its authority in the Missions. The defeat of Artigas in 1820, and the fall of Francisco Ramírez the following year, signaled the end of *federal* domination in the region. On the other hand, the porteños withdrew their attention from the area because their priority was now to mitigate internal conflicts in order to counter the growing Brazilian presence in the Río de la Plata. Brazil, in turn, attempting to ensure Paraguay's continued neutrality, adopted a nonantagonistic policy and restrained its armies from operating in the Missions.

Yet the elimination of these major forces did not completely alleviate the Missions' plight, for bands of armed deserters and wandering remnants of the *federal* armies were still a threat. Some of these interlopers, natives of the area for the most part, although not necessarily former inhabitants of the pueblos, attempted to settle in the most devastated pueblos and support themselves by harvesting yerba from the abandoned yerbales of the former Jesuit communities. They were attracted not only by the prospect of subsistence, but, more important, by the considerable profits to be made selling yerba in the regional markets.

Although the expense and effort required to maintain an administration in the Missions proved prohibitive, Paraguay still considered the entire region sovereign national territory and its rich yerbales a natural resource. Of greatest concern to Francia was the danger that the region—critical to national defense and to any possible overland commerce with Brazil—might fall under the control of the intruders, who, with the profits from their yerba sales, could establish themselves as a powerful force capable of challenging Paraguay's claims to the region and disrupting the free flow of commercial traffic from Itapúa to the Brazilian town of San Borja.

If the Mission could be kept free of outside control, Paraguay would have a secure southern buffer zone. The Argentine blockade, furthermore, necessitated a new supply route for war matériel and other essentials which could not be produced in Paraguay. In 1821, in order to secure this desirable control, Francia began dispatching reconnaissance patrols into the area. The first of these patrols discovered a sizable group of squatters. Francia's concern is evident in his orders to the subdelegate of Itapúa, who had requested instructions concerning the intruders:

> Concerning these Indians, who were followers of Artigas, and who have come from the region of San Xavier to establish themselves with their families and rabble in the ruins of San Ynami, they should be of no worry. What they desire is to be allowed to remain there, harvesting yerba to support themselves, and even enriching themselves with the trade. They already have had the gall to wish to exchange the product of soil which is ours, and which they are stealing; for indeed, all that other bank of the river is well known to be old territory of the Republic.
>
> They want us to tolerate their intrusion; but if we let them stay any longer they may well be able to buy munitions and even firearms with the profits they make out of the commerce in yerba; furthermore, some of the armed deserters of the dispersed troops that roam about on the other side [of the river] might join them on hearing that

with the yerba that is grown there, they can supply themselves with clothes and money. Then it could be really difficult to get rid of them; besides, from the start we should demonstrate [that we have] no intention of allowing a band of bandit Indians to appropriate the territory and yerbales of the Republic. . . .

In the same letter Francia concerned himself with another recent intruder, Aimé Jacques Alexandre Bonpland, who "doubtless has also come and mixed with the Indians under the pretext of finding plants and perhaps medical herbs, but with the chief intention of obtaining a fortune by harvesting yerba there."[4]

Bonpland, the celebrated French naturalist and travel companion of Baron von Humboldt, had arrived in Buenos Aires in 1817 and set to work in the employ of the porteño government as Naturalist of the United Provinces of the Río de la Plata. But in 1820 he expanded his pursuits, and with the financial backing of the French merchants Philibert Voulquin and Dominique Roguin, Bonpland received a concession from the government of Entre Ríos to establish a yerba maté plantation. Failing in this commercial enterprise, Bonpland next enlisted the aid and protection of Francisco Ramírez, which allowed him, in mid 1821, to set up a large operation at the Missions pueblo of Santa Ana. Causing considerable concern to Francia during the most critical period of the Great Conspiracy, the encampment, situated almost directly across the Paraná River from Itapúa, loomed as a potential invasion base for the Ramirista forces. But even the defeat of Ramírez, and the departure of Commander Cáceres, did not discourage the scientific entrepreneur, for he immediately allied himself with the local caudillo Nicolás Aripí, who for the past four years had menaced Paraguay and the Missions.[5]

Needless to say, Bonpland's series of alliances with virtually all of Paraguay's enemies raised grave suspicions concerning the Frenchman—suspicions heightened not only by the French restoration government's promotion of the reconquest of the former Spanish colonies in the name of Ferdinand VII, but also by the clumsy endeavor several years earlier of the French agent, Pierre Saguier, to gain El Dictador's confidence under the pretext of negotiating commercial relations between his nation and blockaded Paraguay.* Although Francia's suspicions that Bonpland's strategic settlement also figured in Ramírez's military plans would not be confirmed until correspondence from the Entrerriano caudillo was found among the Frenchman's personal papers, the fact that Bonpland "proposed to rear extensive plantations of the yerba tree, so as to provide the provinces with the tea, of which such scanty and precarious supplies were now received from Paraguay,"[6] was enough to convince Francia that the enterprise must be halted.[7]

Thus determined to dismantle the operation of Bonpland and his allies, El Dictador ordered the subdelegate of Itapúa to prepare an expedition to cross the Paraná to "round them all up and bring them to this side [of the river] and distribute them among the different towns." In an obvious reference to the anticipated overland trade with Brazil, Francia concluded his order, "The accomplishment of the mission that I order will smooth the way for the things that I am preparing to guarantee the defense of the Republic and its commerce in the future."**

On December 8, 1821, 400 Paraguayan soldiers crossed the Paraná, captured the Frenchman and a number of his employees, brought them back across the river, and dispersed them among a number of southern Paraguayan towns.[8] The capture and detention of the celebrated naturalist created the most notorious scandal of the Francia era. It elicited missives on Bonpland's behalf from, among others, Baron von Humboldt, Simón Bolívar, the Brazilian secretary of state, the English

---

*Chavez, El Supremo Dictador, p. 335. As most European governments did not have diplomatic relations with the Americans, they relied upon information gathered by "confidential emissaries" engaged in a variety of activities, including commerce and scientific pursuit. Because the information provided by these spies was of the most basic nature (such as reports on political and economic developments, the composition and strength of the militaries, and the attitudes and sympathies of the social classes toward the new American governments as well as toward the European governments), it was critical for European policy making.

**ANA, SH, leg. 255, Francia a Ortellado, November 23, 1821. Reflecting the gravity with which Francia viewed such incursions, particularly this settlement, which, under the leadership of Aripí, had actually assumed the title of "a sister province" of Paraguay, he pointedly instructed that they "should be dealt with as enemies" and that "if they do decide to make a defense . . . you shall warn them through some Indian that you take along with you that if they fire a single shot, or offer the slightest resistance, they will all be cut to pieces."

chargé d'affaires in Buenos Aires, and President Antonio José de Sucre of Bolivia.

In mid August 1824, another French naturalist, Jean Etienne Richard de Grandsire, a colleague of Bonpland under commission from the French Scientific Institute, arrived in Itapúa claiming to be on a scientific mission.* In light of the suspicious activities of his fellow countrymen Saguier and Bonpland, Grandsire, unable to produce official documents from the French government, soon found himself expelled from Paraguay.[9]

Although Grandsire failed to secure Bonpland's release, the astute scientist did gain a valuable insight into his colleague's detention. While informing the French minister of Foreign Relations, Baron de Damas, that the French and the English were mistaken to think that Francia refused to release Bonpland because of personal enmity, Grandsire explained that if it were not for Paraguay's precarious situation of being surrounded by turbulent and hostile forces, and its consequent desire to utilize the influence of European powers to strengthen its position, Bonpland would never have been detained for so long. What Francia had hoped for, Grandsire said, was some type of official recognition, even in the form of an official correspondence from a bona fide French authority, such as the consul in Rio de Janeiro, asking for the release of the Frenchman.[10] In any case, the French government completely ignored Grandsire's advice. It never sent any official request for the release of Bonpland, thus adhering to its reactionary policy toward the Latin American republics.

Regardless of the protests and complex machinations surrounding Bonpland's detention,** the French naturalist received remark-

---

*BNRJ, CRB, 1-30, 6, leg. 91, Francia a Ortellado, September 10, 1824. Grandsire claimed that his mission was to locate the juncture of the Amazon and Plata rivers. Francia angrily answered Grandsire's request for a personal interview. While pointing out the commercial advantages that would accrue if France were to adopt as fraternal a stance toward Paraguay as it had toward the United States of America, he denounced the European nation's hostile acts against the new Latin American republics. In particular, he doubted the credibility of the scientists's motives in coming to Paraguay, and speculated that "the emissary, under the pretext of being from the Institute, could be attempting to make observations, gather knowledge or enter into some activitiy harmful to the security and tranquillity of the Republic" (BNRJ, CRB, 1-30, 6, leg. 91, Francia á Ortellado, August 25, 1824).

**If the dictator of Paraguay used Bonpland as a pawn in the international chess game of

ably cordial treatment during his nine years in Paraguay. He was permitted to travel freely and conducted a survey of the natural history of the region surrounding the town of Santa María, where he had been assigned a residence by El Dictador.[11] Within a few years Bonpland had married and become, as he later described himself, "a wealthy farmer," owning 400 cattle plus other livestock and employing forty-five people growing cotton, sugarcane, and yerba. In addition, he ran a small distillery, a carpentry and blacksmith shop, and a four-room hospital which he built along with a small pharmacy, where he prepared medicines for his patients.[12] Everything went so well for Bonpland, in fact, that immediately after his release in early 1831 he informed his friend and financial backer, Dominique Roquin, not only that Francia had accorded him the greatest liberty and that the officials in the area where he lived had treated him with benevolence, but that the rewards of his enterprising activities had enabled him to live in great comfort.[13] Indeed, John Parish Robertson was somewhat dismayed to find that when he interviewed Bonpland the following year in Buenos Aires, the doctor "only regretted, over and over again, that there was no chance of the Dictator's *allowing him to return to Paraguay.*"[14]

---

the era, so, too, did the newly proclaimed dictator of Peru, Simón Bolívar. A personal friend of the French naturalist, Bolívar first wrote Francia in late 1823, threatening to march his army into Paraguay, if necessary, to secure Bonpland's release (Bolívar a Francia, October 22, 1823, as found in Vicente Lecuna, *Cartas del Libertador*, 3:264. For an in-depth analysis of Bolívar's participation in this affair, see Efraím Cardoso, *Bolívar y el Paraguay*). Receiving no reply from Francia, Bolívar let the matter rest until shortly after the final defeat of the royalist forces at the battle of Ayacucho, at which time he again began promoting the idea of invading Paraguay. He ordered his agent in Buenos Aires, Deán Funes, to present an invasion plan to the porteño government (Bolívar a Funes, May 28, 1825, as found in *Revista de la Biblioteca Nacional de Buenos Aires*, 1:164, as cited by Chaves, *El Supremo Dictador*, p. 393). At this same time, Bolívar wrote the chief executive of his native Gran Colombia, Francisco de Paula Santander, extolling the merits of the project (Bolívar a Santander, May 30, 1825, as found in Lecuna, *Cartas*, 4:344). At first undeterred by Buenos Aires's objections to his armed presence (Biblioteca Nacional de Buenos Aires, Colección Funes, 541 and 542, Funes a Bolivar, September 28, 1825, as cited in Chaves, *El Supremo Dicatador*, p. 393), the Libertador pressed for an invitation, insisting that he wanted nothing more from Paraguay "except to return it to the United Provinces" (Alvear y Díaz Vélez al M.R.E. de las Provincias Unidas, October 21, 1825, as found in Gregorio Rodríguez, *Contribución documental . . .*, as cited by Chaves, *El Supremo Dicatador*, p. 394). But faced with resolute porteño opposition, and Santander's protest against aiding Buenos Aires "in its intestinal disorders" (Santander a Bolívar, January 21, 1826, as found in *El Archivo de Santander*, 14: 35, as cited in Chaves, *El Supremo Dictador*, p. 395), Bolívar was forced to abandon his ambitions to intervene in the affairs of the Río de la Plata.

Throughout the early 1820s the Paraguayan government vigorously pursued its policy of depopulating the Missions of all intruders, especially those from nearby Corrientes, who were attracted by the nearby yerbales.[15] While securing the Missions in the hopes of establishing a new trade route with Brazil, Francia also concerned himself with the relentless harassment by Buenos Aires and the other river provinces which had devastated the nation's commerce.

In a mid 1822 letter to the commander of Concepción, Francia reviewed relations with Buenos Aires and analyzed Paraguay's continued dependence:

> Buenos Aires, for its own ends, evil desires, and with reprehensible intentions, has been committing the evil deed and injustice of intercepting the commerce of Paraguay. This it does not only to keep prices for the products of the commerce high and to deprive Paraguay of the liberty to provide itself with arms and munitions, but also to steal and swallow up the whole income of the estates, and products, of Paraguay by means of imposing excessive and intolerable taxes. Buenos Aires has thus been stealing and absorbing the products of Paraguay for eight years, shamelessly failing to comply with the treaties that deal with this specific matter.
>
> Paraguay has thus been put in such a vile and truly infamous dependency that the situation has reached the point where each small town or port on the route to Buenos Aires (having observed Paraguay's submission and shameful resignation), wishes to force all the Paraguayan ships that stop there to pay tribute in products, under the pretext of transit taxes, as if the river were not a free artery of commerce, and as if they were sovereign rulers or masters of Paraguay.

In an analysis remarkably similar to that of Governor Pinedo nearly a half-century before, Francia elaborated on the porteños' intermediary position:

> In Buenos Aires there are always a great number of ships of different nations which come to trade and sell cheaply, and in abundance, not only arms and munitions of every kind, but all kinds of goods and commercial articles. There,

they load even the products of Paraguay, from where they are transported to be sold in the South Sea, in Chile, Lima, and other ports of those seacoasts. It would be much more advantageous and profitable, both for them and for us, if they could come directly to Paraguay to trade; because without the extra charge of the barbarous and exorbitant taxes that one and all are obliged to pay to Buenos Aires, it would be possible to trade far more cheaply and in greater quantitites not only in arms and munitions, which the porteños have prohibited being brought here, but also in all other types of goods and articles of commerce.

El Dictador continued his missive by further explaining the consequences of Paraguayan dependence:

Because of this many have wondered why Paraguay should continue subject to such an ignominious and prejudicial procedure, which is destructive of its prosperity, and which in time may cause its slow ruin by the dependency on the porteños. The porteños keep it in absolute servitude and make it live in tutelage, without allowing it to have more commerce than they wish and when they so desire, prohibiting all communication, correspondence, and commerce with other [nations] after having swallowed up *the product of its labor*.

I am now taking measures and preparing to liberate Paraguay from such burdensome servitude; for otherwise, in spite of its title of sovereign and independent Republic, it will not be considered but as a Republic of Guanás whose subsistance and sweat only serve to fatten others.*

Thus, in spite of its declaration of political independence, the nation had not escaped its colonial heritage of economic dependence. In fact, the reasons behind Francia's future actions are found in his belief that Paraguay could not develop until it freed itself from its traditional dependence: "Not until Paraguay liberates itself from this vile dependency and infamous yoke, freeing its general commerce from such unjust obstacles diametrically

---

*ANA, SH, leg. 235, Francia al Comandante de Concepción, Fernando Acosta, August 12, 1822. Italics added. The Guaná indigenous nation was conquered and held in servitude by the Mbyá indigenous nation, to whom they were forced to pay tribute.

opposed and contrary to its happiness, will it ever be able to prosper, or have the progress that its circumstances and the great production of its soil promise."[16]

After six more months of political and economic pressures caused by the blockade, Francia announced the details of his plan to liberate Paraguay from its dependency:

> The Government has decided to send a force of three thousand soldiers to the other bank [of the river] in order to establish free navigation and eliminate the obstacles, piracy, and exaction imposed upon commercial traffic by the towns of the river coast; for these towns arbitrarily attempt to abrogate for themselves control of the river, to succor and benefit themselves by their atrocious depredations, so as to keep the Republic in the most infamous and servile dependency, and in this manner they prepare its backwardness, diminution, and ruin.[17]

Since the expedition required considerable expenses which could not be covered by the resources of the treasury, the government deposition continued by announcing that the state would have to resort to collecting extraordinary taxes. Reasoning that "although the so-called Europeans residing in this country never perform military service, due to the profession and capacity which their power gives them, they also share in the advantages and profit derived from the defense of commerce and navigation," Francia levied the enormous "contribution" of 150,000 pesos upon the Spaniards of Asunción.*

But before the money could be collected the following year, the turns of international politics had once again removed the necessity of Paraguayan involvement in the Argentine civil wars.[18] Under the shadow of the growing war clouds which would soon burst into the Cisplatine War (1825–28), both Buenos Aires and Brazil attempted to improve relations with Paraguay.

The porteños relaxed the blockade in an effort to secure the necessary Paraguayan ratification of a preliminary peace agree-

---

*BNRJ, CAS, 4-17, 2, leg. 8, Auto Supremo de 20 de enero de 1823. It should be noted that by levying such a large tax, Francia was not only securing finances for the expedition, but was also attacking the economic foundation of the Spaniards' power (see chapter 6).

ment with Spain, and in the hope of fashioning a military alliance with Paraguay before the outbreak of war with Brazil. Yet regardless of the offer to reestablish commercial and diplomatic relations,[19] none of the correspondence sent Francia by the porteño emissary in Corrientes, Juan García de Cossío, over the course of a year's time (November 1823–October 1824) even elicited a reply.[20]

Of far greater importance was the action of Brazil, which in early 1823, only four months after declaring independence from Portugal, reversed its commercial policy toward Paraguay. Freed from European political considerations, and hence no longer required to regard Paraguay as a Spanish possession, Brazil—in an attempt to drive a wedge into the porteño effort to reconstruct the political and economic structure of the old viceroyalty—officially requested commercial relations with Paraguay.[21] Francia, seeking commerce with other independent states, accepted the Brazilian offer. "For our part," he replied, "there is no objection to trading with the Portuguese in the same way that other peoples of America who have constituted themselves into independent states have done, and are doing."[22]

In response to this opportunity to reap lucrative profits, Brazilian merchants, who traditionally had been excluded from direct trade with "the giant province," swarmed into the southeastern border town of Itapúa to participate in the new commerce. In enormous wagons made of durable lapacho hardwood capable of holding well over a ton of yerba or tobacco, the traders carried Paraguayan products across the Missions to the Brazilian town of San Borja. From there, the goods were transported to Pôrto Alegre, which served as the distribution point for Montevideo, Buenos Aires, and Rio de Janeiro. Even the prohibition on exporting precious metals[23] did not dampen the merchants' enthusiasm, for in the five-week period from late July to the beginning of September 1823, Itapúa authorities registered export license requests for more than 21 tons of tobacco and 131 tons of yerba.[24]

Whereas in Paraguay's previous commercial capitalist economy foreign and Paraguayan merchants had dominated trade for their own benefit, Francia now subordinated their interests to those of the local and national governments. Both the municipal and central governments collected a considerable portion of their taxes in yerba and tobacco.* But because the municipalities often were unable to sell all these products locally, and did not have the facilities to transport them to Itapúa for international sale, they frequently incurred losses of revenue.[25] Therefore, Francia required all merchants engaged in the lucrative Asunción-Itapúa traffic to purchase yerba from the city of Asunción, in the amount of at least one-third of their cargo's total value. In this way, since the price of the yerba bought from the government in Asunción was exactly the same as the amount it was sold for in Itapúa,[26] the state "taxed" the Paraguayan merchants in the form of free transportation for government products. In fact, during the years of greatest trade (1834–37), the state even levied an additional "tax" in the form of establishing "contributions" from the merchants engaged in the Asunción-Itapúa commerce.[27]

Moreover, Paraguayan merchants were forced to compete with the Mission pueblos, who could now contract directly with the Brazilian traders.[28] While depopulating the outlying region, in 1823 Francia brought the pueblos north of the Paraná, and those close enough to the river to be protected by Paraguayan military patrols, under the direct supervision of the central government. Limiting the powers of the mayordomos,[29] he reorganized the local economies by employing the Mission inhabitants in the manufacture of cotton cloth, shoe soles, and hats, as well as in the production of tobacco, yerba, and hides, much of which was traded with the Brazilians.[30] By 1828 the Missions' economy—as demonstrated by the remittance of thousands of pesos to the Paraguayan central treasury (see Appendix A)—began to share in the general prosperity of Paraguay. For the first time since the expulsion of the Jesuits sixty years before, the Missions enjoyed an honest administration and actually produced a surplus from their economic activities.

During times of decreased trade, such as the period of the conflict with Corrientes (see below), the government refused licenses to merchants, giving priority to the actual producers of yerba, tobacco, and other exportable products. The state even

---

*Taxes of all types were often paid in kind; indeed, some tax records were actually kept in arrobas of yerba rather than in pesos. For examples, see ANA, NE, leg. 1865, Receptoría de San Estanislao, 1828–32; ANA, NE, leg. 1863, Receptoría de la Villa de San Isidro, 1832 y 1833; and ANA, NE, leg. 1879, Receptoría de la Villa de San Pedro, año 1835.

regulated export licenses among these farmers according to the district in which they lived. Thereby, the government not only ensured that all producers had an equal opportunity to benefit from their labor, but it also prevented flooding the export market by controlling the amount of products that were available for export.[31]

If merchants received the lowest priority under Francia's economic policies, the national government occupied first place. Collecting a considerable portion of its revenue in kind, the state, in addition to its monopoly on hardwoods and shoe soles, possessed large quantities of yerba and tobacco as well as surplus cattle and hides from its estancias. It collected these various products from the state estancias and tax collectors located throughout the republic, and transported them on its own fleet of river craft to the trading centers.[32]

While the state conducted a vigorous trade in metals, textiles, clothing, and other manufactured goods, of greatest importance was the traffic in arms and munitions. As an economic incentive to private merchants who would risk bringing war matériel up the Río de la Plata, Francia in 1814 had declared arms and munitions free of import duties.[33] Shortly thereafter he even authorized such merchants to export precious metals or other highly valued products without paying sales or export taxes.[34] The monopoly on the hardwood trade provided the state with its most powerful economic inducement. Because of the relatively small bulk and high resale value of these hardwoods, traders stood to gain enormous profits by selling them in Buenos Aires, where they were prized for the manufacture of fine furniture. Consequently, the government only granted hardwood export licenses in exchange for arms and munitions. By applying these economic incentives in varying combinations—depending upon the quality of the war matériel, merchants were exempted from specific taxes and granted a percentage of their exports in hardwoods—Paraguay managed to acquire considerable amounts of armaments, in spite of the Spanish, *federal*, and porteño blockades. For example, in 1818 alone the state was able to purchase imported articles of war worth nearly 16,000 pesos.*

During the mid 1820s much war matériel continued to make

---

*ANA, NE, leg. 1230, Cuenta General . . . para el año de 1818, entry for December 31. Demonstrating Francia's complex policy of economic incentives, among the arms imported

its way up the Río de la Plata in spite of the harassment of the lower river provinces. During this period trading vessels were occasionally permitted to come directly to Asunción,[35] but in order to maintain stringent national security and to exercise tighter control over commerce, Francia gradually shifted the terminal port of entry from the capital to the small southwestern border town of Pilar.[36] But by the late 1820s most military supplies, as well as all other imports, unquestionably came by way of Itapúa and the overland Brazilian trade route. Although incomplete documentation makes it difficult to determine precisely the extent of the state arms trade—which continued throughout Francia's administration*—its volume can be gauged by the purchase of 1,000 high-quality rifles and another 1,000 high-quality sabers in mid 1832.[37]

The commonly accepted idea of Paraguayan autarky during the

---

during this year were twenty high-quality rifles at 12.5 pesos each (the merchant was permitted to export the full 250 pesos in hardwoods without paying any import, export, or sales taxes); 1,062 pounds of high-grade gunpowder (the merchant was permitted to export its full 265-peso value in hardwoods while enjoying full tax exemption); 149 sabers at a little over 10 pesos each (the merchant was permitted to export one-third of their 1,508-peso value in hardwoods without paying any taxes); 300 rifles at 10.5 pesos each (the merchant was permitted to export one-third of their 3,150-peso value in hardwoods without paying import or sales taxes, but was required to pay the full export tax on the hardwoods); 300 poor-quality rifles at approximately 6.66 pesos each (the merchant was permitted to export one-third of their 2,000-peso value in hardwoods, but obtained no tax exemption whatsoever); 95 inferior sabers at 7 pesos each (although the merchant was permitted to import the sabers free of sales or import taxes, due to their poor quality he was not granted a license to export any hardwoods and was required to pay the export tax on the items he did export); and 17 inferior-quality cannons at 100 pesos each (as these weapons were of such low quality, the merchant was granted neither a license to export any hardwoods nor any tax exemptions). The poor quality of these cannons elicited a policy statement which noted that "in the future the exportation of wood will only be permitted by those who bring good and serviceable arms" (ANA, NE, leg. 1224, Cuenta general . . . año 1818 . . . enero hasta noviembre . . . quotation taken from the January 20 entry).

*Beginning in the early 1830s, the international merchants placed such a high demand upon Paraguayan shoe soles (due to their compact size, fine quality, and high resale value) that the state rationed the export of this product much as it did with hardwoods. For an example of such dealings, see ANA, NE, leg. 1273, El Delegado de Itapúa á Francia, November 16, 1831. For other examples of the Itapúa arms traffic, see ANA, SH, leg. 240, Francia al Comandante de Itapúa, June 24, 1829; ANA, SH, leg. 242, Francia al Delegado de Itapúa, February 27, 1833; ANA, SH, leg. 242, Francia al Delegado de Itapúa, September 3, November 28, and December 27, 1834; ANA, SH, leg. 377, Roxas a Francia, Feburary 4, 1837; ANA, NE, leg. 1893, Roxas a Francia, May 29, 1837; and ANA, SH, leg. 244, Francia a Roxas, May 25, 1840.

last half of Francia's rule has no basis in fact. An examination of the sales tax receipts for Pilar and Itapúa show continuing commerce through both of these ports during this entire period (see Appendixes D and E). As table 3 demonstrates, a steady, if modest, trade continued through the river port of Pilar during the entire last decade of Francia's tenure. But it was the Itapúa trade that proved to be Paraguay's major source of international commerce, reaching its peak in 1835, when exports amounted to, in monetary value, 35 percent of total Paraguayan exports during the record year of 1816; when private-sector Pilar commerce is added, total private-sector Paraguayan exports reached 38 percent of 1816 exports.

In addition to the exports from the private sector of the economy, an accurate estimate of total Paraguayan exports during these years must include the considerable state trade. Just as with the state arms commerce, incomplete documentation makes it impossible to determine the precise volume. But its magnitude can be appreciated by the fact that of the Itapúa commerce in 1837, state trade accounted for at least 35 percent of total exports, and the following year, 1838, for a remarkable 65 percent of all exports (see table 3, and Appendixes C and F). Even though these years were exceptional (see chap. 9), a conservative estimate based upon the available documentation establishes the state as the nation's largest exporter, with an average annual volume of 15–20 percent of total national exports. When state exports, approximated at 17.5 percent, are added to the private sector exports, total Paraguayan exports for 1835 were at least 46 percent of the nation's "most prosperous" year, 1816.

Aside from being the single most important exporter, the government was also the nation's principal importer. It not only utilized imported articles in the state industries and to equip the armed forces, it also sold many of them to the public through the state store in Asunción. All imports came under state regulation, from necessities such as ponchos[38] to luxury items such as snuff.[39] Assuming the function of consumer advocate, Francia forbade the importation of products of inferior quality.[40] Even consumer preferences became a consideration, as exemplified by El Dictador's order to the delegate of Itapúa to notify the merchants not to bring any more green or yellow ribbons as "the [state] storekeeper here tells me that these two colors are not

Table 3. Paraguayan Exports, 1826–39
(in Pesos)

	1826	1829	1832	1835	1837	1838	1839
Private Sector Exports, Itapúa[a]	39,038	48,353	86,830	135,546	83,095	35,810	17,370
Private Sector Exports, Pilar[b]	NA	16,551	7,051	14,367	20,840	12,253	8,995
Total Private Sector Exports		64,904	93,881	149,913	103,935	48,063	26,365
State Exports, Itapúa		10,256[c]	18,417[c]	28,749[c]	45,249[d]	66,624[d]	
State Exports, Pilar		3,510[c]	1,496[c]	3,047[c]	11,347[e]	22,791[f]	
Total State Exports		13,766	19,913	31,796	56,596	89,415	
Total Paraguayan Exports		78,670	113,794	181,709	160,531	137,478	

a. See Appendix E for archival references
b. See Appendix D for achival references
c. Approximated as 17.5 percent of private sector exports
d. See Appendix F for archival references
e. Approximated as 35 percent of private sector exports
f. Approximated as 65 percent of private sector exports

being purchased."[41] Indeed, state imports included not only essentials such as copper, iron, steel, cauldrons, knives, hatchets, scissors, locks, and nails, but also a variety of nonessential items such as books, hats, chocolate, violin strings, playing cards, and even "513 little wooden dolls, all painted in colors, to be children's toys, and composed of figures of men and women, and various little animals such as horses, tigers, [and] birds. . . ."[42]

Commensurate with the importance of the Brazilian trade, however, were the problems accompanying it. At first both Paraguay and Brazil attempted to maintain cordial relations. While continuing to expel Correntine intruders from the Missions, Francia modified his orders concerning Brazilian interlopers found harvesting yerba, who were simply to be escorted, with their possessions and a warning not to return, to the other side of the Uruguay River.[43] Brazil, for its part, in 1824, seeking to guarantee Paraguayan neutrality in the imminent Cisplatine War with Argentina, assigned a commercial consul to reside in Asunción. Upon the arrival of Antônio Manuel Correia da Câmara in mid 1825, Francia pressed for an end to the continuing Portuguese-indigenous raids on the northern frontier.

Evidently in compliance with his instructions "to separate the relations that exist between that government [of Paraguay] and that of Buenos Aires,"[44] Correia da Câmara recognized the legitimacy of the Paraguayan grievances. Before leaving for consultation with his superiors in Rio de Janeiro early the following year, the Brazilian consul assured the Paraguayan government that the violations would be halted, but nothing had been done to alleviate the situation by the time of his return in 1827. Consequently, Francia refused to permit Correia da Câmara to resume residence in the capital, restricting him to Itapúa. The Brazilian remained there until mid 1829, when he finally abandoned the country in frustration.[45]

Throughout the following decade, despite the continued and expanding commerce in the south, the imperial government did nothing to alleviate tensions in the north. Even so, both nations recognized the reciprocal advantages of avoiding further friction, and therefore throughout the 1830s the Brazilian empire not only scrupulously refrained from any hostile activites in the Missions, but actively cooperated with the Paraguayan authorities in their efforts to keep the trade route open.

While the government took a lenient attitude toward Brazilians found in the Missions district, it maintained an inflexible severity with all other activity there that might interfere with Paraguay's commercial lifeline. With the help of Paraguay's military patrols, and through information provided by Brazilian merchants crossing the region, Francia remained informed of activities in the Missions.

Notified that Buenos Aires had sold the territory between the Aguapey and Uruguay rivers to an English company that intended to establish a colony of settlers,[46] El Dictador took immediate action. In reply to the delegate of Itapúa's confusion over the significance of the news, Francia analyzed the situation:

> The lands between the Aguapey and the Uruguay belong to Paraguay and not to Buenos Aires, which for the past twenty years has not even thought about them. It now seems obvious that Buenos Aires is scheming to appropriate the lands and feign their sale to these Englishmen only to impede and cut the Brazilian commerce with Paraguay, which has hurt them as much as they envy it.[47]

Francia ordered the delegate to inform the Brazilian merchants—who would in turn pass the information along to the commander of the Brazilian town of San Borja and ultimately to the English company itself—that Paraguay would never consent to any such agreement. He warned the English to abandon their project "because according to the declarations and instructions of their own government, they should not come to America to enter into, or take part in, the fights or disputes of one country with another, and least of all in such bad faith as to ally with Buenos Aires to obstruct and cut the commerce between Brazil and Paraguay."[48] Leaving no doubt as to Paraguay's commitment to keep the Missions free of obstacles, Francia asked the merchants the following week to let it be known in Buenos Aires that "the Paraguayans, knowing that the intruders want to eliminate their commerce, are ready to destroy and lay waste to any settlement in those places."[49]

Even though Paraguayan threats were sufficient to discourage the English company from attempting to establish its colony, they proved less impelling to other outsiders than the lure of the Missions' wealth. During the late 1820s the region had grown so peaceful that Brazilian merchants no longer found it necessary to carry arms while making the journey from San Borja to Itapúa, but by 1830 they were demanding that Paraguay provide an armed escort through the increasingly troublesome pueblos.[50] With the peace agreements accompanying the formal end of the Cisplatine War, the regional economy again began to function; not only were trade routes reestablished between the warring neighbors, but the disengaged human and capital resources could now be utilized to produce the many goods that Platine consumers had so long been denied. Once again the wealth of the Missions provided the motivation for yet another conflict in the region's tumultuous history, for during the early 1830s, increasing numbers of adventurous Correntinos began to infiltrate the region in order to harvest clandestinely the valuable yerba, so highly prized on the regional market.

By entering the Missions after making a wide swing south of the Uruguay River the bands of yerba thieves easily avoided the scrutiny of Paraguayan fortifications such as the Campamento de Salto and the Tranquero de Loreto, which Francia finally abandoned as useless.[51] Instead of maintaining these obsolete forts, by mid 1832 El Dictador had decided upon a system of periodic expeditions to contain the interlopers, who, among other disruptive activities, took to destroying the merchants' stopping places and stealing the provisions which they left behind for their return journey.[52] Furthermore, not only were the intruders menacing the entire region—by disrupting commercial traffic and endangering the only reliable communications link with the world east of the Uruguay River—but Correntine merchants had recently appeared in San Borja selling large amounts of Mission yerba.[53]

As it had been years since Paraguayan patrols had policed some of the distant pueblos, Francia instructed the first expedition to take no Correntine prisoners, but rather to permit the intruders to leave with their possessions and to warn them that they would be apprehended if discovered again.[54] Not all of the yerba raiders, however, were so easily persuaded to abandon their lucrative enterprise, and the subsequent apprehension of several Correntinos in a remote corner of the Missions provided the incident which shattered more than a decade of cordial relations between Paraguay and Corrientes.

The threat of Brazilian intervention was finally put to rest by the empire's defeat in the Cisplatine War (1828). With the United Provinces under the firm control of the *federal* administration of Juan Manuel de Rosas, the governor of Corrientes seized the opportunity to challenge Paraguay's control of the Missions. Perhaps the most important reason behind Brigadier General Pedro Ferré's decision, as the French consul in Buenos Aires, Aimé Roger, later recalled, was the fact that increasing quantities of Paraguayan tobacco and yerba—in direct competition with the same products from his own province—had begun arriving in the markets of Montevideo and Buenos Aires.[55] In any event, after dispatching a patrol to investigate the situation, Ferré sent a letter to the Paraguayan government declaring that the area in which the prisoners were taken belonged to Corrientes.[56]

Francia replied by reiterating Paraguayan claims to the entire Missions territory, offering to negotiate with Corrientes the cession of the disputed area which included the two outlying pueblos of La Cruz and Yapeyu. But he left no doubt that Ferré was expected "not to permit his citizens to come to steal yerba, hunt, or do other things in the territories belonging to Paraguay, keeping in mind that Paraguay will not tolerate such agitations and usurpations."[57] Denouncing Francia's position as an act of aggression, Governor Ferré declared war on Paraguay.[58]

The ensuing conflict never assumed the dimensions characteristic of Platine military history. The "Paraguayan-Correntine War" consisted primarily of menacing troop movements, punctuated by occasional skirmishes; there was never a full-scale battle. Initiating hostilities, Corrientes occupied the abandoned Paraguayan fortifications and, to Francia's irate astonishment, the Missions' capital of Candelaria, from which the commander of Itapúa withdrew his small detachment at the first sight of Correntine troops.[59] Ferré, recognizing that his forces lacked the strength to invade the Paraguayan heartland, called for the assistance of the littoral provinces in accordance with the mutual aid pact of January 4, 1831.[60] But to the governor's chagrin, despite the enthusiastic rhetoric spewing from the sister provinces,[61] Corrientes received no material support from its *federal* allies.

Regardless of the relative weakness of the Correntine forces stationed in the Missions, Paraguayan troops did not immediately attempt to retake the area. Lacking combat experience and effective leadership, thoughout 1833 the Paraguayan army limited its activities to harassing the enemy through meticulously planned—yet often disastrous—raids and ambushes.[62] But in December 1833, after tolerating the disruption of the Itapúa trade for more than a year,[63] Paraguayan forces reoccupied Candelaria and provided military escorts for the merchant caravans crossing the Missions.[64]

Once again attempting to invoke the mutual aid pact, Ferré issued a desperate call for support while, in deference to the superior forces, he avoided engaging the Paraguayan army.[65] The Paraguayan offensive sent shock waves throughout Argentina, causing such alarm that a number of provinces immediately began military preparations. Buenos Aires actually outfitted an entire naval squadron in anticipation of the momentous conflict with the fabled Paraguayan army.[66]

It was in just such a situation as this that Francia's secrecy about, and public exaggeration of, Paraguay's military establishment proved useful. During this period the regular army consisted of no more than fifteen hundred regular soldiers, augmented by perhaps another five thousand reserve militia (see fig. 4, above). Yet the French consul in Buenos Aires, in an unwitting testimony to the effectiveness of El Dictador's strategy, informed the home office that the Argentines believed that "Francia constantly maintains more or less 15,000 regular troops which, if necessary, can be augmented by an equal number in a very short time." Cautioning that these estimates were "perhaps exaggerated by fear," Roger further noted, "It is said that the militias are organized in such a form that they can mobilize another 40,000 men at a moment's notice."[67]

To the general relief of the United Provinces, Francia, after establishing two more forts at the strategic pueblos of San Carlos and Santo Tomás, assumed a defensive posture, maintaining his troops in their positions.[68] With this confirmation that the Paraguayan offensive presented no tangible threat, but was intended only to reopen its trade route, Corrientes's sister provinces once again refused to offer material support. Furthermore, the vitriolic criticism in the porteño press of Corrientes's previously cordial relations with Paraguay,[69] and the opposition within his own army to full-fledged war,[70] forced Ferré to abandon his ambitions and accept Paraguayan hegemony in the Missions. By mid 1834 all Correntine troops had left the area, thus permitting the resumption of commercial traffic,[71] which continued unhampered for the remainder of Francia's tenure.

As long as the vital overland commercial artery remained open, it served as an escape valve for the powerful political and economic pressures that might otherwise have driven even Paraguay to abandon its foreign policy of neutrality. But with its commercial lifeline once again secured, the nation harbored no ambitions of becoming involved in Platine affairs. As the porteño press succinctly put it, "Paraguay did not want peace, nor war, with anyone."[72]

9 | THE ECONOMICS OF INDEPENDENCE

At the same time that Francia was developing the new overland trade with Brazil, he continued attempts to secure the free navigation of the Platine river system. These unsuccessful efforts of the mid 1820s make the positions of England, Buenos Aires, and Paraguay strikingly clear.

In 1824 the newly appointed British consul in Buenos Aires, Woodbine Parish, wrote to Francia. Explaining that his function was to promote better relations with all peoples in the old viceroyalty, Parish offered to enter into negotiations which would lead to "reciprocal and uniform sentiments of recognition and friendship" between his nation and the blockaded Paraguay. After planting this hint of recognition of Paraguayan independence,* which, if realized, would mean that English warships would escort commercial vessels up the hazardous Río de la Plata if necessary, Parish formally requested that the British subjects being held in Paraguay be permitted to leave with their property.[1]

The Paraguayan government replied by expressing its desire to "maintain a sincere friendship, harmony, and mutual correspondence between the generous English nation and the Paraguayan state." After reiterating the principle of free navigation as the prerequisite for trade, Francia suggested that if "for the benefit of English merchants, who in such circumstances

---

*It should be noted that during the entire Francia era, Paraguayan independence was not formally recognized by any nation. The first recognition of Paraguay as a sovereign nation came from Brazil on September 14, 1844.

could engage in extensive commerce, the British crown wants to send a commercial consul to protect their interests in Paraguay, the government will admit him with pleasure and satisfaction." El Dictador apologized for the "suspension" of the English subjects, explaining that such extraordinary measures were made necessary by the crisis situation into which Paraguay had been thrown by the blockade of the river. In any case, Francia concluded, the government had already decided to release the Englishmen, with their property, and in fact his letter was being carried by one of them in his own vessel.[2]

At this same time, the Paraguayan government released not only the English subjects, but also several French and Italians, totaling about forty people, all of whom—with the exception of Rengger, Longchamps, and an English physician—were merchants.[3] His immediate objective accomplished, the astute British consul, in a classic example of nineteenth-century English machinations in Latin America, proceeded with his attempt to "open Paraguay for free trade." Emphasizing that future correspondence would result in reciprocal advantage by creating commercial relations, Parish assured Francia that he would recommend to the crown that a commercial consul be named to reside in Asunción.[4]

Regardless of the British consul's apparent sincerity, the qualifying conditions he imposed made it clear that the "champion of free navigation" was actually in league with the porteño *unitarios*. English diplomacy at this time had no interest in provincial or regional self-determination; rather, it centered upon forming alliances with the South American metropolises based upon their mutual interest in reconstructing the administrative units of the old viceroyalties into politically and economically unified neocolonial nations. Realizing that a stable political economy was essential in a country that was to supply primary materials to industry and to serve as a sustained market for manufactured goods, England saw the metropolitan centers as the only force capable of stabilizing the political chaos and economic dislocations of the American economies. In turn, through their monopoly on international trade, the metropolises were able to maintain their domination of the provincial economies, which thus remained dependent upon the commercial centers to market their exports and purchase their imports.

Consequently, in keeping with England's diplomatic design, the British consul now pressured Paraguay to abandon its independent course. Including a copy of the commercial treaty recently signed with the United Provinces, Parish suggested that a similar arrangement could be reached with Paraguay if only it would agree to one crucial condition:

> But in order to proceed with the establishment of such relations, it is necessary that he who suscribes to this plan be aware that the geographical location of Paraguay makes it absolutely essential that first of all a preliminary accord be reached between the government of said State and that of the United Provinces of the Río de la Plata, through whose territories must pass all foreign commerce.[5]

In other words, the Englishman wanted Paraguay to sacrifice its hard-won independence for the sake of British trade.* Francia did not even consider the British proposition. Indeed, it was precisely such deviousness—on the part of not only the Spanish and French, in their attempts to resubjugate the Americans, but also the English, who sought to establish their preeminence in the emerging neocolonial order—that led Francia to distrust all Europeans; as he later counseled the delegate of Itapúa: "You should never believe the Europeans, nor trust in them, whichever nation they are from."[6]

To understand Francia's nationalistic philosophy, it is essential to review several key aspects of his economic policy. Most important, El Dictador did not consider foreign trade to be simply the domain of the owners of the means of production and commerce. Consequently, commerce—no longer conducted by, and for, the oligarchy—was regulated by the state to benefit the entire nation, that is, the Paraguayan people.

As the first economic expression of this revolutionary priority, the government prohibited the export of gold and silver specie to meet Paraguay's habitually unfavorable balance of trade pay-

---

*Although England was a major force in the June 1815 Congress of Vienna, which bound its members to the principle that "the navigation of rivers is totally free and commerce shall not be obstructed on them," Britain selectively employed, or refused to employ, its naval might to enforce the agreement according to its own diplomatic design.

ments. Under the traditional dependent trade, not only did commerce suffer from the heavy taxation of the lower river provinces—which resulted in depressing the prices of exports while inflating the cost of imports—but, because the constant siphoning off of specie left Paraguay with a chronic shortage of capital, dependency was increased by the related need of Paraguayan merchants to rely upon the porteño credit merchants. Consequently, as Francia decreed shortly after being elected dictator in 1814, and reiterated numerous times during the years of his tenure, the export of precious metals was absolutely forbidden.[7]

Francia clearly recognized that "there is no doubt that the wealth of nations is a nerve and a basis of their defense; and therefore all nations wish to multiply the sources of their riches and the channels which transport them, believing that the lack of such auxiliary facilities can bring about their ruin and dissolution." He insisted, however, that

> The export of precious metals is not essential to maintain external commerce if the exportable fruits and products that come from the different regions of the Republic are always greater than the imports that they consume. Consequently, the exportation of specie is therefore certainly useless, disadvantageous, and prejudicial because, as it does not favor an equal balance of trade, it would debilitate the State by diminishing its resources.[8]

In later years Francia moved to eliminate private, as well as public, foreign debt by actually forbidding Paraguayan merchants to contract foreign debts in the course of their business.[9] In cases where such indebtedness was incurred, the government not only prohibited the violator from discharging the debt, but also levied a fine of an equal amount to be paid to the state treasury.[10]

In conjunction with the above policies, the state regulated external commerce by initiating a stringently enforced system of trade licenses which required all Paraguayans to secure government authorization to export local products, upon which the state set a minimum price.[11] Through these and other regulations, the government established a planned economy, thereby providing Paraguay with the means of breaking its traditional economic dependence and maintaining an equitable balance of trade.

While still enjoying the advantages of their dominant position, members of the oligarchy had found it advantageous to circumvent such regulations;[12] for Paraguay's traditional monocultural economy, through its superexploitation of the nation's labor force, had constituted the economic foundation of their privileged, although dependent, status. By the mid 1820s, however, with the elimination of the elite as the dominant economic, political, and social force, the traditional dependent commerce was no longer acceptable; indeed, it was intolerable.

Within the context of these nationalist priorities, the unexpected arrival at Pilar of a porteño trading vessel several months after the frustrating events with the British consul was viewed with deep suspicion. As most of the great quantities of goods that the ship carried were destined for consignment and did not have the proper Paraguayan trade licenses, it appeared that the entire matter might be an attempt to subvert Paraguay's commercial policies. Fearing that the acceptance of the goods would "give grounds to those who wish to imply that our government is inconsistent," Francia ordered the schooner to return downstream without unloading its cargo.[13] He suspected that the considerable quantity of unlicensed goods belonged to the English, who, with the porteños, planned to enmesh the nation in commercial conflicts. El Dictador believed that in reality the incident was a porteño machination "to keep Paraguay in dependency, and to see if finally they can obtain its submission."[14]

Once again reiterating the demand for free navigation, Francia underscored his commitment to his nation's economic independence in his message to the porteño merchants:

> When the flag of the Republic is allowed free navigation to the sea, all that come to trade will be admitted, and then commerce will be organized as is most suitable and in a manner that is beneficial to the Paraguayans, and not only as it has been until now, for the exploitation and profit of the foreigners.[15]

It is this critical distinction between free navigation and the organization of Paraguayan commerce in a manner beneficial to Paraguay which is the key to understanding the nation's economy. Francia did not equate the concepts of free navigation and free trade. While consistently demanding the right of free navigation for Paraguayan vessels—a central aspect of breaking its dependency upon foreign transportation of its exports and imports—El Dictador never confused this concept with that of free trade. In the thousands of documents written by Francia reviewed in the preparation of this work, there is not a single defense of free trade.

Francia consistently maintained that independent "nations only have trade with whom they want, when and how they want, and when it accommodates them, stopping when they find it convenient for whatever reason." Indeed, upon learning that the commander of Concepción had informed the Brazilians that the object of the American "*causa común*" was unrestrained commercial trade, Francia severely admonished him. In the words of El Dictador: "If anyone makes a similar response, and knows all of the meaning and significance that can be given to such an expression, without doubt he has done so in profound and extreme malice; and if not, it is necessary to say that he is an idiot, that without knowing what this means he has impertinently rattled off an absurdity."[16]

Exemplifying the priorities and functioning of Paraguayan commerce is a transaction conducted with a female Spanish merchant who arrived at Pilar in late 1825 with a large shipment of imports which she wished to trade for yerba.* Following standard procedure, the delegate of Pilar sent a detailed report to Francia listing the quantities and quality of the merchandise, the price that the Andulusa claimed to have paid for them in Buenos Aires, and her declaration that she was prepared to accept the yerba at whatever price El Dictador assigned.[17] Francia reviewed the prices of the imports, and even though they were greatly inflated, according to the published prices found in the

---

*Even though most of the Pilar commerce was conducted with the neighboring province of Corrientes, other merchants who conformed to Paraguayan trade regulations were permitted to engage in commmercial activities. For examples of trade with Corrientes in 1826, see ANA, LC, Vol. 24, entry for August 3; ANA, LC, Vol. 26, entries for February 23 and March 21; ANA, SH, leg. 393, Gill a Francia, February 8 and September 10; and ANA, NE, leg. 1846, Libro Manuel de la Tesorería de Guerra . . . 1826, entries for April 22 and December 5. For examples of trade with several porteño merchants in 1826, see ANA, LC, Vol. 24, both entries for August 30. Also see ANA, NE, leg. 2568, Gill á Francia, June 29, 1827, for details of a commercial transaction with a French merchant in Pilar.

porteño gazettes that he regularly received, he agreed to a transaction. Authorizing the delegate to exchange specified amounts of state yerba for each of her products, Francia noted the exaggerated prices, but, as he explained, *"this does not matter, because the contract that is offered her is not based upon the concept of fixed values."*[18] And by "fixed values" Francia meant the price that items would fetch on the open market.

In organizing Paraguayan international commerce, Francia rejected the classic liberal concept of the marketplace, where the law of supply and demand determines the prices of commodities. Indeed, the liberal capitalist economic institution of "free trade" served as the basis of nineteenth-century economic imperialism. Although generally viewed as progressive by the oligarchs of the former colonies, who had suffered the economic restrictions of Spanish and Portuguese imperialism, such trade was inherently disadvantageous to the new Latin American nations. The world metropolises, due to their industrial and technological advantages, could "naturally" set the prices of their manufactured goods low enough to undersell local production—thereby prohibiting the development of industry in the neocolonies—yet high enough so that client nations chronically incurred a negative balance of trade payment. Consequently, the deficit had to be discharged by transferring specie and capital; and by this constant siphoning off of accumulated wealth, the metropolises prospered while the Latin American nations found themselves without the necessary capital to develop their economies.

Clearly, economic imperialism could only function with the cooperation of the local oligarchy. The elite, owning the means of production, were able to force the superexploitation of the nation's workers in order to produce sufficient primary products—at an "acceptable" price—to meet the negative balance of payments which, together with the expenses of their consumption of luxury imports, grew to staggering sums. In short, the foreign imperialists and the local oligarchies collaborated to benefit themselves at the expense of the nation, for although both the imperialists and the oligarchies reaped profits and luxuries, this wealth was the product of the labor of the local population.

José Antonio Vázquez captured the fundamental nature of nineteenth-century economic liberalism when he observed, "Liberalism in Europe, in the mouth of Victor Hugo, is

Liberalism. Liberalism in the former Spanish colonies, in the mouth of Rivadavia or Mitre, is only colonialism."[19]

With the elimination of the oligarchy as the dominant national force, Francia was able to control Paraguay's commerce; he refused to base international commerce on open market prices, or in his own words, "upon the concept of fixed values." Although the price of imports certainly was a contributing factor, the classic capitalist practice of exchanging commodities on the basis of their prices exercised only minimal influence, for Francia did not permit the terms of Paraguayan trade to be determined by regional or world market prices. Instead, he organized the exchange of the native products of Paraguay—defined explicitly by El Dictador as "the product of its labor[20]—upon their actual cost of production, or *labor value*, in relation to the utility, or *use value*, of the imports.

In the case of state trade, the mechanism for accomplishing this was relatively simple. El Dictador set by fiat the amounts of each native product that would be exchanged for specified amounts of imports after evaluating their usefulness.* For all remaining trade the government assured an equitable exchange by adjusting the price of exports to the price of imports.

The application of this economic principle is best illustrated in the price differentials found in Itapúa and Pilar. As overland transportation was considerably more expensive and time consuming than river traffic, the price of imports at Itapúa was accordingly greater than in Pilar. Consequently, rather than basing the Itapúa commerce upon the fixed prices of Paraguayan exports—which, considering the high cost of Itapúa imports, would have meant accepting significantly fewer imports or incurring a deficit in the balance of trade—Francia gradually raised the price of exports to compensate for the expensive imports. In 1823 the prices of Paraguay's principal exports—yerba and tobacco—were 80 and 200 pesos a ton respectively, both in Pilar and Itapúa. While the price of these products in Pilar did not increase throughout the years of Francia's tenure, by 1826 the government had raised them to 120 and 320 pesos respectively

---

*Indeed, as particular products were no longer necessary due to the development of the Paraguayan economy, which came to produce many traditionally imported items, Francia simply prohibited their further importation. See ANA, SH, leg. 394, Castro á Francia, February 27, 1830, for such a prohibition on flour, oil, and olives.

in Itapúa, and to 180 and 400 pesos respectively by 1829—an increase of 125 percent in the price of yerba and 100 percent in the price of tobacco at Itapúa over the cost of these same products being sold in Pilar at the same time (see Appendixes D and E). Additionally, Francia forced the Brazilian merchants to accept both old and fresh yerba, and tobacco, without allowing any price distinction,[21] while the merchants trading at Pilar were subjected to such regulations only in the case of tobacco, being permitted to purchase the yerba *fuerte* at a mere 40 pesos a ton (see Appendix D).

Thus, by basing commerce not on open market prices but rather upon the utility of imports in relation to the amount of labor required to produce the exports, Paraguay acquired its imports in exchange for its exports without incurring a deficit in the balance of trade. Furthermore, by thus organizing commerce "in a manner beneficial to the Paraguayans," the nation necessarily did not provide an "open" market where the industrialized European countries could sell their products without limit as to price or utility. It is only in this sense that Paraguay was "closed" to international commerce.

While the idea of Paraguayan autarky is historically incorrect, it is true that the nation's state-controlled economy excluded the establishment of the classic capitalist "free market." Francia's economic nationalism not only led Paraguay out of the dependent status of formal Spanish colonialism, but, by rejecting the structurally inequitable concept of free trade, it prevented capitalist penetration of the economy, thereby denying the new imperialists the opportunity to reduce Paraguay to the status of a dependent neocolony. Therefore, it is understandable that Paraguay, unique in its successful opposition to the emerging neocolonial order, became the object not only of porteño aggression, but also of English ambition.

With the end of the Cisplatine War (1825–28), renewed agitation for war against Paraguay swept Buenos Aires. Although partially motivated by internal political considerations,* the invasion

---

*As Julio César Chaves pointed out (*El Supremo Dictador*, p. 406), the governor of Buenos Aires, Colonel Manuel Dorrego, proposed to use the victorious army of Fructuoso Rivera, which had just completed the Missions campaign against Brazil, to invade Paraguay, for even if it were to be unsuccessful in resubjugating the republic, Rivera would still be prevented from using his army to intervene in Uruguay or Buenos Aires.

would, as the British consul informed the Foreign Office, serve the double purpose of "rich Plunder," and, more important as far as Woodbine Parish was concerned, of "assuring once more an intercourse with that rich Country and the rest of the World."[22] Of course, the British consul was interested in such intercourse not in the abstract but because his nation planned to dominate the potentially enormous markets of Paraguay; Mr. Hope, an English agent in Corrientes, had informed him in a confidential report the previous year, "I suppose, was the trade open, about one Million and a half dollars [i.e., pesos] worth chiefly of British Manufactures might be annually introduced there."[23]

It is no accident, then, that the intense propaganda campaign conducted in the porteño press was led by the influential *British Packet and Argentine News*,[24] which enthusiastically supported the "expedition to liberate Paraguay." Emphasizing the commercial opportunities to be gained from the new markets that would be "opened," the paper's October 1, 1828, editorial pressed for the attack against Paraguay: "We think that those who reflect upon these advantages, will agree that the attempt to open the trade of Paraguay is worth a few sacrifices."[25]

In recognition of the scope of such an invasion, Francia mobilized the nation's armed forces to defend the republic against both Buenos Aires and Brazil.[26] Regardless of the recent war between the regional superpowers, El Dictador harbored no illusions about Paraguay's imperial neighbor to the east, itself also a neocolony of the British Empire. As the resident Brazilian consul in Paraguay, Correia da Câmara, informed his superiors: "El Dictador has the most vehement suspicions that the empire will ally itself with Buenos Aires in a defensive and offensive Alliance Treaty."[27] Although such an alliance was not consummated at this time, Francia's fears proved prophetic of the War of the Triple Alliance (1864–70), in which Brazil, Argentina, and Uruguay, financed by enormous English loans, waged a savage war of genocide against Paraguay.*

---

*Indeed, as early as 1830, in perhaps the first indication of the policy that Brazil would adopt in the War of the Triple Alliance, Correia da Câmara informed his secretary of state, "The only manner (as I have already had the honor of telling you) of finishing with that nacent colossus [Paraguay] would be by a rapid and well coordinated invasion" (Correia da Câmara a Miguel Calmon du Pin e Almeida, Ministro e Secretario de Estado, April 2, 1830, as found in the *Anais do Itamarati,* 4: 166).

In fact, even the British-supported Argentine invasion failed to materialize at this time, owing to another outbreak of civil war which drew attention away from efforts to resubjugate Paraguay. The triumph of the powerful caudillo Juan Manuel de Rosas (1829–31 and 1835–52), who, under the *federal* banner, pursued a policy of consolidating power in the so-called United Provinces, resulted in a shift of Argentine policy toward Paraguay. With his resources taxed by Platine faction fighting, military campaigns against the native inhabitants of the interior, and international conflicts, Rosas deemphasized the reincorporation of Paraguay. His primary concern, in fact, was that the republic remain neutral. To this end, in April 1830, shortly after taking control of the porteño government, Rosas dispatched an emissary to confer with Francia. Although the Argentine caudillo refused to relinquish claims to the former province, the Asunción conference seemed to have resulted in an understanding between the two governments.[28] Satisfied that Francia had no intention of breaking his long-standing policy of nonintervention in Argentina's civil disputes, Rosas sought to assure Paraguayan neutrality by also assuming a nonantagonistic position, thus laying the basis for more than a decade of reduced hostilities between Buenos Aires and Paraguay.[29]

Regardless of the improved relations with the port, the harassment of the lower river provinces kept the Pilar trade at a modest level throughout the 1830s. During the latter half of the decade, the Itapúa trade suffered a decline due to the Farroupilho Revolt (1835–45), a bloody seccessionist movement in the southern Brazilian state of Rio Grande do Sul, through which all of Itapúa's commerce passed. Further, leading to a new round of civil war which engulfed the entire Río de la Plata by 1838, Uruguayan factional strife, which began several years earlier, had merged with the continuing autonomists' struggle to oppose porteño domination in the Argentine Confederation. Completing this already complex picture, the French, irritated by Rosas's refusal to extend them the privileges of the 1825 British-Argentine commercial treaty, blockaded Buenos Aires and supplied military aid to anti-Rosas forces both in Uruguay and Argentina from 1838 to 1840.

The principal effect of these upheavals upon Paraguayan commerce was the disruption of its supplies of European-manufactured goods, for foreign ships found it increasingly difficult to work their way into the harassed and often blockaded ports of Pôrto Alegre, Montevideo, and Buenos Aires. Consequently, beginning in 1836, Brazilian merchants arriving at Itapúa, unable to acquire sufficient imported commodities, began bringing greater amounts of gold to exchange for Paraguayan products.[30]

In turn, the private export sector of the Paraguayan economy, stagnating because of the scarcity of imports, suffered a drastic decline (see table 3 and Appendix E). Normally, in a free market export economy governed by the law of supply and demand, such conditions can not only inflate the prices of scarce imports but, owing to the saturation of specie, can also cause the prices even of local commodities to rise. Although, as discussed above, the roots of economic dependence extend deep into structural inequities, it is precisely such crises—whether they are the result of "normal readjustments" in the world economy or are due to "unrelated political developments"—that show the dependency of export economies, vividly demonstrating that their prosperity is dependent upon forces completely outside their control. If controlled only by the functioning of the capitalist world market economy, dependent national economies can be severely depressed even by such apparently accidental incidents as civil strife along trade routes—to say nothing of deliberate economic manipulations. It is a testimony to the effectiveness of Paraguay's economic policies, and the subsequent strength of the national economy, that the value of Paraguayan exports actually increased during the last years of the decade.

Like all the former colonies, Paraguay had chronically suffered from a scarcity of specie. But under state control, the internal exchange rate of gold remained constant during the last fifteen years of Francia's administration at 17.3 pesos *fuertes** to the ounce of gold.[31] As a means of acquiring more hard currency, the government set the international exchange rate at 17.75 pesos *fuertes* per ounce of gold,[32] thereby providing merchants

---

*During this entire period Paraguay did not issue a national currency, but continued using the Spanish-minted *peso fuerte* and *peso corriente*. The relationship between the two remained constant throughout Francia's tenure, with the *peso corriente* being valued at 3 percent less than the *peso fuerte*. For examples of conversions, see ANA, NE, leg. 1232, Cuenta de Mayordomo de Proprios, 1815; ANA, LC, vol. 38, entry 49, February 6, 1835; and ANA, LC, vol. 43, entry 393, August 1, 1840.

with an incentive to trade in gold, as they would realize a 2.6 percent appreciation over the value of Paraguayan currency. For example, in the yerba trade at Itapúa, merchants exchanging their gold at the international exchange rate could then purchase yerba at an effective price of 175.3 pesos per ton rather than the established price of 180 pesos per ton.[33]

By the mid 1830s, owing to the cumulative effects of Francia's policies, the national economy no longer suffered from a shortage of hard currency, and therefore the government actually depreciated the value of the increasing amounts of gold that began flowing into Itapúa. Beginning in 1836, Francia reduced the amounts of native products that would be exchanged for each ounce of gold.[34] Again Itapúa yerba serves as a convenient example. Rather than exchanging yerba at an effective price of 175.3 pesos per ton in transactions conducted for gold, from this date onward Francia set an effective price of 204 pesos per ton[35]—thus appreciating the value of Paraguayan yerba by a full 16 percent. Even though price fluctuations are common in export economies, the significance of the appreciation in the value of Paraguayan exports lay in the fact that the increase was the result of an active policy on the part of the Paraguayan state, rather than a passive reflection of external forces.

An even more important demonstration of the effectiveness of Paraguay's state-controlled economy was the fact that the severity of the depression suffered in the private sector—which grew increasingly worse as the decade came to a close in spite of the elimination of the special tax on the Asunción-Itapúa traffic[36]— did not extend to the overall national economy. Although in 1837 and 1838 private sector exports declined 31 and 68 percent respectively in relation to their 1835 level, total national exports delined only 11 percent in 1837 and 30 percent in 1838 (see table 3 and Appendix C).

In order to achieve such remarkable economic stabilization, the state intervened where the private sector had failed to fulfill the nation's needs; it provided marketing and transportation facilities for Paraguay's widespread internal trading centers. This was accomplished by utilizing its commercial fleet of fifteen vessels,[37] which transversed the republic buying local products and transporting them to Itapúa.[38] The government—in possession of these additional quantities of yerba, tobacco, and hides, which augmented the already considerable amounts normally collected from its own estancias and through taxation—was thus able to offset the collapse of the private sector by increasing state exports to account for at least 35 percent of all national exports in 1837, and 65 percent of total exports in 1838 (see table 3 and Appendixes C and F).

Further mitigating the effects of the economic crisis, the government filled its vessels on their return voyages with imports, and with products from Paraguay's diverse regions, which it then offered for sale to the public.[39] The magnitude of state control of, and participation in, the national economy during these years is demonstrated by the massive increase in state sales. In inverse proportion to the declining commerce in the private sector, in relation to its 1835 level profits from state sales increased 98 percent by 1837, rising to 168 percent in 1838, temporarily dipping to 88 percent in 1839, before growing to an incredible 244 percent in 1840 (see fig. 7 and Appedix A).

It was this massive state intervention and the corresponding degree of control that such participation provided—combined with the rejection of the inherently unequal concept of free trade—that distinguished Paraguay's economy from those of all other Latin American nations of the epoch. Unlike its semiindependent, neocolonial sister states, whose dependent economies served to enrich the local elite and the capitalist world metropolises, Paraguay, by establishing an autonomous economic as well as political system, had truly won its full independence.

Through the destruction of the oligarchy's dominant position and the radical reorientation of its international commerce, popular Paraguay did not permit its riches to be consumed by the elite or siphoned off to the regional or world metropolises. By thus organizing commerce in a manner beneficial to the entire nation, the state assured that the product of Paraguay's labor—the nation's wealth—remained within Paraguay to benefit the original producers of that wealth—the people of Paraguay.

CONCLUSION

As extraordinary as Paraguay's popular revolution may appear to be, it is consistent with the ideological currents and historical realities of the era. Of obvious influence were the basic ideas of eighteenth- and early nineteenth-century Enlightenment thought. Such early Enlightenment philosophers as John Locke (1632–1704) rejected the assumption that society's structure derived from divine rights granted to monarchs and declared that human beings belonged to an order based upon nature. This led to the view not only that people possessed the natural rights of life and liberty, but, since products of nature derived their value from the human labor that went into producing them, that people also had a right to the fruits of their own labor.

Equally evident is the influence of Jean Jacques Rousseau (1712–78), who reasoned that sovereignty ultimately rested with the people, who, from their natural state of freedom and equality, had entered into a "social contract" to protect their natural rights. In the event that the established social order should fail to perform this function satisfactorily, the people possessed the ultimate authority to overthrow it and establish a new order which assured the maximum fulfillment of their inherent rights. While such concepts are generally accepted today, in early nineteenth-century Paraguay they constituted a powerful revolutionary doctrine not only against Spanish imperial rule and the Catholic Church, but against any attempt by the Argentine metropolis or the Paraguayan elites to deny the people their sovereignty.

The various schools of Enlightenment thought reveal other similarities with the principal tenets of popular Paraguay. Although it is unclear exactly which of the ideological currents Francia was most familiar with, as all drew upon the same basic body of knowledge, the overlap of ideas demonstrates the major historical forces which dominated the epoch.

Based upon the concept that all wealth was derived from the land, the first modern school of economists, founded by François Quesnay (1694–1774), took the name of physiocracy, meaning the "rule of nature." Physiocracy shortly found expression in such eminent figures as Anne Robert Jacques Turgot, Louis XVI's controversial finance minister, and Pierre Samuel Du Pont, who served as an aide to President Thomas Jefferson, himself greatly influenced by the physiocratic doctrine. While the physiocratic idea that in the natural order the value of all products, including manufactured goods, derived from the labor consumed in their production was consistent with Francia's own economic philosophy, their other major precepts stand in direct contradiction to his. The elitist doctrine condoned large landowning and advanced a society in which most of the land was owned by those who did no manual labor themselves—a belief completely inconsistent with Paraguay's radical land reform. Another fundamental difference is seen in the fact that physiocracy, the first doctrine to utilize the term and policy of laissez faire, held that any deviation from the "natural order"—such as taxes upon commerce or even organized relief for famine victims—constituted a violation of natural law and therefore was strictly to be avoided.

As the first great thinker to interpret Enlightenment thought in a manner explicitly favorable to the consolidating capitalist order, Adam Smith (1723–90), in his monumental work, *The Wealth of Nations* (1776), contended that the only source of wealth was the production resulting from labor and resources, and that the real value of all products could only be measured by the labor expended in their production. Here, again, a similarity to Francia's beliefs is apparent, as is the case with many of Smith's political ideas, such as that the function of government consisted in provision for the national defense, public works, the general protection of foreign commerce, subsidization of primary schools for the masses, and taxation levied in proportion to the level of prosperity enjoyed under the protection of the state.

Yet the other major aspects of Smith's doctrine were either

not applicable, or totally contradictory, to popular Paraguay. As the principal synthesizer of capitalist theory, Smith advanced the idea that production increased through the division of labor and by the introduction of machinery—essential concepts for the development of the industrializing metropolises, but of little importance to early nineteenth-century Paraguay. Of greater significance, Smith's concept of the laws of capitalist supply and demand—out of which grew the liberal doctrine of "free trade"—proved to be not only inapplicable, but antithetical. According to Smith, the unrestricted industrial and commercial activities of private entrepreneurs—although motivated only by a selfish quest for personal gain—were guided by the "invisible hand" of the marketplace so as to result in more efficient production of goods; thus, through laissez faire—or, as Smith put it, "the obvious and simple system of natural liberty"—the "invisible hand" of capitalism would ultimately serve to promote the overall best interests of society. And while the inhumane exploitation of the European working class testifies to the shortsightedness of Smith's analysis even in the capitalist metropolises, the acceptance of these principles in the economic dependencies of those metropolises proved to be the "invisible hand" of neocolonialism, which only promoted the interests of the oligarchy and the imperialists at the expense of the Latin American people.

Within decades, Adam Smith's contemporaries and followers, such as Jean Baptiste Say (1767–1823) and David Ricardo (1772–1823), had eliminated social welfare and moral considerations from the developing theory of capitalism. The dismal ideas of Thomas Robert Malthus (1766–1834), first presented in his *Essay on the Principle of Population* (1798), were quickly adopted as a rationalization of capitalism's brutality. Malthus advanced the theory that because population increased geometrically while food supply grew only arithmetically, the earth faced imminent overpopulation. Malthus recommended that absolutely no charity or relief be granted to the suffering masses, for he contended that their misery resulted from the law of nature, not from capitalist exploitation; therefore the responsibility of alleviating their condition lay with themselves, and not the upper classes.

These classic economists presented the basic assumptions of

the Enlightenment in a manner that served to support the liberal capitalist economic and social order by their emphasis upon the self-seeking individual as the essential social unit. Although Francia drew upon their ideas, the differences between early nineteenth-century Paraguay's socioeconomic system and that derived from these theories far outweighed the similarities. Francia's beliefs are more closely identified with those of Constantin François Volney (1757–1820), who, in *Les Ruines* (1791), rejected the liberal ideas that society comprised essentially unconnected individuals and put forth the concept of society as an organic whole, that is, the sum total of all its people and their actions. Indeed, as exemplified by such fundamental precepts as working in community and subordinating individual interest to public welfare, the priorities of popular Paraguay show much greater similarity to the interpretations promulgated by the contemporary critics of capitalism, who placed the greatest importance upon the social aspects of Enlightenment thought.

Emphasizing not only political equality—which the capitalist liberals theoretically advanced in the form of representative government—but also social and economic equality, these philosophers believed in the ultimate perfectability of human nature. They saw the compétititve concept of laissez faire, of "war of everyone against everyone," as the antithesis of the natural willingness of people to cooperate. Also drawing upon the works of Locke and Rousseau, these idealists, while incorporating the reformist aspects of their "establishment" counterparts, went far beyond them and advanced radical theories of social organization. The first of the Utopians, François Noël Babeuf (1760–97), proposed the nationalization of all large industries and the eventual elimination of private property by abolishing inheritance. In a similar vein, Count Henri de Saint-Simon (1760–1825) advocated the equality of opportunity for all. In his *Nouveau Christianisme* (1825), Saint-Simon argued not only for the destruction of the old order, but also for its replacement by a new pacifist order based upon the concept that "all men ought to regard each other as brothers."

None of these theories could actually have served as models for nineteenth-century Paraguay, principally because they all developed within the historical context of the world metropolises and not in their superexploited dependencies. Considering, however, the two principal currents of Enlightenment thought—the pragmatic supporters and the idealist critics of capitalism—popular Paraguay is unquestionably more closely related to the latter.

The acceptance of capitalist economic doctrine and its supporting ideology profoundly influenced the course of events in early nineteenth-century Latin America. Adopting its precepts, the American metropolitan elites formed alliances with their European counterparts not only in order to overthrow the old colonial order, but also to establish themselves at the top of the new neocolonial order. The creole elites thereby became the new dominators, against whom the dominated necessarily directed their struggle for liberation. In fact, the root cause of the Río de la Plata's protracted civil wars is found in this most basic of all historical dynamics—the conflict between the oppressed and the oppressors.

Supporting Paraguay's struggle against its dependence, the other provinces of the Río de la Plata absorbed the brunt of the porteños' efforts to maintain control over the region, thus preventing an actual invasion which might have crushed Paraguay's autonomous revolution. Just as important, furthermore, Paraguay's heritage gave the country all the elements necessary for the coalescence of modern mass nationalism—a popular consciousness in which large segments of the population, identifying their interests as those of the nation, recognize the great advantages of the unitary nation-state to which they pledge their loyalty and active support. Paraguay's people, biologically homogeneous as a result of centuries of miscegenation, also shared a common language, religion, and culture. Its national territory—a relatively compact and densely populated area—was not divided into regions with conflicting interests, and therefore, unlike the larger Latin American nations, Paraguay did not have to await the development of such cohesive technology as the steamship, telegraph, and railroad. Furthermore, while the imperialist aggressions of its age-old antagonist, Brazil, and, even more important, of its American metropolis, Buenos Aires, provided an external threat around which a consensus of political ideology could readily form, the Spanish and creole elites provided an internal "Other" which served as an even more immediate focus for the emerging social identity of the people.

Even so, had these been the only historical factors operating in the young nation, nationalism in Paraguay might very well have taken the traditional form of elite, intellectual, and urban-based nationalism characteristic throughout Latin America during the nineteenth century. Unlike the other Latin American nations, however, Paraguay occupied an extreme peripheral position within the Spanish empire. This effectively prohibited the development during the colonial period of a powerful and sophisticated creole elite which could forcibly implant itself at the top of the new national social order. Wracked by internal divisions and suffering the effects of Spanish, Portuguese, and porteño aggressions, the inexperienced creole elite found itself nearly paralyzed, incapable of effectively governing the province. Given this historical deadlock, Francia's leadership, which gave nationalistic form to the people's aspirations and power, proved to be the decisive factor in enacting, and maintaining, the popular social revolution.

Yet—as exemplified by such contemporaries as José Artigas in the Río de la Plata and Fathers Miguel Hidalgo and José María Morelos in Mexico—popular movements, complete with revolutionary leadership, extended far beyond the borders of Paraguay. Furthermore, as the examples of Túpac Amaru II in eighteenth-century Peru and Emiliano Zapata in twentieth-century Mexico demonstrate, such popular movements are not limited to this or to any other period of American history. In itself, the fusion of revolutionary leadership with popular forces in nineteenth-century Paraguay certainly cannot be regarded as unique; what is distinctive is its success.

Although no process of social change can serve as a model for any other, Paraguay's radical revolution includes several fundamental components necessary to any successful revolution in Latin America. In dismantling their traditional dependent society, the Paraguayans denied both the Spanish and creole elites their dominant social, political, and economic status, thus preventing them from continuing to direct the affairs of the nation in their upper-class interests. Along with eliminating the domination of the oligarchy, Paraguay refused to yield to the aggressions of Argentine imperialism, thus escaping the new dependency suffered by the other provinces of the old viceroyalty that continued to be dominated by Buenos Aires as it emerged as the

American submetropolis of the neocolonial order in the Río de la Plata. Through stringent state control and a sweeping land reform, moreover, Paraguay diversified its traditional monocultural economy and developed a balanced economy designed to provide adequately for the fundamental needs of all the people—the first nation in all of American history to achieve such a radical goal.

The implementation of these four fundamentals—the removal of the elites, the liberation from imperialist domination, the enactment of an egalitarian land reform, and the institution of rational state direction of the economy—provided Paraguay with the means of breaking out of its traditional dependence and establishing a truly autonomous nation. Indeed, the successful enactment of these basic measures—as much today as 150 years ago—is the foundation of independence and development; for political independence alone, without economic independence, historically has resulted in nothing more than what today is called underdevelopment.

CHRONOLOGY

1536	Buenos Aires founded by Pedro de Mendoza.
1537	Asunción founded by an expedition from Buenos Aires led by Juan de Salazar y Espinola.
1541	Buenos Aires abandoned.
1580	Buenos Aires refounded by an expedition from Asunción led by Juan Garay.
1607	The first Jesuit Missions established in Paraguay.
1618	Spanish Crown establishes a customs barrier at Córdoba.
1622	Spanish Crown withdraws permission for its American colonies to trade with Brazil.
1680	Portuguese establish the Colônia do Sacramento in the Banda Oriental (Uruguay).
1719–1735	Communeros Revolt in Paraguay.
1759	Jesuits expelled from the Portuguese domains.
1763	Jesuits expelled from the French domains.
1767	Jesuits expelled from the Spanish domains.
1776	Creation of the Viceroyalty of La Plata.
1777 & 1778	Free Commerce Regulations enacted to facilitate interprovincial trade within the Spanish-American Empire.
1796–1806	Administration of Governor Lázaro de Rivera of Paraguay.
1806–1811	Administration of Governor Bernado de Velasco of Paraguay.
1806	British expedition occupies Buenos Aires; expelled by creole militia.
1807	British expedition occupies Montevideo and attacks Buenos Aires; creole militia successfully defend the city, forcing the British to capitulate.
1808	Napoleon invades the Iberian Peninsula, forcing the Portuguese court, transported by the British fleet, to flee to Rio de Janeiro; captures the Bourbon Monarch Ferdinand VII and appoints his brother, Joseph Bonaparte, as the new king of Spain.
1810	May 25: The porteño cabildo deposes Viceroy Baltasar Hidalgo de Cisneros and establishes the Provisional Junta of the Río de la Plata to "govern in the name of Ferdinand VII."
	July 24: Royalist Asunción cabildo abierto rejects Buenos Aires's proclamation of authority and pledges allegiance to the Supreme Regency Council in Spain.
	December: The porteño "Liberation Army," under the command of General Manuel Belgrano, invades Paraguay.
1811	January 19: Belgrano defeated by the Paraguayan creoles at Paraguarí.
	March 9: Belgrano defeated again by the Paraguayan creoles at Tacuarí.
	May 9: Portuguese emissary arrives in Asunción to negotiate the conditions of military aid with the Paraguayan royalists.

May 14–15: Asunción barracks coup in reaction to the royalists' agreement to recognize the Portuguese queen's claims to the Spanish Crown. Creoles force Governor Velasco to accept Francia and another associate to cogovern.

June 17: Creole general assembly establishes a five-member junta, including Francia, to govern Paraguay.

August 1: Francia retires from the junta to protest continuing military interference in governmental affairs.

September 3: Francia returns to the junta after forcing the expulsion of its most conservative member.

October 11: Treaty between the Paraguayan and porteño governments.

December 15: Francia once again retires from the junta to protest further military interference.

1812 November 12: Racked by internal divisions and threatened by renewed porteño aggressions, the creole elite begs Francia to return to the government; he accepts only after one-half of the armed forces are placed under his direct command and the two porteñista members of the junta are prevented from taking independent action.

1813 The secretary of the Buenos Aires government, Nicolas de Herrera, arrives in Asunción to promote a union of the two provinces. First popular congress called to decide the major issues.

September 30: Popular congress convened. It annuls the Treaty of October 1811, refuses to send delegates to the Constitutional Congress of the Río de la Plata, declares independence, proclaims Paraguay a republic, and establishes a consulship, with Francia and Fulgencio Yegros as heads of state, to govern the nation.

1814 José Artigas emerges as champion of the *federal* cause against the *unitarios*.

Francia begins building a popular administration, attacking the socioeconomic foundations of the old Spanish ruling class, and consolidates his control over the military.

October 3: The popular congress abolishes the consulship and elects Francia supreme dictaor of the republic.

November 13: Export of specie prohibited.

December 12: Imports of arms and munitions declared free of taxes.

1815 Artigas reaches his apex as standard bearer of the *federal* cause; beginnings of *federal* harassment of Paraguayan commerce.

July 2: Church placed under state authority; abolition of the Holy Office of the Inquisition.

December 21: High Spanish church officials replaced by Paraguayans.

1816 June 5: The Popular Congress elects Francia perpetual dictator of the republic.

1817 January: The supreme director of the United Provinces of the Río de la Plata, Juan Martín de Pueyrredón, orders the blockade of all Paraguayan commerce and dispatches Colonel Juan Baltazar Vargas to Paraguay in an unsuccessful attempt to foment a revolt among the upper class.

1819 Bishop Pedro Garcia de Panés retires.

Reacting to the paralysis of commerce and to their political disenfranchisment, the Paraguayan elite begin conspiring to assassinate Francia and overthrow the government.

Chronology 175

1820   March 28: Immediately following the discovery of the Great Conspiracy, Francia begins arresting the subversives.

June 8: Religious brotherhoods banned.

August 4: Abolition of the traditional ecclesiastical exemption from civil courts.

September: Artigas and a small band of followers receive asylum in Paraguay.

October: Francisco Ramírez and his army arrive at the Paraguayan border.

November: Leaving a sizable force in the Missions, Ramírez is forced to return to the south in a futile attempt to crush a rebellion in the *federal* ranks.

1821   June: Paraguayan border patrol captures royalist correspondence to the commander of the Ramírista forces; the next morning the Asunción Spaniards are arrested and remain in prison for nearly nineteen months, released only after paying an enormous "contribution."

July 3: Paraguayan border patrol intercepts a letter of the Ramírista chieftain to the Paraguayan conspirators.

July 10: Unbeknownst to Francia or the conspirators, Francisco Ramírez is killed at the battle of Córdoba.

July 17: Francia begins executing the leading conspirators; within a week, as many as twenty-one people have lost their lives.

December 21: Capture of the French naturalist Aimé Jacques Alexandre Bonpland.

1823   February: Four months after declaring its independence from Portugal, Brazil initiates commercial relations with Paraguay.

March 23: The defunct Royal Seminary of San Carlos formally closes and its lands are confiscated.

1824   December 30: Secularization of the monasteries and confiscation of their lands.

December 30: Abolition of the Asunción cabildo.

1825   The Cisplatine War between Brazil and the United Provinces, which terminates in the creation of the buffer state of Uruguay in 1828.

General release of foreigners "suspended" in Paraguay.

August: After several months of clarifying his credentials, the Brazilian commercial consul, Antonio Correa da Câmara, arrives in Asunción, where he spends the next five months negotiating Brazilian-Paraguayan relations.

September: Royal land grants annulled.

1827   September: Second mission of Correa da Câmara, during which he is restricted to the trading town of Itapúa until his departure in June 1829.

1829   The beginning of the long rule of the porteño *federal* caudillo, Juan Manuel de Rosas (1829–31 and 1835–52).

1830   April: The Asunción conference between Francia and Rosas's emissary, in which the two governments reach an informal agreement to reduce tensions.

October 24: Major tax reductions, followed in 1835 and 1837 by further reductions.

1831   January 4: Mutual aid pact of the Litoral Provinces.

February 14: Bonpland released.

May 19: Export of livestock prohibited.

1832   October 6: Corrientes declares war against Paraguay and occupies the Missions' capital of Candelaria.

1833	December: Paraguay retakes Candelaria and reestablishes hegemony over the Missions.
1834	August 30: The government standardizes the salaries of the nation's primary school teachers.
1835	Establishment of the state pharmacies.
	The beginning of the Farroupilho Revolt in the Brazilian southern state of Rio Grande do Sul, which lasts until 1845.
1836	Inauguration of Paraguay's first public library.
	Uruguayan factional strife leads to a new round of civil war, which engulfs the entire Río de la Plata by 1838.
1838	The French blockade Buenos Aires and extend military aid to the anti-Rosas forces (1838–40).
	July 15: With only months to live, Panés is reinstated as Bishop of Paraguay.
1840	September 20: Francia dies.
	September 24: Provisional junta established.
1841	January 22: Military overthrow the junta and establish a triumvirate.
	February 9: Military overthrow the triumvirate.
	March 11: General congress convened.
	March 12: Councilor government established by the congress.
1844	March 13: General congress elects Carlos Antonio López president of Paraguay.
1862	September 10: Carlos Antonio López dies. Provisional government of Francisco Solano López.
	October 16: General congress elects Francisco Solano López president of Paraguay.
1864	November 12: War of the Triple Alliance begins.
1870	March 1: Francisco Solano López killed at Cerro Corá. The end of War of the Triple Alliance and Paraguay's autonomous revolution.

ABBREVIATIONS

The following abbreviations are examples of those used in citations of archival documents and of newspapers. Since these materials are explained here, they are not included in the bibliography.

Archives

AGI	Archivo General de Indias, Seville, Spain
ABA, leg. 323	Audiencia de Buenos Aires, legajo 323
AGN	Archivo General de la Nación, Buenos Aires, Argentina
10-1, 19, leg. 13	room 10, cabinet 1, shelf 19, legajo 13
AGPC	Archivo General de la Provincia de Corrientes, Corrientes, Argentina
CO, EA, leg. 2	Correspondencia Oficial, Expedientes Administrativos, legajo 2
ANA	Archivo Nacional, Asunción, Paraguay
LC, vol. 40	Libro de Caja, volume 40
NE, leg. 3410	Nueva Encuadernación, legajo 3410
SC, leg. 81*	Sección Civil, legajo 81. During the late 1940s the Archivo Nacional was reorganized in a more chronological manner. Consequently, the nine documents marked with asterisks, as they were taken from secondary sources written before the reorganization, are no longer to be found in their original legajos.
SH, leg. 229	Sección Historica, legajo 229
BNRJ	Biblioteca Nacional, Rio de Janeiro, Brazil
CAS, 4-17, 2, leg. 8	Cuaderno de Autos Supremos, room 4, cabinet 17, shelf 2, legajo 8
CDA, 1-28, 36, leg. 22	Coleção de Angelis, room 1, cabinet 28, shelf 36, legajo 32
CRB 1-30, 2, leg. 80	Coleção Rio Branco, room I, cabinet 30, shelf 2, legajo 80
RP, 2-36, 27, leg. 9	Relações Paraguaias, room II, cabinet 36, shelf 27, legajo 9

Newspapers

GBA	*Gazeta de Buenos Aires*
GM	*Gazeta Mercantile de Buenos Aires*

APPENDICES

	Page
Appendix A, Paraguayan National Budgets	180
Appendix B, Cash Held in Deposit	215
Appendix C, Paraguayan Exports	225
Appendix D, Pilar Exports	238
Appendix E, Itapúa Exports	245
Appendix F, State Exports	254
Appendix G, Paraguayan Import Taxes: 1816-1824	258
Appendix H, Paraguayan Army	259
Appendix I, State Estancias	263

APPENDIX A

PARAGUAYAN NATIONAL BUDGETS

	Page
1816	181
1818	183
1820	185
1822	187
1823	189
1828	191
1829	193
1831	195
1832	197
1833	199
1834	201
1835	203
1837	205
1838	207
1839	209
1840	211
Archival Locations of Paraguayan National Budgets	213

-1816-

RECEIPTS		Pesos	
Taxes		222,131	(83.92%)
Import	83,640		
Export	61,537		
Excise	35,312		
Tithe	30,024		
Warehouse tax	6,221		
Official Legal Paper	4,969		
Anchorage	428		
Sale of State Products to Troops		21,154	(7.99%)
Rents of State Property		5,683	(2.15%)
State Inheritance		4,220	(1.59%)
Payment for Previous Sale of Offices		3,100	(1.17%)
Buena Cuenta		2,902	(1.10%)
Collection of Papal Bulls		2,492	(.94%)
Forfeited Bond		1,068	(.40%)
Willed to State		896	(.34%)
Confiscations		831	(.31%)
Collection of Debts		107	(.04%)
Sale of State Products to Public		81	(.03%)
Fines		62	(.02%)
Total		264,727	

-1816-

EXPENDITURES		Pesos	
Military		133,123	(83.88%)
Salaries	88,928		
Provisions for troops	33,807		
Construction of ships	8,551		
Lighting, masses & doctor	1,837		
State Works		10,737	(6.77%)
Government Salaries		9,306	(5.86%)
Treasury staff	4,954		
Francia	4,352		
Church		5,102	(3.22%)
General Expenses		443	(.28%)
Illegible	250		
Purchase of slave	103		
Rent of treasury building	80		
Total		158,711	

	Pesos
TOTAL RECEIPTS	264,727
TOTAL EXPENDITURES	158,711
SURPLUS	106,016

ANA, LC, Tomo 15, Libro Manual de la Caxa de Hazienda... para la Cuenta del año 1816.

-1818-

RECEIPTS		Pesos	
Taxes		150,652	(52.51%)
Import	58,480		
Export	47,770		
Excise	40,285**		
Official Legal Paper	3,508		
Anchorage	331		
War tax	235		
Tithe	43		
Confiscations.........(336 + 89,771)*		90,107	(31.41%)
Sale of State Products to Troops		24,941	(8.70%)
State Inheritance		15,417	(5.37%)
Collection of Papal Bulls		2,901	(1.01%)
Administration of Mail		1,876*	(.65%)
Rents of State, State Property, and Lands		336	(.12%)
Collection of Debts		284	(.10%)
Sale of State Products to Public		251	(.09%)
Fines.................(49* + 62)		111	(.04%)
Willed to State		49	(.02%)
Payment for Previous Sale of Offices		6	
Total		286,932	

*These figures are found in Deposito, ANA, NE#1230, Cuenta General de las Entradas y Salidas ocurridas en la Tesorería General de Hacienda de la República del Paraguay para todo el año de 1818.

**This sum includes 10,100 pilfered pesos which were repaid from Alcabala funds.

-1818-

EXPENDITURES		Pesos	
Military		150,947	(77.33%)
Salaries	96,650		
Provisions for troops (including lighting and medicines)	47,675		
Construction of ships	6,622		
State Works		15,170	(7.77%)
Government Salaries		13,370	(6.85%)
Francia	9,270		
Treasury staff	4,100		
Buena Cuenta		11,433	(5.86%)
Church		3,869	(1.98%)
General Expenses		431	(.22%)
Purchase of land	381		
Bookkeeping error	50		
Total		195,220	

	Pesos
TOTAL RECEIPTS	286,932
TOTAL EXPENDITURES	195,220
SURPLUS	91,712

Unless otherwise indicated, the figures for 1818 are found in ANA, NE#1230, Cuenta General de las Entradas y Salidas ocurridas en la Tesorería General de la República del Paraguay para todo el año de 1818.

-1820-

RECEIPTS		Pesos	
Taxes..		114,094	(69.27%)
Imports...................	69,674		
Excise....................	33,445		
Exports...................	8,146		
Official Legal Paper......	2,210		
War tax...................	489		
Anchorage.................	130		
Sale of State Products to Troops...........		31,001	(18.82%)
Sale of State Products to Public...........		8,379	(5.09%)
Agricultural products and animals.............	7,729		
Merchandise...............	650		
Repayment of Salary Advances......................		6,559	(3.98%)
Collection of Debts..........................		1,576	(.96%)
State Inheritance............................		1,515	(.92%)
Confiscations................................		1,410*	(.86%)
Rents of State Property......................		146	(.09%)
Fines..		43	(.03%)
Total.................................		164,723	

*This figure is the difference between the sums found in ANA, NE#1839, <u>Libro Manual de la Caxa de Hazienda -- para la Cuenta del Año 1820, Depósito</u>, and ANA, NE#1119, <u>Libro Manual de la Caxa de Hazienda -- para la Cuenta desde 16 de Abril a fin de Diciembre 1819, Depósito</u>.

-1820-

EXPENDITURES		Pesos	
Military		175,200	(80.55%)
Army salaries (including doctor)	122,650		
Provisions for troops	30,115		
Construction of ships	13,615		
Musicians, lighting, masses, and construction of barracks	8,820		
State Works		30,334	(13.95%)
Salaries and materials	30,334		
Government Salaries		8,501	(3.91%)
Francia	4,054		
Treasury staff and miscellaneous	3,063		
War treasurer and staff	1,184		
Church		3,469	(1.60%)
Total		217,504	

	Pesos
TOTAL EXPENDITURES	217,504
TOTAL RECEIPTS	164,723
DEFICIT	52,781

Unless otherwise indicated, the figures for 1820 are found in ANA, LC, Tomo 17, <u>Libro Manual de la Caxa de Hazienda... para la Cuenta del año 1820</u> (a copy is found in NE#1839), and ANA, LC, Tomo 18, <u>Libro Manual de la Tesorería de Guerra...para la Cuenta corriente desde 15 de Noviembre de 1819, y todo el año siguiente de 1820</u> (a copy is found in NE#3104).

-1822-

RECEIPTS		Pesos	
Confiscations		121,123	(66.48%)
Sale of State Products to Troops		15,272	(8.39%)
Taxes		14,336	(7.88%)
Excise	7,910		
Imports	4,824		
Official Legal Paper	1,440		
Exports	162		
State Inheritance		12,797	(7.03%)
Willed to State		7,345	(4.04%)
Repayment of Salary Advances		3,979	(2.19%)
Collection of Debts		2,885	(1.59%)
Sale of State Products to Public		2,372	(1.30%)
Inventory Adjustment		1,699	(.93%)
Fines		40	(.02%)
Rents of State Property		31	(.02%)
Total		181,879	

-1822-

EXPENDITURES		Pesos	
Military		121,409	(79.87%)
Army salaries (including doctor and bleeder)	94,454		
Provisions for troops	16,616		
Construction of ships	6,295		
Musicians, lighting, and masses	4,040		
State Works		22,570	(14.85%)
Salaries and materials	22,570		
Government Salaries		4,108	(2.7%)
Treasury staff and miscellaneous	2,895		
War treasurer and staff	1,213		
Church		2,793	(1.84%)
General Expenses		1,110	(.73%)
Destroyed houses due to public works	595		
José Artigas and followers' pension	515		
Total		151,990	

	Pesos
TOTAL RECEIPTS	181,879
TOTAL EXPENDITURES	151,990
SURPLUS	29,889

ANA, LC, Tomo 20. Although the title page is missing, and regardless of the mislabeled cover which reads 1821, this volume is the Libro Manual de la Caxa de Hazienda -- para la Cuenta del año de 1822. And ANA, LC, Tomo 21, Libro Manual de la Tesorería de Guerra -- para la Cuenta corriente desde 1 de Enero hasta fin de Diciembre del año de 1822 (a copy is found in NE#1841 and 1842).

-1823-

RECEIPTS		Pesos	
Taxes...................................		38,952	(45.49%)
Imports..................	19,808		
Excise.....................	11,082		
Tannery Tax.................	3,588		
Exports.................	1,853		
Official Legal Paper.........	1,348		
Tithe......................	1,273		
Sale of State Products to Troops.............		16,874	(19.71%)
State Inheritance...........................		10,824	(12.64%)
Collection of Debts.........................		5,651	(6.60%)
Forced Contributions........................		5,494	(6.42%)
Inventory Adjustment........................		3,193	(3.73%)
Sale of State Products to Public............		1,845	(2.15%)
Repayment of Salary Advances................		1,721	(2.01%)
Confiscations...............................		404	(.47%)
Fines.......................................		306	(.36%)
Rents of State Property.....................		164	(.28%)
Miscellaneous...............................		195	(.23%)
Sale of city lot........	195		
Total.....................................		85,623	

-1823-

EXPENDITURES   Pesos

Military..................................... 104,865 (84.57%)
    Army salaries (including
      doctor and bleeder)..... 54,287
    Provisions for troops.... 41,212
    Construction of ships....   7,787
    Musicians, lighting, and
      masses..................   1,579

State Works................................... 12,482 (10.07%)
    Salaries and materials... 12,482

Church..   3,102 (2.5%)

Government Salaries...........................   3,045 (2.42%)
    Treasury staff...........   2,067
    War treasurer and staff..   978

General Expenses..............................   278 (.22%)
    José Artigas pension.....   155
    Pension to unidentified
      individual..............   56
    Expenses of a confiscation   37
    Goods to Francia.........   30

    Total................................. 123,772

                                                                        Pesos

TOTAL EXPENDITURES................................. 123,772

TOTAL RECEIPTS..................................... 85,623

    DEFICIT.. 38,149

ANA, LC, Tomo 22, Libro Manual de la Caxa de Hazienda...
para la Cuenta del año de 1823 (a copy is found in NE#3106),
and ANA, LC, Tomo 23, Libro Manual de la Tesorería de
Guerra...para la Cuenta del año 1823 (a copy is found in
NE#1844).

-1828-

RECEIPTS		Pesos	
Sale of State Products to Public............		59,809	(39.75%)
Merchandise..............	50,507		
Agricultural products and animals.............	9,101		
Taxes..		44,548	(29.61%)
Tithe.....................	38,296*		
Excise....................	2,733		
Official Legal Paper (1,493 + 498*).......................	1,991		
Tannery Tax...............	1,487		
Miscellaneous............	41		
Sale of State Products to Troops............		23,616	(15.7%)
Rents..		8,517	(5.66%)
State lands...............	8,507		
State property...........	10		
State Inheritance...........................		4,542	(3.02%)
Transfer from Mayordomos....................		3,648	(2.42%)
Collection of Debts.........................		3,202	(2.13%)
Confiscations (1,648* + 925)................		2,573	(1.71%)
Illegible...................................		13	(.01%)
Total................................		150,468	

*These figures are the difference between the sums found in ANA, NE#1851, Dinero Efectivo en Depósito, Diciembre 15, 1828 and ANA, NE#1849, Dinero Efectivo en Depósito, Diciembre 15, 1827.

-1828-

EXPENDITURES		Pesos
Military.....................................		87,816 (83.63%)
Army salaries (including musicians)..........	79,227	
Provisions for troops (includes state operating expenses).........	7,476	
Lighting and masses......	783	
Sailors' salaries........	330	
State Works................................		12,326 (11.74%)
Salaries.................	11,576	
Charcoal.................	759	
Government Salaries.......................		3,193 (3.04%)
Treasury staff...........	1,533	
Crews of state ships.....	1,190	
Primary School Teacher........	300	
Public Defender for Minors and the Poor.................	86	
Lamplighter..............	84	
Church......................................		1,552 (1.03%)
General Expenses...........................		232 (.22%)
Maintenance of prisoner..	108	
José Artigas pension.....	99	
Miscellaneous and illegible...............	25	
Total..................................		105,119

	Pesos
TOTAL RECEIPTS.....................................	150,468
TOTAL EXPENDITURES.................................	105,119
SURPLUS..	45,449

Unless otherwise indicated, the figures for 1828 are found in ANA, LC, Tomo 30, <u>Libro Manual de la Tesorería General</u>... <u>año 1828</u>.

-1829-

RECEIPTS		Pesos	
Sale of State Products to Public		46,402	(32.07%)
Merchandise	35,226		
Agricultural products and animals	11,124		
Sale of State Products to Troops		36,547	(25.26%)
Taxes		25,447	(17.59%)
Tithe	20,125*		
Excise	3,565		
Tannery Tax	1,090		
Official Legal Paper	359*		
War tax	275		
Miscellaneous	33		
Confiscations........(19,751* + 241)		19,992	(13.82%)
State Inheritance		7,838	(5.42%)
Rents		6,170	(4.27%)
State lands	6,041		
State property	129		
Fines		1,208	(.84%)
Transfer from Pueblos		446*	(.31%)
Collection of Debts		403	(.28%)
Miscellaneous		215	(.15%)
Correction of bookkeeping error	125		
Illegible	78		
Sale of school materials to Itapúa	12		
Total		144,668	

*These figures are the difference between the sums found in ANA, NE#1854, <u>Dinero Efectivo en Depósito, Diciembre 15, 1829</u>, and ANA, NE#1851, <u>Dinero Efectivo en Depósito, Diciembre 15, 1828</u>.

-1829-

EXPENDITURES		Pesos
Military		116,215 (89.4%)
Army salaries	99,867	
Provisions for troops (includes state operating expenses)	13,690	
Deployment of troops	1,504	
Lighting and masses	724	
Sailors' salaries	334	
Doctor	96	
State Works		10,488 (8.07%)
Salaries	9,710	
Charcoal	778	
Government Salaries		3,100 (2.38%)
Treasury staff	1,405	
Crews of state ships	1,182	
Primary School Teacher	300	
Public Defender for Minors and the Poor	129	
Lamplighter	84	
Church		52 (.04%)
General Expenses		310 (.24%)
Maintenance of prisoner	108	
Expenses of treasury inventory and audit	103	
José Artigas pension	99	
Total		130,165

	Pesos
TOTAL RECEIPTS	144,668
TOTAL EXPENDITURES	130,165
SURPLUS	14,503

Unless otherwise indicated, these figures for 1829 are found in ANA, LC, Tomo 32, <u>Libro Manual de la Tesorería General -- desde Enero hasta Septiembre de 1829</u>, and ANA, LC, Tomo 33, <u>Libro Manual de la Tesorería General -- Septiembre hasta el fin de Diciembre de 1829</u>.

-1831-

RECEIPTS		Pesos	
Sale of State Products to Troops		34,646	(34.54%)
Sale of State Products to Public		27,103	(27.02%)
Agricultural products and animals	13,661		
Merchandise	13,442		
Taxes		25,260	(25.18%)
Agriculture	8,867*		
Itapúa	8,736		
Abolished Tithe	2,818*		
Excise	2,656		
Tannery Tax	2,183		
Transfer from Pueblos		3,407*	(3.4%)
Confiscations (2,420* + 850**)		3,270	(3.26%)
Rents		3,209	(3.2%)
State lands	3,149		
State property	60		
State Inheritance		2,964	(2.95%)
Collection of Debts		163	(.16%)
Miscellaneous		292	(.29%)
Sale of city lot	206		
Overpayment	82		
Willed to state	4		
Total		100,314	

*These figures are one-half of the difference between the sums found in ANA, NE#1865, Dinero Efectivo en Depósito, diciembre 15, 1832, and ANA, NE#1850, Dinero Efectivo en Depósito, febrero 15, 1831.

**This figure is the difference between the sums found in ANA, NE#1850, Dinero Efectivo en Depósito, febrero 15, 1831, and ANA, NE#1857, Dinero Efectivo en Depósito, diciembre 15, 1830.

-1831-

EXPENDITURES		Pesos
Military		83,352 (86.11%)
Army salaries	81,460	
Lighting and masses	710	
Provisions for troops	611	
Doctor and bleeder	324	
Sailors' salaries	247	
State Works		8,629 (8.91%)
Salaries	7,845	
Charcoal	784	
Government Salaries		2,485 (2.53%)
Treasury salaries	1,280	
Crews of state ships	692	
Primary School Teacher	300	
Public Defender for Minors and the Poor	129	
Lamplighter	84	
State Operating Expenses		1,702 (1.76%)
Church		250 (.26%)
General Expenses		375 (.39%)
Aid to an individual	206	
Maintenance of prisoner	77	
Hire slaves	70	
Commission to tax collector	22	
Total		96,793

	Pesos
TOTAL RECEIPTS	100,314
TOTAL EXPENDITURES	96,793
SURPLUS	3,521

Unless otherwise indicated, these figures for 1831 are found in ANA, LC, Tomo 34, Libro Manual de la Tesorería General... año 1831.

-1832-

RECEIPTS   Pesos

Taxes.. 27,789 (28.1%)
    Itapúa export taxes...... 9,177
      (3,495 + 5,628*)
    Agriculture................ 8,867*
    Excise..................... 4,224
    Abolished Tithe............ 2,819*
    Official Legal Paper....... 2,702
      (1,897 + 805*)

Sale of State Products to Troops............ 35,646 (36.05%)

Sale of State Products to Public............ 24,619 (24.9%)
    Merchandise............... 12,980
    Agricultural products
      and animals............ 11,639

Rents....................................... 4,518 (4.57%)
    State lands............... 4,444
    State property...........   74

Transfer from Pueblos....................... 3,408* (3.45%)

Confiscations............................... 2,420* (2.45%)

Collection of Debts.........................   300 (.3%)

State Inheritance...........................   165 (.17%)

Miscellaneous...............................   23 (.02%)
    Breakage of state
      property...............   23
                                                                                             ———

    Total................................ 98,888

*These figures are one-half of the differences between the sums found in ANA, NE#1865, Dinero Efectivo en Depósito, diciembre 15, 1832, and ANA, NE#1850, Dinero Efectivo en Depósito, febrero 15, 1831.

-1832-

EXPENDITURES		Pesos
Military.............................		98,601 (87.26%)
Army salaries............	96,824	
Lighting and masses......	698	
Doctor and bleeder.......	459	
Sailors' salaries........	270	
Provisions for troops....	221	
Expenses for recruits....	129	
State Works.........................		8,143 (7.21%)
Salaries.................	7,594	
Charcoal.................	549	
Government Salaries..................		3,025 (2.68%)
Treasury staff...........	1,308	
Crews of state ships.....	1,151	
Primary School Teacher...	340	
Jailer...................	99	
Lamplighter..............	84	
Public Defender for Minors and the Poor.................	43	
State Operating Expenses.............		2,277 (2.02%)
Church...............................		250 (.22%)
General Expenses.....................		751 (.66%)
Destroyed houses due to public works.........	370	
Aid to two individuals...	309	
Maintenance of prisoner..	72	
Total............................		113,047

	Pesos
TOTAL EXPENDITURES..................................	113,047
TOTAL RECEIPTS......................................	98,888
DEFICIT...	14,159

Unless otherwise indicated, these figures for 1832 are found in ANA, LC, Tomo 35, <u>Libro Manual de la Tesorería General...año 1832</u>.

-1833-

RECEIPTS		Pesos	
Sale of State Products to Troops		19,573	(41.39%)
Taxes		13,644	(28.85%)
Agriculture	6,485*		
Abolished Tithe	3,739*		
Excise	1,945		
Official Legal Paper	902*		
Itapúa export taxes	573*		
Rents		5,543	(11.72%)
State lands	5,527		
State property	16		
Sale of State Products to Public		4,642	(9.82%)
Agricultural products and animals	4,642		
Confiscations		2,574*	(5.44%)
State Inheritance		735	(1.55%)
Forced Contributions		200	(.42%)
Transfer from Pueblos		180*	(.38%)
Fines		107	(.23%)
Collection of Debts		67	(.14%)
Miscellaneous		24	(.05%)
Breakage of state property	24		
Total		47,289	

*These figures are the differences between the sums found in ANA, NE#1869, Dinero Efectivo en Depósito, Diciembre 15, 1833, and ANA, NE#1865, Dinero Efectivo en Depósito, Diciembre 15, 1832.

-1833-

EXPENDITURES		Pesos
Military		68,558 (85.29%)
Army salaries	57,950	
Expenses for recruits	7,072	
Provisions and aid for troops	2,072	
Lighting and masses	695	
Sailors' salaries	390	
Doctor	306	
Leatherworker	73	
State Works		7,842 (9.76%)
Salaries	7,575	
Charcoal	267	
Government Salaries		1,865 (2.32%)
Treasury staff	1,180	
Primary School Teacher	360	
Crews of state ships	142	
Jailer	99	
Lamplighter	84	
State Operating Expenses		1,794 (2.23%)
Church		250 (.31%)
General Expenses		72 (.09%)
Maintenance of prisoner	72	
Total		80,381

	Pesos
TOTAL EXPENDITURES	80,381
TOTAL RECEIPTS	47,289
DEFICIT	33,092

Unless otherwise indicated, these figures are found in ANA, LC, Tomo 36, <u>Libro Manual de la Tesorería General...año 1833</u>.

-1834-

RECEIPTS   Pesos

Forced Contributions ..(27,295 + 283*)...... 27,578 (35%)

Sale of State Products to Public............ 24,128 (30.63%)
    Merchandise............... 18,480
    Agricultural products
      and animals............ 5,048
    Steel....................   600

Confiscations..........(5,109* + 283**)..... 5,392 (6.84%)

Rents....................................... 5,361 (6.81%)
    State lands............... 5,357
    State property............   4

Sale of State Products to Troops............ 5,204 (6.61%)

Taxes....................................... 5,197 (6.6%)
    Excise.................... 3,094
    Agricultural.............. 1,481*
    Official Legal Paper......   622*

Collection of Debts......................... 3,356 (4.26%)

State Inheritance........................... 1,993 (2.53%)

Miscellaneous...............................   568 (.72%)
    Francia paid for two
      slaves' liberty.........   550
    Breakage of state
      property...............   18

    Total............................... 78,777

*These figures are the differences between the sums found in ANA, NE#1875, Dinero Efectivo en Depósito, Abril 15, 1834, and ANA, NE#1869, Dinero Efectivo en Depósito, Diciembre 15, 1833.

**ANA, NE#1871, Cuaderno... Contribución de los Negociantes.

-1834-

EXPENDITURES		Pesos
Military...............................		42,819 (76.43%)
Army salaries (including musicians)..........	28,334	
Expenses for recruits....	13,336	
Lighting and masses......	461	
Sailors' salaries........	355	
Doctor...................	250	
Provisions for troops....	69	
Leatherworker............	14	
State Works..............................		8,685 (15.51%)
Salaries.................	8,464	
Charcoal.................	221	
State Operating Expenses..................		2,393 (4.27%)
Government Salaries.......................		1,626 (2.9%)
Treasury staff...........	1,116	
Primary School Teacher....	285	
Jailer...................	99	
Lamplighter..............	84	
Public Defender for Minors and the Poor..............	42	
Church....................................		320 (.57%)
General Expenses..........................		276 (.54%)
Houses damaged due to public works.........	125	
Reward to diligent judges	76	
Maintenance of prisoner..	72	
Miscellaneous............	3	
Total................		56,119

	Pesos
TOTAL RECEIPTS...........................	78,777
TOTAL EXPENDITURES.......................	56,119
SURPLUS..............................	22,658

Unless otherwise indicated, these figures are found in ANA, LC, Tomo 37, <u>Libro Manual de la Tesorería General...año 1834</u>.

-1835-

RECEIPTS	Pesos

Taxes.. 19,031 (27.93%)
    Agriculture................... 7,136*
    Itapua................... 5,935*
    Excise....................... 4,920
    Official Legal Paper......... 1,026*
    Abolished Tithe.............. 14*

Sale of State Products to Public............. 16,481 (24.19%)
    Merchandise..............13,847
    Agricultural products
      and animals.............. 2,393
    Iron..................... 170
    Medicines................ 71

Sale of State Products to Troops............. 9,229 (13.55%)

Confiscations................................ 7,978* (11.71%)

Rents.. 5,835 (8.57%)
    State lands............... 5,816
    State property........... 19

State Inheritance......(2,552 + 1,856*)..... 4,408 (6.47%)

Transfer from Pueblos........................ 2,890* (4.24%)

Forced Contributions...(1,407 + 214**)...... 1,621 (2.38%)

Collection of Debts.......................... 615 (.9%)

Miscellaneous................................ 38 (.06%)
    Breakage of state
      property................ 31
    Illegible................ 7

    Total................................. 68,126

*These figures are the difference between the sums found in ANA, NE#1880, Dinero Efectivo en Depósito, Junio 15, 1835, and ANA, NE#1875, Dinero Efectivo en Depósito, Abril 15, 1834. The "State Inheritance" figure of 1,856 pesos is adjusted to account for the return of funds from this category since 1832.

**ANA, NE#1871, Cuaderno...Contribución de los Negociantes.

–1835–

EXPENDITURES		Pesos
Military..		62,456 (85.29%)
Army salaries (including musicians)..........	37,755	
Expenses for recruits....	23,215	
Sailors' salaries........	511	
Lighting and masses......	402	
Doctor...................	300	
Provisions for troops....	200	
Leatherworker............	73	
State Works...............................		5,422 (7.4%)
Salaries.................	5,312	
Charcoal.................	110	
State Operating Expenses....................		2,999 (4.1%)
Government Salaries.........................		1,546 (2.11%)
Treasury staff...........	1,116	
Primary School Teacher........	247	
Jailer...................	99	
Lamplighter..............	84	
Church.....................................		320 (.44%)
General Expenses...........................		484 (.66%)
Purchase of city lot.....	412	
Maintenance of prisoner..	72	
Total.................................		73,227

	Pesos
TOTAL EXPENDITURES...................................	73,227
TOTAL RECEIPTS.......................................	68,126
DEFICIT...	5,101

Unless otherwise indicated, these figures are found in ANA, LC, Tomo 38, Libro Manual de la Tesorería General...año 1835. The first 21 entries of this ledger are missing.

-1837-

RECEIPTS	Pesos
Confiscations...............................	40,291*(37.41%)
Sale of State Products to Troops...........	28,419 (26.39%)
Sale of State Products to Public...........	22,609 (20.99%)
Merchandise............. 16,869	
Agricultural products	
and animals............ 2,999	
Glassware and crockery.. 1,938	
Medicines............... 803	
Taxes.......................................	9,553 (8.87%)
Agriculture.................. 5,429*	
Itapúa....................... 1,827*	
Excise....................... 1,568	
Official Legal Paper......... 722*	
Abolished Tithe.............. 7*	
Rents.......................................	5,148 (4.79%)
State lands............. 5,140	
State property.......... 8	
Collection of Debts........................	613 (.57%)
Transfer from Pueblos......................	515*(.48%)
State Inheritance..........................	323 (.3%)
Miscellaneous..............................	182 (.17%)
Sale of city lot........ 90	
Breakage of state	
property............... 71	
Audit, overpay, etc..... 21	
Forced Contributions.......................	48**(.04%)
Total............................	107,701

*These figures are the difference between the figures found in ANA, NE#2607, Dinero Efectivo en Depósito, Noviembre 15, 1837, and ANA, NE#1883, Dinero Efectivo en Depósito, Octubre 15, 1836.

**ANA, NE#1871, Cuaderno...Contribución de los Negociantes.

-1837-

EXPENDITURES		Pesos
Military........		115,627 (91.48%)
Army salaries (including musicians)..........	113,448	
Lighting and masses......	701	
Sailors' salaries........	532	
Escort of state ships....	402	
Doctor...................	289	
Provisions to troops.....	182	
Leatherworker............	73	
State Works..........		4,620 (3.66%)
Salaries.................	4,549	
Charcoal.................	71	
State Operating Expenses........		3,347 (2.65%)
Government Salaries.............		1,782 (1.41%)
Treasury staff...........	864	
Public Defender for Minors and the Poor (2½ years salary)...................	313	
Primary School Teacher........	247	
Police...................	175	
Jailer...................	99	
Lamplighter..............	84	
Church..........		320 (.25%)
General Expenses.............		667 (.53%)
Purchase of city lots....	667	
Total............		126,363

	Pesos
TOTAL EXPENDITURES................	126,363
TOTAL RECEIPTS....................	107,701
DEFICIT.......................	18,662

Unless otherwise indicated, these figures are found in ANA, LC, Tomo 40, Libro Manual de la Tesorería General...año 1837. (A register of receipts from November 30, 1837-June 23, 1841 is found in NE#1290.)

-1838-

RECEIPTS		Pesos	
Sale of State Products to Troops............		37,810	(28.49%)
Sale of State Products to Public............		30,254	(22.8%)
Merchandise...............	22,782		
Medicines.................	2,931		
Animals...................	1,862		
Glassware and crockery..	1,600		
Iron (also small quantity of copper)........	1,079		
Taxes..		20,295	(15.29%)
Agriculture...............	11,132*		
Itapúa (3,191* + 1,210).................	4,401		
Excise....................	2,474		
Official Legal Paper........	2,288*		
Transfer from Pueblos......................		13,609*	(10.26%)
Confiscations.......(3,302* + 10,186)......		13,488	(10.16%)
Rents.......................................		7,037	(5.3%)
State lands..............	6,919		
State property..........	118		
Collection of Debts........................		6,822	(5.14%)
State Inheritance...(1,113* + 412).........		1,525	(1.15%)
Forced Contributions......................		1,236	(.93%)
Fines.......................................		98	(.07%)
Miscellaneous.............................		527	(.4%)
Audit, overpay, etc.....	389		
Breakage of state property...............	138		
Total...............................		132,701	

*These figures are the differences between the sums found in ANA, NE#1896, Dinero Efectivo en Depósito, Diciembre 15, 1838, and Dinero Efectivo en Depósito, Noviembre 15, 1837. The "State Inheritance" figure of 1,113 pesos is adjusted to account for the return of funds from this category in 1836 and 1837.

-1838-

EXPENDITURES		Pesos	
Military		120,594	(94.51%)
Army salaries (including musicians)	114,670		
Cloths and materials	4,262		
Lighting and masses	718		
Escort of state ships	362		
Sailors' salaries	303		
Doctor	206		
Leatherworker	73		
State Works		3,373	(2.64%)
Salaries	3,272		
Charcoal	101		
State Operating Expenses		1,714	(1.34%)
Government Salaries		1,592	(1.25%)
Treasury staff	1,092		
Primary School Teacher	247		
Jailer	99		
Lamplighter	84		
Police	70		
Church		320	(.25%)
General Expenses		31	(.02%)
Purchase of city lot	25		
Miscellaneous	6		
Total		127,624	

	Pesos
TOTAL RECEIPTS	132,701
TOTAL EXPENDITURES	127,624
SURPLUS	5,077

Unless otherwise indicated, these figures are found in ANA, LC, Tomo 41, <u>Libro Manual de la Tesorería General...año 1838</u>. The first 21 entries are missing.

-1839-

RECEIPTS		Pesos	
Sale of State Products to Troops............		26,381	(29.17%)
Sale of State Products to Public............		21,935	(24.25%)
Merchandise................	11,134		
Medicines..................	4,097		
Cattle.....................	3,000		
Glassware & crockery.......	2,800		
Iron.......................	806		
Salt.......................	98		
Taxes.......................................		18,576	(20.54%)
Itapúa (1,849* + 8,240)..	10,089		
Agriculture................	6,604*		
Official Legal Paper.......	991*		
Excise.....................	892		
Confiscations......(8,538* + 966)..........		9,504	(10.51%)
Rents.......................................		6,319	(6.99%)
State lands...............	6,157		
State property...........	162		
Forced Contributions.......................		3,000	(3.32%)
State Inheritance....(933* + 1,302)........		2,235	(2.47%)
Transfer from Pueblos......................		1,068*	(1.18%)
Collection of Debts........................		429	(.47%)
Fines.......................................		26	(.03%)
Miscellaneous..............................		969	(1.07%)
Forfeit for mistreatment of slaves..........	630		
Sale of city lots........	172		
Breakage of state property...............	117		
Total.............................		90,442	

*These figures are the differences between the sums found in ANA, NE#1899, Dinero Efectivo en Depósito, Diciembre 15, 1839, and ANA, NE#1896, Dinero Efectivo en Depósito, Diciembre 15, 1838.

-1839-

EXPENDITURES		Pesos	
Military............................		96,629	(88.75%)
Army salaries (including musicians)..........	94,371		
Lighting and masses......	814		
Expenses for recruits....	745		
Doctor...................	288		
Sailors' salaries........	225		
Escort of state ships....	186		
State Works.........................		4,595	(4.22%)
State Operating Expenses.............		4,649	(4.27%)
Salaries.................	4,566		
Charcoal.................	83		
Government Salaries.................		1,570	(1.44%)
Treasury staff...........	1,140		
Primary School Teacher........	247		
Jailer...................	99		
Lamplighter..............	84		
Church..............................		320	(.29%)
General Expenses....................		1,109	(1.01%)
Purchase of city lots....	1,052		
Expenses of state lawsuit	36		
Care of orphan...........	21		
Total......................		108,872	

	Pesos
TOTAL EXPENDITURES................................	108,872
TOTAL RECEIPTS....................................	90,442
DEFICIT..	18,430

Unless otherwise indicated, these figures are found in ANA, LC, Tomo 42, <u>Libro Manual de la Tesorería General...año 1839</u>.

-1840-

RECEIPTS		Pesos
Sale of State Products to Public..........		47,736 (25.63%)
Merchandise (including glassware & crockery)...	33,475	
Cattle...................	5,429	
English linen & steel....	3,059	
Medicines................	3,000	
Iron.....................	2,773	
State Inheritance......(35,618* + 5,008)...		40,626 (21.59%)
Sale of State Products to Troops...........		35,148 (18.68%)
Taxes......................................		31,084 (16.52%)
Itapúa (22,253 + 71*)....	22,324	
Agriculture..................	5,711*	
Excise.......................	1,191	
Official Legal Paper.........	1,053*	
Cattle...................	805	
Confiscations..........(6,295* + 4,064)....		10,359 (5.5%)
Fines......................................		8,440 (4.48%)
Lawsuit against Señora Machain................	8,240	
Miscellaneous............	200	
Rents......................................		7,268 (3.86%)
State lands..............	7,219	
State property...........	49	
Transfer from Pueblos.....................		4,902*(2.6%)
Sale of State Livestock to Brazilians......		2,344 (1.25%)
Collection of Debts.......................		8
Miscellaneous.............................		308 (.16%)
Sale of city lots........	155	
Breakage of state property................	138	
Overpay and audit........	15	
Total................................		188,223

*These figures are the differences between the sums found in ANA, NE#2622, Dinero Efectivo en Depósito, Diciembre 15, 1840, and ANA, NE#1899, Dinero Efectivo en Depósito, Diciembre 15, 1839.

-1840-

EXPENDITURES		Pesos	
Military		112,553	(89.22%)
Army salaries (including musicians)	111,296		
Lighting and masses	866		
Sailors' salaries	205		
Doctor	186		
State Works		4,973	(3.94%)
Salaries	4,890		
Charcoal	83		
State Operating Expenses (includes lamplighter)		3,978	(3.15%)
Government Salaries		2,926	(2.32%)
Treasury staff	1,199		
Four Members of the Junta (Oct.-Dec.)	813		
President of Junta (Oct.-Dec.)	407		
Primary School Teacher	247		
Jailer	99		
Secretary (Oct.-Dec.)	72		
Recording Clerk (Oct.-Dec.)	51		
Librarian (Oct.-Dec.)	38		
General Expenses		1,507	(1.19%)
Purchase of yerba for state employees	1,273		
Expenses of Francia's funeral	152		
Care of orphan	41		
Aid to individual	41		
Church		285	(.23%)
Total		126,222	

	Pesos
TOTAL RECEIPTS	188,223
TOTAL EXPENDITURES	126,222
SURPLUS	62,001

Unless otherwise indicated, these figures are found in ANA, LC, Tomo 43, <u>Libro Manual de la Tesorería General...año 1840</u>.

Archival Locations of Paraguayan National Budgets

1816   ANA, LC, Tomo 15, Libro Manual de la Caxa de Hazienda ...para la Cuenta del año 1816.

1818   ANA, NE#1230, Cuenta general de las Entradas y Salidas ocurridas en la Tesorería General de Hacienda de la República del Paraguay para todo el año de 1818.

1819   ANA, LC, Tomo 16, Libro Manual de la Caxa de Hazienda ...para la Cuenta desde 16 de Abril a fin de Diciembre 1819. A copy is found in NE#1119.

1820   ANA, LC, Tomo 17, Libro Manual de la Caxa de Hazienda ...para la Cuenta del año 1820. A copy is found in NE#1839.

ANA, LC, Tomo 18, Libro Manual de la Tesorería de Guerra... para la Cuenta corriente desde 15 de Noviembre de 1819, y todo el año siguiente de 1820. A copy is found in NE#3104.

1821   ANA, LC, Tomo 19, Libro Manual de la Caxa de Hazienda ...para la Cuenta del año de 1821. A copy is found in NE#1840.

1822   ANA, LC, Tomo 20. Although the title page is missing, and regardless of the mislabeled cover which reads 1821, this volume is the Libro Manual de la Caxa de Hazienda... para la Cuenta del año de 1822.

ANA, LC, Tomo 21, Libro Manual de la Tesorería de Guerra... para la Cuenta corriente desde 1 de Enero hasta fin de Diciembre del año de 1822. A copy is found in NE#1841 and NE#1842.

1823   ANA, LC, Tomo 22, Libro Manual de la Caxa de Hazienda ...para la Cuenta del año de 1823. A copy is found in NE#3106.

ANA, LC, Tomo 23, Libro Manual de la Tesorería de Guerra... para la Cuenta del año 1823. A copy is found in NE#1844.

1824   ANA, NE#1844, Cuenta General del año 1824.

1826   ANA, LC, Tomo 25, Libro Manual de la Tesorería de Guerra... desde Enero 1 hasta el fin de Julio de 1826. Tomo 26 is a copy of Tomo 25.

1826 cont. ANA, LC, Tomo 24, Libro Manual de la Tesorería de Guerra... desde Julio 31 hasta el fin de Diciembre de 1826.

1827 ANA, LC, Tomo 27, Libro Manual de la Tesorería General... desde Mayo 30 hasta el fin de Diciembre de 1827. Tomos 28 and 29 are copies of Tomo 27.

1828 ANA, LC, Tomo 30, Libro Manual de la Tesorería General... año 1828 (mislabeled 1827).

1829 ANA, LC, Tomo 32, Libro Manual de la Tesorería General... desde Enero hasta Septiembre de 1829. Tomo 31, which is mislabeled 1828, is a copy of Tomo 32.

ANA, LC, Tomo 33, Libro Manual de la Tesorería General... Septiembre hasta el fin de Diciembre de 1829.

1830 ANA, LC, Tomo 39, Libro Manual de la Tesorería General... desde Enero hasta Noviembre 6, 1831 (mislabeled 1836)..

1831 ANA, LC, Tomo 34, Libro Manual de la Tesorería General... año 1831.

1832 ANA, LC, Tomo 35, Libro Manual de la Tesorería General... año 1832.

1833 ANA, LC, Tomo 36, Libro Manual de la Tesorería General... año 1833.

1834 ANA, LC, Tomo 37, Libro Manual de la Tesorería General... año 1834.

1835 ANA, LC, Tomo 38, Libro Manual de la Tesorería General... año 1835. The first 21 entries of this ledger are missing.

1837 ANA, LC, Tomo 40, Libro Manual de la Tesorería General... año 1837. A register of receipts from November 30, 1837 to June 23, 1841 is found in NE#1290.

1838 ANA, LC, Tomo 41, Libro Manual de la Tesorería General... año 1838. The first 21 entries are missing.

1839 ANA, LC, Tomo 42, Libro Manual de la Tesorería General... año 1839.

1840 ANA, LC, Tomo 43, Libro Manual de la Tesorería General... año 1840.

APPENDIX B

CASH HELD IN DEPOSIT

	Page
1818	216
1819	216
1820	217
1821	217
1827	218
1828	218
1829	218
1830	219
1831	219
1832	220
1833	220
1834	221
1835	221
1836	222
1837	222
1838	223
1839	223
1840	224

CASH HELD IN DEPOSIT - 1818*

	Pesos
Individuals	85,456
Sacred Places of Jerusalem	2,813
Administration of Mail	1,876
Conspirators	1,158
Priest	344
Department of Commerce	180
Fines	49
Total	91,876

CASH HELD IN DEPOSIT - 1819**

	Pesos
Individuals	87,722
Sacred Places of Jerusalem	4,202
Administration of Caazapá	2.392
Administration of Mail	1,876
Conspirators	1,158
Debts	1,052
Franciscans	611
Department of Commerce	180
Fines	49
Total	99,242

* ANA, NE#1230, Cuenta General... de la República del Paraguay para todo el año de 1818.

** ANA, NE#1119, Libro Manual de la Caxa de Hazienda... para la Cuenta desde 16 de Abril a fin de Diciembre 1819.

CASH HELD IN DEPOSIT - 1820*

	Pesos
Individuals	88,593
Sacred Places of Jerusalem	4,325
Administration of Caazapá	2,392
Administration of Mail	1,876
Conspirators	1,158
Franciscans	611
Priest	416
Department of Commerce	180
Fines	49
Total	99,600

CASH HELD IN DEPOSIT - 1821**

	Pesos
Individuals	89,946
Sacred Places of Jerusalem	4.333
Administration of Caazapá	2,392
Administration of Mail	1,876
Conspirators	1,158
Franciscans	611
Priest	416
Department of Commerce	180
Fines	49
Total	100,961

* ANA, NE#1839, Libro Manual de la Caxa de Hazienda... para la Cuenta del año 1820.

** ANA, NE#1840, Libro Manual de la Caxa de Hazienda... para la Cuenta del año 1821.

CASH HELD IN DEPOSIT - 1827*	Pesos
Tithe	25,697
Official Legal Paper	915
Town of Yuti	446
Total ...	27,058

CASH HELD IN DEPOSIT - 1828**	Pesos
Tithe	63,993
Church	1,648
Official Legal Paper	1,413
Town of Yuti	446
Prisoner	103
Total ...	67,603

CASH HELD IN DEPOSIT - 1829***	Pesos
Tithe	20,125
Confiscations from Foreigners	8,652
Churches (7 Churches and 1 Chapel)	7,769
Priests	6,636
Official Legal Paper	359
Town of Yuti	446
Prisoner	103
Total ...	44,090

* ANA,NE#1849, Dinero Efectivo en Depósito, diciembre 15,1827.
** ANA,NE#1851, Dinero Efectivo en Depósito, diciembre, 1828.
*** ANA,NE#1854, Dinero Efectivo en Depósito, diciembre 15,1829.

CASH HELD IN DEPOSIT - 1830*	Pesos
Abolished Tithe	60,628
Confiscations from Foreigners	14,473
Churches (12 Churches and 1 Chapel)	11,115
State Inheritance	7,866
Priests	6,286
Official Legal Paper	1,903
Agricultural Tax	124
Total	102,395

CASH HELD IN DEPOSIT - 1831**	Pesos
Abolished Tithe	60,628
Confiscations from Foreigners	14,473
Churches (14 Churches and 1 Chapel)	11,965
State Inheritance	7,866
Priests	6,202
Agricultural Tax	124
Official Legal Paper	99
Total	101,357

* ANA, NE#1857, <u>Dinero Efectivo en Depósito, diciembre 15,1830</u>.
** ANA, NE#1850, <u>Dinero Efectivo en Depósito, febrero 15,1831</u>.

CASH HELD IN DEPOSIT - 1832*

	Pesos
Abolished Tithe	66,265
Agricultural Tax	17,858
Churches (18 Churches and 1 Chapel)	16,805
Confiscations from Foreigners	14,267
State Inheritance	7,626
Missions (3 Towns)	6,815
Priests	5,650
Itapúa Export Tax	5,628
Official Legal Paper	904
Total	141,818

CASH HELD IN DEPOSIT - 1833**

	Pesos
Abolished Tithe	70,004
Agricultural Tax	24,343
Churches (21 Churches and 1 Chapel)	19,379
Confiscations from Foreigners	14,267
State Inheritance	7,745
Missions (4 Towns)	6,995
Itapúa Export Tax	6,201
Priests	5,561
Official Legal Paper	1,806
Debt owed to English merchant	1,100
Total	157,401

*ANA, NE#1865, <u>Dinero Efectivo en Depósito, diciembre 15,1832</u>.
**ANA, NE#1869, <u>Dinero Efectivo en Depósito, diciembre 15,1833</u>.

CASH HELD IN DEPOSIT – 1834*

	Pesos
Abolished Tithe	70,004
Agricultural Tax	25,824
Churches (22 Churches and 1 Chapel)	19,800
Confiscations from Foreigners	14,067
State Inheritance	7,595
Missions (4 Towns)	6,995
Itapúa Export Tax	6,200
Priests	5,534
Prisoners	5,109
Official Legal Paper	2,428
Debt owed to English merchant	1,100
Total	164,656

CASH HELD IN DEPOSIT – 1835**

	Pesos
Abolished Tithe	70.018
Agricultural Tax	32.960
Churches (29 Churches and 1 Chapel)	26,082
Confiscations from Foreigners	14,067
Itapúa Export Tax	12,135
Missions (6 Towns)	9,885
State Inheritance	9,722
Prisoners and Debts	6,805
Priests	5,390
Official Legal Paper	3,454
Debt owed to English merchant	1,100
Transport Tax on Products brought to Itapúa	427
Total	192,045

* ANA, NE#1875, Dinero Efectivo en Depósito, abril 15, 1834.

** ANA, NE#1880, Dinero Efectivo en Depósito, junio 15, 1835.

CASH HELD IN DEPOSIT - 1836*

	Pesos
Abolished Tithe	70,787
Agricultural Tax	40,347
Itapúa Export Tax	29,005
Churches (31 Churches and 2 Chapels)	27,561
Missions (7 Towns)	17,855
Confiscations from Foreigners	14,067
State Inheritance	9,529
Prisoners and Debts	7,576
Priests	5,225
Official Legal Paper	4,695
Debt owed to English merchant	1,100
Transport Tax on Products brought to Itapúa	630
Total	228,377

CASH HELD IN DEPOSIT - 1837**

	Pesos
Abolished Tithe	70,794
Prisoners and Debts	47,177
Agricultural Tax	45.776
Itapúa Export Tax	30,832
Churches (32 Churches and 2 Chapels)	28,251
Missions (7 Towns)	18,370
Confiscations from Foreigners	14,067
State Inheritance	9,513
Official Legal Paper	5,417
Priests	5,092
Debt owed to English merchant	1,100
Transport Tax on Products brought to Itapúa	630
Total	277,019

* ANA, NE#1883, Dinero Efectivo en Depósito, octubre, 1836.

** ANA, NE#2607, Dinero Efectivo en Depósito, noviembre 15, 1837.

CASH HELD IN DEPOSIT - 1838*

	Pesos
Abolished Tithe	70,794
Agricultural Tax	56,908
Prisoners and Debts	48,175
Itapúa Export Tax	34,023
Missions (9 Towns)	31,979
Churches (35 Churches and 2 Chapels)	30,555
Confiscations from Foreigners	14,067
State Inheritance	10,835
Official Legal Paper	7,705
Priests	4,978
Debt owed to English merchant	1,100
Transport Tax on Products brought to Itapúa	630
Total	311,749

CASH HELD IN DEPOSIT - 1839**

	Pesos
Abolished Tithe	70,794
Agricultural Tax	63,512
Prisoners and Debts	52,122
Itapúa Export Tax	35,872
Churches (38 Churches and 2 Chapels)	35,146
Missions (10 Towns)	33,047
Confiscations from Foreigners	14,067
State Inheritance	11,768
Official Legal Paper	8,696
Priests	4,978
Debt owed to English merchant	1,100
Transport Tax on Products brought to Itapúa	678
Total	331,780

* ANA,NE#1896, Dinero Efectivo en Depósito, diciembre 15,1838.
** ANA,NE#1899, Dinero Efectivo en Depósito, diciembre 15,1839.

CASH HELD IN DEPOSIT - 1840*

	Pesos
Abolished Tithe	70,794
Agricultural Tax	69,223
Prisoners and Debts	55,983
State Inheritance (Including 36,646 pesos from Francia)	47,386
Missions (11 Towns)	37,949
Churches (39 Churches and 2 Chapels)	37,580
Itapúa Export Tax	35,943
Confiscations from Foreigners	14,067
Official Legal Paper	9,749
Priests	4,978
Debt owed to English merchant	1,100
Transport Tax on Products brought to Itapua	678
Total	385,430

* ANA, NE#2622, Dinero Efectivo en Depósito, diciembre 15, 1840.

APPENDIX C

PARAGUAYAN EXPORTS
                                          Page

             1800...................... 226
             1816...................... 227
             1818...................... 228
             1819...................... 229
             1820...................... 230
             1829...................... 231
             1832...................... 232
             1835...................... 233
             1837...................... 234
             1838...................... 235
             1839...................... 236
Asuncion-Buenos Aires Exports 1827.... 237

PARAGUAYAN EXPORTS - 1800

Yerba*	2,739	tons
Cascara**	200	tons
Sugar	19.7	tons
Honey	17.9	tons
Sweets	15.8	tons
Woods	19,084	yards
Leather	2,697	hides
	2,134	soles
Cash	15,775	pesos

Plus small quantities of crockery, oranges, starch, pepper, salt, and one black slave named Tomás.

ANA, NE#3360, <u>Libro de Asiento de Guías para el año de 1800</u>. As tobacco was a royal monopoly, licenses were not issued for its exportation and it is therefore not included in the ledger. Judging from incomplete information, approximately 300 to 400 tons of tobacco were exported.

*Calculated by multiplying:
$$\frac{28{,}948 \text{ tercios} \times 7.5 \text{ arrobas} \times 25 \text{ pounds}}{2{,}000 \text{ pounds}}$$

**The bark of the curupay tree, or <u>Cáscara de Curupaí</u>, was widely used in the curing of hides.

PARAGUAYAN EXPORTS - 1816

				Pesos	
Yerba..........	3,624	tons*	....	289,920	(74.10%)
Tobacco........	414.95	tons..............		82,990	(21.21%)
Soles..........	5,644	soles.............		13,405	(3.43%)
Sweets.........	64.60	tons..............		3,876	(.99%)
Aguardiente....	1,389	barrels...........		1,042	(.27%)
				391,233	

Plus small quantities of ship planks, ship cables, crockery, oranges, sugar, honey, watermelons, wax, sugar cane, and starch, amounting to approximately another 2 percent of total exports.

Export quantities are calculated upon their respective export taxes found in ANA, NE#1826, Cuadernos de Recaudación ...por el Derecho de Sisa sobre los frutos exportados, año 1816. As Paraguayan hardwoods were a state monopoly, export taxes were not collected on them and they are therefore not included in the ledger.

The peso value of yerba, tobacco, sweets, and aguardiente (80 pesos, 200 pesos, 60 pesos per ton, and 6 reales per barrel respectively) are calculated upon 1829 Pilar export prices found in ANA, NE#1853, Pilar Alcabala Receipts, 1829. The peso value of soles (19 reales each) is calculated upon their 1818 export value found in ANA, SH#229, Cuaderno de Venta, Compras y Gastos... año de 1818.

*Calculated at 7.5 arrobas per tercio.

PARAGUAYAN EXPORTS - 1818

			Pesos	
Yerba	2,568.53	tons*	205,482	(70.23%)
Tobacco	339.23	tons	67,846	(23.19%)
Soles	4,864	soles	11,552	(3.95%)
Sweets	104.10	tons	6,246	(2.13%)
Aguardiente	1,917	barrels	1,438	(.49%)
			292,564	

Plus small quantities of oranges, honey, wood, ship cables, crockery, starch, corn, sugar, baskets, stone, rice, and sugar cane, amounting to approximately another 4 percent of total exports.

Export quantities are calculated upon their respective export taxes found in ANA, NE#1230, <u>Cuenta General de las Entradas y Salidas ocurridas en la Tesorería General... para todo el año de 1818</u>, using the 1816 tax structure found in ANA, NE#1826, <u>Cuadernos de Recaudación... por el Derecho de Sisa sobre los frutos exportados, año 1816</u>. As Paraguayan hardwoods were a state monopoly, export taxes were not collected on them and they are therefore not included in the ledger.

The peso value of yerba, tobacco, sweets, and aguardiente (80 pesos, 200 pesos, 60 pesos per ton, and 6 reales per barrel respectively) are calculated upon 1829 Pilar export prices found in ANA, NE#1853, <u>Pilar Alcabala Receipts, 1829</u>. The peso value of soles (19 reales each) is calculated upon their 1818 export value found in ANA, SH#229, <u>Cuaderno de Venta, Compras y Gastos... año de 1818</u>.

*Calculated at 7.5 arrobas per tercio.

PARAGUAYAN EXPORTS - 1819

				Pesos	
Yerba	1,369	tons*		109,520	(57.09%)
Tobacco	359.42	tons		71,884	(37.47%)
Soles	3,811	soles		9,051	(4.72%)
Sweets	21.12	tons		1,267	(.66%)
Aguardiente	173	barrels		130	(.07%)
				191,852	

Plus small quantities of wood and stones, amounting to approximately another 1 percent of total exports.

Export quantities are yearly projections calculated upon their respective five months' (July-November) export taxes found in ANA, NE#1119, Libro Manual de la Tesorería General... para la cuenta desde 16 de Abril a fin de Diciembre 1819, using the 1816 tax structure found in ANA, NE#1826, Cuadernos de Recaudación... por el Derecho de Sisa sobre los frutos exportados, año 1816. As Paraguayan hardwoods were a state monopoly, export taxes were not collected on them and they are therefore not included in the ledger.

The peso value of yerba, tobacco, sweets, and aguardiente (80 pesos, 200 pesos, 60 pesos per ton, and 6 reales per barrel respectively) are calculated upon 1829 Pilar export prices found in ANA, NE#1853, Pilar Alcabala Receipts, 1829. The peso value of soles (19 reales each) is calculated upon their 1818 export value found in ANA, SH#229, Cuaderno de Venta, Compras y Gastos... año de 1818.

*Calculated at 7.5 arrobas per tercio.

PARAGUAYAN EXPORTS - 1820

			Pesos	
Yerba	529.55 tons*		42,364	(73.68%)
Tobacco	68.45 tons		13,690	(23.81%)
Soles	608 soles		1,444	(2.51%)
			57,498	

Plus small quantities of oranges, ship cables, sweets, stones, starch, and crockery, amounting to approximately another 1 percent of total exports.

Export quantities are calculated upon their respective export taxes found in ANA, NE#1839, <u>Libro Manual de la Caxa de Hazienda...para la Cuenta del ano 1820</u>, using the 1816 tax structure found in ANA, NE#1826, <u>Cuadernos de Recaudación...por el Derecho de Sisa sobre los frutos exportados, ano 1816</u>. As Paraguayan hardwoods were a state monopoly, export taxes were not collected on them and they are therefore not included in the ledger.

The peso value of yerba and tobacco (80 pesos and 200 pesos per ton respectively) are calculated upon 1829 Pilar export prices found in ANA, NE#1853, <u>Pilar Alcabala Receipts, 1829</u>. The peso value of soles (19 reales each) is calculated upon their 1818 export value found in ANA, SH#229, <u>Cuaderno de Venta, Compras y Gastos...año de 1818</u>.

*Calculated at 7.5 arrobas per tercio.

PARAGUAYAN EXPORTS - 1829

			Pesos	
Tobacco.....	80.68	tons.....	28,292	(43.36%)
Yerba.......	140.28	tons.....	15,845	(24.28%)
Livestock...	2,565	animals..	13,201	(20.23%)
Salt........	23.92	tons.....	2,870	(4.39%)
Wagons......	63	wagons...	2,520	(3.86%)
Aguardiente.	1,816	barrels..	1,405	(2.15%)
Honey.......	17.73	tons.....	1,105	(1.69%)
			65,238	

Plus small quantities of corn, crockery, sugar, sweets, and hides, amounting to approximately another 4 percent of total exports.

Compiled from Appendices <u>Pilar Exports 1829</u> and <u>Itapúa Exports 1829</u>.

PARAGUAYAN EXPORTS - 1832

			Pesos	
Yerba..........	325.23	tons..............	55,228	(58.39%)
Tobacco........	77.21	tons..............	28,888	(30.54%)
Livestock......	1,435	animals..........	5,760	(6.09%)
Salt...........	14.02	tons..............	1,682	(1.77%)
Aguardiente....	1,784	barrels...........	1,614	(1.70%)
Wagons.........	35	wagons............	1,400	(1.48%)
			94,572	

Plus small quantities of hides, cigars, sweets, honey, soap, starch, corn, and crockery, amounting to approximately another 4 percent of total exports.

Compiled from Appendices <u>Pilar Exports 1832</u> and <u>Itapúa Exports 1832</u>.

PARAGUAYAN EXPORTS - 1835

			Pesos	
Tobacco........	300.20	tons...............	115,406	(76.69%)
Yerba..........	145.97	tons...............	17,283	(11.48%)
Hides.......... 7,843		hides..............	6,566	(4.36%)
Salt...........	42.62	tons...............	5,114	(3.39%)
Wagons.........	83	wagons.............	4,565	(3.03%)
Aguardiente.... 1,861		barrels............	1,535	(1.02%)
			150,469	

Plus small quantities of sweets, honey, corn, cigars, starch, soap, crockery, cheese, and bacon, amounting to approximately another 3 percent of total exports.

Compiled from Appendices Pilar Exports 1835 and Itapúa Exports 1835.

PARAGUAYAN EXPORTS - 1837

		Pesos	
Tobacco........	155.45 tons............ (+ 6.60 tons*) = 162.05 tons total**....	56,639 59,279**	(54.51%) (39.73%)**
Yerba..........	219.43 tons............ (+123.66 tons*) = 343.09 tons total**....	24,552 46,811**	(23.63%) (31.37%)**
Hides..........	9,347 (+10,323*)....... = 19,670 total**.......	8,693 18,180**	(8.36%) (12.18%)**
Wagons.........	123....................	6,765 6,765	(6.51%) (4.53%)**
Salt...........	37.90 tons.............	4,548 4,548	(4.37%) (3.04%)**
Corn...........	468 fanegas............	1,404 1,404	(1.35%) (.94%)**
Aguardiente....	1,778 barrels..........	1,334 1,334	(1.28%) (.89%)**
Soles..........	3,621*.................	10,863**	(7.28%)**
		103,935 149,184**	

Plus small quantities of cigars, honey, sweets, rice, starch, sugar, soap, dried manioc, onions, cheese, crockery, and hams, amounting to approximately another 6 percent of total exports.

Compiled from Appendices <u>Pilar Exports 1837</u> and <u>Itapúa Exports 1837</u>.

*State exports from Itapúa. See Appendix <u>State Exports Itapúa 1837</u>.

**These figures include state exports from Itapúa.

PARAGUAYAN EXPORTS - 1838

		Pesos	
Yerba..........	156.83 tons..............	20,702	(43.07%)
	(+ 195.63 tons*) =		
	352.46 tons total**.....	55,915**	(48.75%)**
Tobacco........	48.56 tons..............	15,593	(32.44%)
	(+ 27.56 tons*) =		
	76.12 tons total**......	26,617**	(23.20%)**
Wagons.........	88......................	4,840	(10.07%)
		4,840	(4.22%)**
Salt...........	23.55 tons..............	2,826	(5.87%)
		2,826	(2.46%)**
Hides..........	2,874 (+ 13,427*).......	2,677	(5.56%)
	= 16,301 total**........	16,104**	(14.04%)**
Aguardiente....	1,900 barrels...........	1,425	(2.96%)
		1,425	(1.24%)**
Soles..........	2,320*..................	6,960**	(6.06%)**
		48,063	
		114,687**	

Plus small quantities of corn, cigars, honey, sweets, rice, starch, sugar, soap, dried manioc, onions, cheese, crockery, and hams, amounting to approximately another 8 percent of total exports.

Compiled from Appendices <u>Pilar Exports 1838</u> and <u>Itapúa Exports 1838</u>.

*State exports from Itapúa. See Appendix <u>State Exports Itapúa 1837</u>.

**These figures include state exports from Itapúa.

PARAGUAYAN EXPORTS - 1839

			Pesos	
Yerba	113.55	tons	14,006	(53.12%)
Tobacco	25.32	tons	7,826	(29.68%)
Salt	13.98	tons	1,678	(6.36%)
Aguardiente	2,004	barrels	1,503	(5.70%)
Hides	918	hides	912	(3.45%)
Wagons	8	wagons	440	(1.66%)
			26,365	

Plus small quantities of corn, cigars, honey, sweets, rice, starch, sugar, soap, dried manioc, onions, cheese, crockery, and hams, amounting to approximately another 10 percent of total exports.

Compiled from Appendices <u>Pilar Exports 1839</u> and <u>Itapúa Exports 1839</u>.

EXPORTS ASUNCION-BUENOS AIRES - 1827

Yerba... 138.94 tons*
Tobacco....................................... 32.11 tons
Leather....................................... 273 hides
                                               85 soles

ANA, LC, Tomo 27, Libro Manual de la Tesorería General...
desde Mayo 30 hasta el fin de Diciembre de 1827. These
figures do not include any exports from January 1 to May
29, 1827. They only represent five large shipments directly from Asunción to Buenos Aires.

*Calculated at 7.5 arrobas per tercio.

APPENDIX D

PILAR EXPORTS

	Page
1829	239
1832	240
1835	241
1837	242
1838	243
1839	244

PILAR EXPORTS - 1829

		Pesos	
Yerba..........	94.06 tons at 80 pesos.....	7,525	(45.46%)
Tobacco........	19.90 tons at 200 pesos....	3,980	(24.04%)
Salt...........	23.92 tons at 120 pesos....	2,870	(17.34%)
Aguardiente....	1,645 barrels at 6 reales..	1,234	(7.45%)
Honey..........	15.70 tons at 60 pesos.....	942	(5.69%)
		16,551	

Plus small quantities of corn, crockery, sugar, and sweets, amounting to approximately another 8 percent of total exports.

ANA, NE#1853, Comprobantes de Alcabala, Pilar, 1829.

PILAR EXPORTS - 1832

		Pesos
Yerba..........	32.02 tons................	2,450 (34.74%)
	29.22 tons of fresh yerba at 80 pesos = 2,338	
	2.8 tons of old yerba at 40 pesos = 112	
Tobacco........	9.98 tons at 200 pesos.....	1,996 (28.30%)
Salt...........	14.02 tons at 120 pesos....	1,682 (23.85%)
Aguardiente....	1,231 barrels at 6 reales..	923 (13.09%)
		7,051

Plus small quantities of sweets, honey, crockery, starch, corn, and cigars, amounting to approximately another 13 percent of total exports.

ANA, NE#1858, Comprobantes de Alcabala, Pilar, 1832.

PILAR EXPORTS - 1835

		Pesos
Yerba..........	78.57 tons.................	5,151 (35.85%)
	50.20 tons of fresh yerba at 80 pesos = 4,016	
	28.37 tons of old yerba at 40 pesos = 1,135	
Salt...........	42.62 tons at 120 pesos....	5,114 (35.59%)
Tobacco........	17.35 tons at 180 pesos....	3,123 (21.73%)
Aguardiente....	1,305 barrels at 6 reales..	979 (6.81%)
		14,367

Plus small quantities of sweets, honey, starch, corn, and crockery, amounting to approximately another 13 percent of exports.

ANA, NE#1881, Comprobantes de Alcabala, Pilar, 1835.

PILAR EXPORTS - 1837

		Pesos
Yerba..........	134.06 tons................	9,185 (44.07%)
	95.56 tons of fresh yerba at 80 pesos = 7,645	
	38.50 tons of old yerba at 40 pesos = 1,540	
Salt...........	37.90 tons at 120 pesos....	4,548 (21.82%)
Tobacco........	24.27 tons at 180 pesos....	4,369 (20.96%)
Corn...........	468 fanegas at 3 pesos.....	1,404 (6.73%)
Aguardiente....	1,778 barrels at 6 reales..	<u>1,334</u> (6.40%)
		20,840

Plus small quantities of honey, sweets, rice, starch, sugar, crockery, and dried manioc, amounting to approximately another 13 percent of exports.

ANA, NE#1886, <u>Comprobantes de Alcabala, Pilar, 1837</u>.

PILAR EXPORTS - 1838

		Pesos	
Yerba..........	64.65 tons.................	4,110	(33.55%)
	38.10 tons of fresh yerba at 80 pesos = 3,048		
	26.55 tons of old yerba at 40 pesos = 1,062		
Tobacco........	19.46 tons at 200 pesos....	3,892	(31.77%)
Salt...........	23.55 tons at 120 pesos....	2,826	(23.06%)
Aguardiente....	1,900 barrels at 6 reales..	1,425	(11.63%)
		12,253	

Plus small quantities of corn, honey, sweets, rice, starch, sugar, crockery, dried manioc, onions, and ponchos, amounting to approximately another 15 percent of exports.

ANA, NE#3128, Comprobantes de Alcabala, Pilar, 1838.

PILAR EXPORTS - 1839

		Pesos
Yerba..........	55.42 tons..................	3,542 (39.37%)
	33.12 tons of fresh yerba at 80 pesos = 2,650	
	22.30 tons of old yerba at 40 pesos = 892	
Tobacco........	11.36 tons at 200 pesos....	2,272 (25.25%)
Salt...........	13.98 tons at 120 pesos....	1,678 (18.65%)
Aguardiente....	2,004 barrels at 6 reales..	<u>1,503</u> (16.70%)
		8,995

Plus small quantities of corn, honey, sweets, rice, starch, sugar, crockery, dried manioc, onions, and ponchos, amounting to approximately another 15 percent of exports.

ANA, NE#3129, <u>Comprobantes de Alcabala, Pilar, 1839</u>.

APPENDIX E

ITAPUA EXPORTS
                                              Page

        1826............................ 246
        1829............................ 247
        1832............................ 248
        1835............................ 249
        1837............................ 250
        1838............................ 251
        1839............................ 252
Itapúa Export Taxes 1829-1840.............. 253

ITAPUA EXPORTS - 1826

		Pesos
Tobacco......	112.21 tons...................	35,787 (91.67%)
	111.46 tons at 320 pesos = 35,667	
	.75 ton of pipe tobacco at 160 pesos = 120	
Yerba........	17.77 tons at 120 pesos......	2,132 (5.46%)
Wagons.......	23 wagons at 25 pesos........	575 (1.47%)
Hides........	1,091........................	544 (1.39%)
	1,077 cueros de Garra at 4 reales = 539	
	14 cueros Redondos at 3 reales = 5	
		39,038

ANA, NE#1243 and 1244, <u>Comprobantes de Alcabala, Itapua, 1826</u>.

ITAPUA EXPORTS - 1829

		Pesos	
Tobacco	60.78 tons at 400 pesos	24,312	(50.07%)
Livestock	2,565 animals	13,201	(27.30%)
Yerba	46.22 tons at 180 pesos	8,320	(17.20%)
Wagons	63 wagons at 40 pesos	2,520	(5.21%)
		48,353	

Plus small quantities of corn, sweets, aguardiente (171 barrels at 1 peso), honey (2.03 tons at 80 pesos), and hides, amounting to approximately another 3 percent of total exports.

ANA, NE#2569 and 2570, Comprobantes de Alcabala, Itapúa, 1829.

ITAPUA EXPORTS - 1832

		Pesos	
Yerba........	293.21 tons at 180 pesos.....	52,778	(60.78%)
Tobacco......	67.23 tons at 400 pesos......	26,892	(30.97%)
Livestock....	1,435 animals................	5,760	(6.63%)
Wagons.......	35 at 40 pesos...............	1,400	(1.61%)
		86,830	

Plus small quantities of hides, cigars, aguardiente (553 barrels at 1.25 pesos), soap, sweets, corn, starch, and honey, amounting to approximately another 4 percent of total exports.

ANA, NE#2583 and 2584, Comprobantes de Alcabala, Itapúa, 1832.

ITAPUA EXPORTS - 1835

		Pesos
Tobacco......	282.85 tons.................	112,283 (82.83%)
	279.28 tons at 400 pesos = 111,712	
	3.57 tons of pipe tobacco at 160 pesos = 571	
Yerba........	67.40 tons at 180 pesos......	12,132 (8.95%)
Hides........	7,843.......................	6,566 (4.84%)
	5,109 cueros Redondos at 6 reales = 3,832	
	2,734 cueros de Garros at 1 peso = 2,734	
Wagons.......	83 wagons at 55 pesos........	4,565 (3.36%)
		135,546

Plus small quantities of aguardiente (556 barrels at 1 peso), cigars, soap, sweets, corn, cheese, honey, starch, and bacon, amounting to approximately another 2 percent of exports.

ANA, NE#2592, 2593, 2596-2599, <u>Comprobantes de Alcabala, Itapúa, 1835.</u>

ITAPUA EXPORTS - 1837

		Pesos
Tobacco......	131.18 tons...................	52,270 (62.90%)
	130.46 tons at 400 pesos = 52,184	
	.72 ton of pipe tobacco at 120 pesos = 86	
Yerba........	85.37 tons at 180 pesos......	15,367 (18.49%)
Hides........	9,347.......................	8,693 (10.46%)
	6,730 cueros de Garra at 1 peso = 6,730	
	2,617 cueros Redondos at 6 reales = 1,963	
Wagons.......	123 wagons at 55 pesos.......	6,765 (8.14%)
		83,095

Plus small quantities of cigars, aguardiente, corn, sugar, salt, onions, rice, sweets, soap, starch, honey, cheese, and hams, amounting to approximately another 4 percent of exports.

ANA, NE#2969-2973, Comprobantes de Alcabala, Itapúa, 1837.

ITAPUA EXPORTS - 1838

		Pesos
Yerba........	92.18 tons at 180 pesos......	16,592 (46.33%)
Tobacco......	29.48 tons...................	11,701 (32.67%)
	29.10 tons at 400 pesos = 11,640	
	.38 ton of pipe tobacco at 160 pesos = 61	
Wagons.......	88 wagons at 55 pesos........	4,840 (13.51%)
Hides........	2,874........................	2,677 (7.47%)
	2,086 cueros de Garra at 1 peso = 2,086	
	788 cueros Redondos at 6 reales = 591	
		35,810

Plus small quantities of cigars, honey, aguardiente, corn, sugar, salt, onions, rice, sweets, soap, starch, cheese, and hams, amounting to approximately another 5 percent of exports.

ANA, NE#1304-1307, Comprobantes de Alcabala, Itapua, 1838.

ITAPUA EXPORTS - 1839

		Pesos	
Yerba........	58.13 tons at 180 pesos......	10,464	(60.24%)
Tobacco......	13.96 tons...................	5,554	(31.97%)
	13.81 tons at 400 pesos = 5,524		
	.15 ton of pipe tobacco at 200 pesos = 30		
Hides........	918..........................	912	(5.24%)
	893 cueros de Garra at 1 peso = 893		
	25 cueros Redondos at 6 reales = 19		
Wagons.......	8 at 55 pesos................	440	(2.53%)
		17,370	

Plus small quantities of cigars, honey, aguardiente, corn, sugar, salt, onions, sweets, soap, starch, cheese, and hams, amounting to approximately another 7 percent of exports.

ANA, NE#1308 and 1309, Comprobantes de Alcabala, Itapúa, 1839.

ITAPUA EXPORT TAXES - 1829-1840

	Tax	Percentage of Value*
Wagons	2 pesos each	3.6%
Aguardiente	.5 real per barrel	6.3%
Yerba	1.5 pesos per tercio	8.1%
Cigars	10 reales per arroba	8.3%
Sugar	4 reales per arroba	9.1%
Tobacco	5 reales per arroba	12.5%
Corn	.5 real per almud	12.5%
Honey	1 real per asumbre	12.5%
Soles	4 reales each	16.7%
Cueros Redondos	1 real each	16.7%
Cattle	1 peso each	20.0%
Cueros de Garra	2 reales each	25.0%

The export taxes on yerba, cigars, tobacco, soles, cattle, and hides were established by the Supreme Decree of June 15, 1829 (ANA, SH#240). Taxes on the other exports were established shortly after and remained constant throughout the 1830's.

*As prices and measures varied slightly during the 1830's, these percentages are close approximations only. In addition, the actual export tax for a given year must also include the Alcabala, which was reduced from 4 to 2 percent by the Supreme Decree of October 24, 1830 (ANA, NE#1862) and further reduced to 1 percent by the Supreme Decree of October 26, 1835 (ANA, NE#1880).

APPENDIX F

STATE EXPORTS

	Page
State Exports Pilar, 1831...............	255
State Exports Itapúa, 1837..............	256
State Exports Itapúa, 1838..............	257

STATE EXPORTS PILAR - 1831

		Pesos	
Yerba*	85.03 tons at 80 pesos	6,802	(81.09%)
Soles	500 at 3 pesos (approximate price)**	1,500	(17.88%)
Hides	86 cueros de Garra at 1 peso	86	(1.02%)
		8,388	

Compiled from the correspondence of Delegado Castro of Pilar to Francia (ANA, SH#394), letters from January 16 to November 22, 1831. These are minimum export figures as the correspondence is obviously incomplete.

*Calculated at 7.5 arrobas per tercio.

**Based upon the price of soles found in ANA, NE#2569, Comprobantes de Alcabala, Itapúa, 1829.

STATE EXPORTS ITAPUA - 1837

		Pesos
Yerba*	123.66 tons at 180 pesos...	22,259 (49.19%)
Soles	3,621 at 3 pesos (approximate price)**	10,863 (24.00%)
Hides	10,323......................	9,487 (20.96%)
	6,978 cueros de Garra at 1 peso = 6,978	
	3,345 cueros Redondos at 6 reales = 2,509	
Tobacco	6.6 tons at 400 pesos......	2,640 (5.83%)
		45,249

Compiled from the correspondence of Delegado Casimiro Roxas of Itapúa to Francia (ANA, SH#377), letters from January 12 to November 30, 1837. These are <u>minimum</u> export figures as the correspondence is obviously incomplete.

*Calculated at 8.5 arrobas per tercio.

**Based upon the price of soles found in ANA, NE#2569, <u>Comprobantes de Alcabala, Itapúa, 1829</u>.

STATE EXPORTS ITAPUA - 1838

		Pesos
Yerba*	195.63 tons at 180 pesos....	35,213 (52.85%)
Hides	13,427 cueros de Garra at 1 peso.....	13,427 (20.15%)
Tobacco	27.56 tons at 400 pesos.....	11,024 (16.54%)
Soles	2,320 at 3 pesos (approximate price)**	6,960 (10.44%)
		66,624

Compiled from the correspondence of Delegado Casimiro Roxas of Itapúa to Francia (ANA, SH#377 and 378) letters from January 8 to December 31, 1838. These are minimum export figures as the correspondence is obviously incomplete.

*Calculated at 8.5 arrobas per tercio.

**Based upon the price of soles found in ANA, NE#2569, Comprobantes de Alcabala, Itapúa, 1829.

APPENDIX G

PARAGUAYAN IMPORT TAXES: 1816-1824

                                                    Import Tax

Year	Import Tax	Ref
1816	83,640 pesos	(A)
1818	58,480 pesos	(B)
1819	42,643 pesos	(C)
1820	69,674 pesos	(D)
1821	44,346 pesos	(E)
1822	4,824 pesos	(F)
1823	19,808 pesos	(G)
1824	27,006 pesos	(H)

A. ANA, LC, Tomo 15, Libro Manual de la Caxa de Hazienda... para la Cuenta del año 1816. (Import taxes from January 1 to March 29 = 8 percent; April to December = 15 percent.)

B. ANA, NE#1230, Cuenta General de las Entradas y Salidas ocurridas en la Tesorería General de Hacienda de la República del Paraguay para todo el año de 1818. (Import taxes for 1818 were 15 percent.)

C. ANA, NE#1119, Libro Manual de la Caxa de Hazienda... para la Cuenta desde 16 de Abril a fin de Diciembre 1819. (Import taxes for 1819 were 15 percent.)

D. ANA, LC, Tomo 17, Libro Manual de la Caxa de Hazienda... para la Cuenta del año 1820. (Import taxes for 1820 were 15 percent.)

E. ANA, LC, Tomo 19, Libro Manual de la Caxa de Hazienda... para la Cuenta del año de 1821. (Import taxes for 1821 were 15 percent.)

F. ANA, LC, Tomo 20. Although the title page is missing, and regardless of the mislabeled cover which reads 1821, this volume is the Libro Manual de la Caxa de Hazienda ...para la Cuenta del año de 1822. (Import taxes for 1822 were 15 percent.)

G. ANA, LC, Tomo 22, Libro Manual de la Caxa de Hazienda... para la Cuenta del año de 1823. (Import taxes were reduced to 12 percent in 1823.)

H. ANA, NE#1844, Cuenta General del año 1824. (Import taxes for 1824 were 12 percent.)

259

APPENDIX H

PARAGUAYAN ARMY

	Page
1828	259
1834	260
1837	261
1839	262

PARAGUAYAN ARMY - 1828*

The Paraguayan army on May 31, 1828, consisted of:

 5 companies of riflemen
 4 companies of mounted grenadiers
 3 companies of infantry
 3 companies of cavalry
 2 companies of artillery

Total Personnel	Pesos Monthly Each	Pesos	
1 captain	25	25	
4 lieutenants	21.5	88	(A)
18 sub-lieutenants	18.5	341	(A)
32 sergeants	9.5	320.5	(A)
77 corporals	6	480	(A)
450 soldiers	5	2,409	(A)
107 cavalrymen	5	535	
35 artillerymen	5	175	
435 recruits	5	2,175	
3 drummers	5	15	
2 buglers	5	10	
1 bleeder	20.5	20.5	
2 helpers	17	34	
1,167 TOTAL		6,628	(B)

*Salary Payment Ledger, May 31, 1828, NE#1038.

A - The 1 lieutenant of the mounted grenadiers was paid 23.5 pesos monthly.
  - The 4 sub-lieutenants of the mounted grenadiers were paid 20.5 pesos monthly.
  - The 11 sergeants of the mounted grenadiers were paid 11 pesos monthly.
  - The 18 corporals of the mounted grenadiers were paid 7 pesos monthly.
  - The 159 soldiers of the mounted grenadiers were paid 6 pesos monthly.

B - This total monthly figure is confirmed by the identical sum paid as military salaries on May 31, 1828. LC, Tomo 30, Libro Manual de la Tesorería General... año 1828.

PARAGUAYAN ARMY - 1834*

The Paraguayan army on April 30, 1834, consisted of:

- 4 companies of infantry
- 3 companies of grenadiers
- 3 companies of riflemen
- 2 companies of artillery
- 1 company of lancers
- 1 new squadron being formed

Total Personnel	Pesos Monthly Each	Bi-Monthly Salaries	
1 captain	25	50	
3 lieutenants	20	120	
6 1st sub-lieutenants	17.5	210	
5 2nd sub-lieutenants	16.5	165	
24 sergeants	9.5	466	(A)
47 corporals	6.5	649	(A)
223 soldiers	5.5	2,653	(A)
70 artillerymen	5.5	770	
13 drummers	4.25	109	(B)
5 fluteplayers	4.25	40.5	(C)
3 buglers	5.5	33	
400 subtotal		5,265.5	(D)
249 recruits**	(approximation)	2,740.0	(E)
649 TOTAL		8,005.5	

---

*Salary Payment Ledger, April 30, 1834, NE#1870.

A - The 5 grenadier sergeants were paid 10.5 pesos monthly.
    The 19 grenadier corporals were paid 7.5 pesos monthly.
    The 100 grenadier soldiers were paid 6.5 pesos monthly.

B - The 1 master drummer was paid 5.5 pesos monthly, while the 2 apprentice drummers were paid 3.25 pesos monthly.

C - The 1 apprentice fluteplayer was paid 3.25 pesos monthly.

D - This bi-monthly figure, after deductions equaling 5,232 pesos, is confirmed by the identical sum paid as military salaries on April 30, 1834. LC, Tomo 37, Libro Manual de la Tesorería General... año 1834.

E - These figures for recruits are based upon the total expenditures for recruits (7.534 pesos) for the 5-1/2-month period (between the beginning of February and mid-July, 1834) calculated at 5.5 pesos monthly per recruit. LC, Tomo 37, Libro Manual de la Tesorería General... año 1834.

PARAGUAYAN ARMY - 1837*

The Paraguayan army on December 31, 1837, consisted of:

4 companies of infantry
4 companies of riflemen
4 companies of cavalry
3 companies of lancers
3 companies of grenadiers
1 company of artillery
1 military band

Total Personnel	Pesos Monthly Each	Bi-Monthly Salaries	
3 lieutenants	20	120	
11 1st sub-lieutenants	17.5	385	
6 2nd sub-lieutenants	16.5	198	
42 sergeants	9.5	796	(A)
103 corporals	6.5	1,367	(A)
1,445 soldiers	5.5	16,127	(A)
107 artillerymen	5.5	1,177	
14 drummers	5	140	
7 fluteplayers	5	70	
3 buglers	5	30	
19-piece band	5	190	
1,760 TOTAL		20,600	(B)

---

*Salary Payment Ledger, December 31, 1837, NE#2607, 2608, and 1893.

A - The 9 lancer sergeants were paid 8.5 pesos monthly, while the 8 grenadier sergeants were paid 10.5 pesos monthly.

- The 16 lancer corporals were paid 6 pesos monthly, while the 22 grenadier corporals were paid 7.5 pesos monthly.

- The 122 lancer soldiers were paid 5 pesos monthly, while the 177 grenadier soldiers were paid 6.5 pesos monthly.

B - This bi-monthly figure, after deductions equaling 19,038 pesos, is confirmed by the identical sum paid as military salaries on December 22, 1837. LC, Tomo 40, Libro Manual de la Tesorería General... año 1837.

PARAGUAYAN ARMY - 1839*

The Paraguayan army on June 30, 1839, consisted of:

- 6 companies of cavalry
- 4 companies of infantry
- 4 companies of riflemen
- 3 companies of grenadiers
- 3 companies of lancers
- 1 company of artillery
- 1 military band

Total Personnel	Pesos Monthly Each	Bi-Monthly Salaries	
3 lieutenants	20	120	
17 1st sub-lieutenants	17.5	595	
4 2nd sub-lieutenants	16.5	132	
43 sergeants	9.5	813	(A)
102 corporals	6.5	1,352	(A)
1,052 soldiers	5.5	11,806	(A)
86 artillerymen	5.5	946	
13 drummers	5	130	
5 fluteplayers	5	50	
2 buglers	5	20	
18-piece band	5	180	
1,345 TOTAL		16,144	(B)

---

*Salary Payment Ledger, June 30, 1839, NE#2617.

A - The 9 lancer sergeants were paid 8.5 pesos monthly, while the 7 grenadier sergeants were paid 10.5 pesos monthly.

- The 14 lancer corporals were paid 6 pesos monthly, while the 20 grenadier corporals were paid 7.5 pesos monthly.

- The 106 lancer soldiers were paid 5 pesos monthly, while the 170 grenadier soldiers were paid 6.5 pesos monthly.

B - This bi-monthly figure, after deductions equaling 14,335 pesos, is confirmed by the identical sum paid as military salaries on June 30, 1839. LC, Tomo 42, Libro Manual de la Tesorería General... año 1839.

APPENDIX I

STATE ESTANCIAS

INTERIOR

    Estancia San Miguel del Ytá
    Estancia Manduvirá del Ytá
    Estancia de Yaguarón
    Estancia de Pirayuby en Ybytimí
    Estancia de Yacá en Ybytimí
    Estancia de Paraguarí
    Estancia de Gausary
    Estancia de Tabapy
    Estancia de Mbuyapey
    Estancia de Quyquyo
    Estancia de Tobatí
    Puesto de Piribebuy
    Puesto del Potero de Bogados
    Estancia de Apychapá en Caapucú
    Estancia de Solís Cué en Caapucú
    Estancia San Solano en Caazapá
    Puesto Mberuyty en Caazapá
    Estancia Belem en Caazapá
    Puesto San Vicente en Caazapá
    Puesto Ybyrugua en Caazapá
    Estancia Jara en Caazapá
    Puesto Pirity en Caazapá
    Estancia Jesús María en Caazapá
    Estancia San Juan en Caazapá
    Puesto San Ysidro en Caazapá
    Estancias de Yuty
    Estancia del Rosario en Santa María
    Estancia de San Roque en Santa Maria
    Estancia de Santa Rosa
    Estancia de San Miguel en Santiago
    Estancia de Atinguy en Santiago
    Estancia de San Francisco en Santiago
    Estancia de Tavayurú en Santiago
    Estancia de San Ysidro en San Ignacio
    Estancia de San Pablo en San Ignacio
    Estancia de Yaguaretá en San Ignacio
    Estancia de San Cosme
    Estancia del Partido del Carmen
    Estancia de San Martín en la Villa de la Encarnación
    Estancia de Santa Teresa en la Villa de la Encarnación

LOWER COAST

    Estancia de Surubíy
    Estancia Estanzuela de la Villa de Oliva
    Estancia de Carayá en Villa Franca
    Estancia de San Fernando en Villa Franca
    Estancia de Yacaré
    Puesto del Partido de Tacuarí
    Puesto de Desmochadas
    Puesto de Isla Ombú
    Puesto de Buazú Cuá
    Estancia de San Francisco Solano
    Puesto de Yabebyry

UPPER COAST

    Puesto de Atyrá
    Estancia de Zaguaa Cuá en los Altos
    Estancia de Ybyracañapá de la Villa del Rosario
    Puesto de Ybyrayú
    Puesto Loma
    Puesto Tuyú
    Puesto Arce Cué
    Estancia de Capii pobó
    Puesto de Tacuarí
    Estancia Catiguá
    Puesto de Mbururú
    Puesto de Isla Yobaí
    Estancia de Mingo en San Joaquin
    Puesto de Bola Cuá en San Joaquin
    Estancia de San Miguel en San Estanislao
    Estancia de la Villa de San Pedro
    Puesto de Tacuatí
    Estancias de la Villa de Concepción
    Estancia de la Villa del Salvador

ANA, SH#229, Razón de las Estancias del Estado, without date. Although this document is found in the volume that contains documents for 1818 and 1819, it certainly is more recent than 1827 as the third and fourth estancias listed under the Lower Coast are located in Villa Franca, which was founded in 1827. Quite probably this document is from the mid-1830's.

NOTES

INTRODUCTION

1. John Parish Robertson and William Parish Robertson, *Four Years in Paraguay*, 2:189.
2. José Antonio Vázquez, *El Doctor Francia, visto y oído por sus contemporaneos*, p. 43.
3. Francisco Wisner de Morgenstern, *El Dictador del Paraguay*, p. 88.
4. Johann Rudolf Rengger, *The Reign of doctor Joseph Gaspar Roderick de Francia, in Paraguay*, p. 205.
5. See Table 2. For a biography of Francia, see Justo Pastor Benítez, *La vida solitaria de Dr. José Gaspar de Francia*, or the appropriate chapters in Julio César Chaves, *El Supremo Dictador*, in which most of the known details of his life are presented.
6. Frey Mariano Velazco, *Proclama de un Paraguayo a sus paysanos*, as quoted in Chaves, *El Supremo Dictador*, p. 185. According to Atilio García Mellid, *Proceso a los falsificadores de la historia del Paraguay*, 1:235n, a copy of *Proclama . . .* can be found at the Biblioteca Nacional, Buenos Aires, #245.071R, but on various occasions during 1973 the staff was unable to locate it. Also see excerpts found in José Antonio Vázquez, *El doctor Francia*, pp. 266–68.
7. Quoted in José Antonio Vázquez, *El doctor Francia*, p. 596.
8. Vicente Pazos Kanki, *A Narrative of Facts connected with the Change Effected in the Political Condition and Relations of Paraguay under the Direction of Dr. Thomas Francia by an Individual who Witnessed many of them, and Obtained Authentic Information Respecting the Rest.*
9. Quoted in Antonio Zinny, *Historia de los Gobernantes del Paraguay, 1553–1887*, p. 386.
10. Charles Darwin, *The Voyage of the Beagle*, p. 119.
11. Wisner de Morgenstern, *El Dictador*, p. 88.
12. For examples of Francista poems, songs, and pamphlets, see Blas Garay, ed., *Descripción de las honras fúnebres que se hicieron al Exmo. Señor Dr. José Gaspar Rodríguez de Francia, Supremo Dictador Perpetuo de la república del Paraguay, primera de la América del Sud.* Also see the reproduction of several popular verses, testimonies, and excerpts from official documents and newspaper articles found in José Antonio Vázquez, *El doctor Francia*, pp. 783–922, and Chaves, *El Supremo Dictador*, pp. 464–77.
13. Manuel Antonio Pérez, "Oración," *GM*, July 22, 1846. "Oración" was reprinted as part of the continuing polemic around Francia, which experienced a dramatic surge in mid 1846. For a list of the newspaper articles and their positions, see Chaves, *El Supremo Dictador*, p. 414n. For a lengthy excerpt from "Oración," see José Antonio Vázquez, *El doctor Francia*, pp. 810–17.
14. Pérez, "Oración," as reproduced in Garay, *Descripción*, p. 51.
15. *Libro que contiene las condiciones patria de los Colegiales, 1772–1810*, Archivo del Colegio Nacional de Monserrat, Córdoba, following the 1783 entry.
16. Thomas Carlyle, "Doctor Francia," in *Carlyle's Complete Works, Critical and Miscellaneous Essays*, 4:205–63.
17. Auguste Comte, *Appel aux conservateurs*; the "Calendrier Positiviste" is found between pp. 114 and 115.

18. García Mellid, *Proceso*, vol. 1.
19. Pablo Neruda, "El Doctor Francia," in *Obras Completas*, pp. 430–31.
20 The single notable exception is the fascinating historical novel by Augusto Roa Bastos, *Yo el Supremo* (1975).

CHAPTER 1

1. AGI, ABA, leg. 322, Pinedo al Rey, January 29, 1777.
2. AGI, ABA, leg. 202, Pinedo al Rey, June 14, 1773.
3. Felix de Azara, *Descripción e historia del Paraguay y del Rio de la Plata*, pp. 204–5.
4. ANA, NE, leg. 3360, *Libro de Asiento de Guias para el año de 1800*.
5. AGI, ABA, leg. 202, Pinedo al Rey, June 14, 1773.
6. AGI, ABA, leg. 322, Rivera al Rey, May 19, 1798.
7. AGI, ABA, leg. 322, Pinedo al Rey, January 29, 1777.
(Italics added.)
8. Ibid.
9. Ibid.
10. Ibid.
11. AGI, ABA, leg. 322, Pinedo al Rey, January 29, 1777.
12. AGI, ABA, leg. 322, Rivera al Rey, May 19, 1798.

CHAPTER 2

1. AGI, ABA, leg. 85, Azara a Avilés, May 8, 1799.
2. For a detailed discussion of Bucareli's decrees, see Pablo P. Hernández, *Organización social de las doctrinas Guaraníes de la Compañía de Jesús*, 2:174–89.
3. The figures for 1750 were submitted by the Jesuit P. Manuel Querini in compliance with the royal cedula of June 17, 1747, as cited in C. E. Corona Baratech, "Notas para un estudio de la sociedad en el Río de la Plata durante el virreinato," *Anuario de Estudios Americanos* 6(1953):144. The figures for 1764 were submitted by Padre Juan Francisco Carrio to his superior, Padre Fugencio Joseph Gonzales, AGI, ABA, leg. 21, Carrio a Gonzales, December 17, 1765. The figures for 1767, 1784, and 1801 are taken from Branislava Susnik, *El indio colonial del Paraguay*, charts in vol. 2, between pp. 172 and 173. Susnik draws upon varied primary sources (see her chapter 2, pp. 107–72, for details).
4. As cited by Cárdif G. Fúrlong, "Las Misiones Jesuíticas," *Historia de la Nación Argentina* 3(1939):420.
5. AGI, ABA, leg. 323, Oficio Real a Avilés, November 30, 1798.
6. As these measures proved to be impractical, they shortly ceased to be enforced.
7. AGI, ABA, leg. 142, Alós al Rey, October 20, 1788.
8. Ibid., Appendix 5, "Estado de los ganados . . . que quedaron el año de 1768 . . . 1769 . . . y en este año de 1788."
9. AGI, ABA, leg. 85, Avilés al Rey, June 8, 1799.
10. AGI, ABA, leg. 85, Azara a Avilés, May 8, 1799.
11. AGI, ABA, leg. 142, Alos al Rey, October 20, 1788, Appendix 6, "Pueblo de Jesús," July 11, 1788.
12. AGI, ABA, leg. 85, Azara a Avilés, May 8, 1799.
13. AGI, ABA, leg. 142, Avilés al Rey, June 8, 1800.
14. Ibid.
15. AGI, ABA, leg. 142, Alós al Rey, October 20, 1788.
16. Ibid.

CHAPTER 3

1. James R. Scobie, *Argentina*, p. 75.
2. ANA, SH, leg. 211, La junta provisional gobernativa de la capital del Río de la Plata a los habitantes de ella y de las provincias de su superior mando, May 26, 1810.
3. John H. Williams, "Dr. Francia and the Creation of the Republic of Paraguay: 1810–1814," Ph.D diss., University of Florida (Gainesville), pp. 118, 119.
4. Pedro Somellera, "Notas a la Introducción que ha puesto el Dr. Rengger a su Ensayo Historico," in *Documentos del Archivo de Belgrano*, vol. 3, p. 316n.
5. Mariano Antonio Molas, *Descripción histórica de la antigua provincia del Paraguay*, p. 97.
6. John Parish Robertson and William Parish Robertson, *Francia's Reign of Terror*, p. 21.
7. During the defense of Buenos Aires and Montevideo against the English, Paraguayans had been drafted in large numbers to fight in the porteño armies.
8. The text of the address is found in Cecilio Báez, *Historia colonial del Paraguay y Río de la Plata*, p. 173.
9. Ibid.
10. BNRJ, CRB, Acto del Congreso del 24 de julio de 1810, as cited in Julio César Chaves, *El Supremo Dictador*, p. 94.
11. ANA, SH, leg. 212, Bando del Gobernador Velasco, August 1, 1810, as cited in Williams, "Dr. Francia," p. 54. The mobilization proved extremely effective, activating approximately 6,000 mounted soldiers; but owing to the lack of arms in the province, only 500 of these had rifles, the remainder being armed with lances, swords, machetes, and clubs. (BNRJ, CRB, 1-29, 22, leg. 9, Acuerdo del Cabildo de Asunción, February 18, 1811, as cited by Williams, "Dr. Francia," p. 50. Also see Somellera, "Notas," p. 319.)
12. Julio César Chaves, *Historia de las relaciones entre Buenos Aires y el Paraguay: 1810–1813*, p. 59.
13. Williams, "Dr. Francia," pp. 78–80.
14. ANA, SH, leg. 184, Pablo Thompson al Gobernador Velasco, December 21, 1810, as cited in Williams, "Dr. Francia," p. 62.
15. Proclama de Belgrano, as published in the *GBA*, February 12, 1811; Belgrano a la Junta Provisional de Buenos Aires, January 24, 1811, as published in the *GBA*, February 12, 1811.
16. Williams, "Dr. Francia," p. 65.
17. Ibid., p. 27.
18. Julio César Chaves, *El Supremo Dictador*, p. 98.
19. AGN, 10-3, 2, leg. 4, Cavañas a Belgrano, March 14, 1811, as cited in Williams, "Dr. Francia," p. 69.
20. AGPC, CO, EA, leg. 1, Belgrano a Galván, March 18, 1811, as cited in Williams, "Dr. Francia," p. 69.
21. Somellera, "Notas," pp. 319, 320.
22. E. Bradford Burns, *A History of Brazil*, pp. 101, 102.
23. The Banda Oriental, claimed by both empires, was called the Cisplatine Province by the Portuguese.
24. Somellera, "Notas," pp. 319, 320.
25. ANA, SH, leg. 215, Velasco al Comandante de Coimbra, February 6, 1811, May 1, 8, and 9, 1811.
26. Informe de José de Abreu sobre el suceso del 14 de mayo, 7 de junio de 1811, as found in Cecilio Baez, *Historia diplomática del Paraguay*, 2:139.
27. Efraím Cardozo, *Afinidades entre el Paraguay y la Banda Oriental en 1811*, pp. 27, 28, as cited in Williams, "Dr. Francia," p. 103.
28. BNRJ, CRB, 1-29, 22, leg. 9, Acuerdo el Cabildo de Asunción, May 13, 1811.

29. Somellera, "Notas," pp. 321–27.
30. Williams, "Dr. Francia," p. 108.
31. Julio César Chaves, *La Revolución del 14 y 15 de Mayo*, p. 28, as cited by Williams, "Dr. Francia," p. 106.
32. Williams, "Dr. Francia," p. 107.
33. ANA, SH, leg. 213-A, Cabellero a Velasco, May 15, 1811.
34. Williams, "Dr. Francia," p. 110; ANA, SH, leg. 213, *Velasco a Caballero*, May 15, 1811.
35. Williams, "Dr. Francia," p. 113.
36. Somellera, "Notas," p. 329.
37. ANA, SH, leg. 213, Bando del 17 de mayo de 1811.
38. ANA, SH, leg. 214, Bando del 30 de mayo de 1811.
39. Velasco, Francia y Zevallos al Capitán General Diego de Souza, May 20, 1811, as found in Báez, *Historia diplomática*, 2:144, 145.
40. Diego de Souza a Velasco, Francia y Zevallos, June 18, 1811, as found in Báez, *Historia Diplomática*, 2:146.
41. Williams, "*Dr. Francia*," pp. 118, 119; Informe de José de Abreu sobre el suceso del 14 de mayo, June 7, 1811, as found in Báez, *Historia Diplomática*, 2:143; ANA, SH, leg. 214, Bando del Comandante y Oficiales del Quartel General . . . , June 9, 1811.
42. For a discussion of relations with Brazil, see R. Antonio Ramos, *La Política del Brasil en el Paraguay*.
43. La junta del Paraguay al Triumvirato de Buenos Aires, May 19, 1812, as found in Benjamin Vargas Peña, *Paraguay-Argentina*.
44. Williams, "Dr. Francia," p. 121.
45. ANA, SH, leg. 214, Bando del 30 de mayo de 1811.
46. ANA, SH, leg. 213, Francia y Zevallos al Comandante de Concepción, May 28, 1811; Williams, "Dr. Francia," p. 134.
47. ANA, SH, leg. 213, Francia al Congreso General, June 17, 1811.
48. ANA, SH, leg. 213, Resolución del Mariano Antonio Molas, June 18, 1811.
49. Ibid.
50. ANA, SH, leg. 214, La Junta del Paraguay a los Excelentísimos Señores Presidente y Vocales de la Junta Guvernativa de Buenos Aires, July 20, 1811.

CHAPTER 4

1. John Hoyt Williams, "Dr. Francia and the Creation of the Republic of Paraguay," Ph.D. diss., University of Florida (Gainesville), p. 144.
2. Julio César Chaves, *El Supremo Dictador*, p. 122.
3. Francisco Wisner de Morgenstern, *El Dictador del Paraguay*, p. 42.
4. ANA, SH, leg. 214, Fulgencio Yegros, Caballero y de la Mora a Francia, August 6, 1811.
5. ANA, SH, leg. 214, Antonio Tomás Yegros a Francia, August 9, 1811.
6. Williams, "Dr. Francia," p. 150.
7. ANA, SH, leg. 214, Antonio Tomás Yegros al Cabildo, September 2. 1811.
8. BNRJ, CRB, 1-29, 22, leg. 9, El Cabildo a Francia, September 9, 1811, found in the Acuerdo del Cabildo, September 8, 1811.
9. ANA, SH, leg. 214, Francia al Cabildo, September 3, 1811.
10. Chaves, *El Supremo Dictador*, p. 125.
11. Pedro Somellera, "Notas a la introducción que ha puesto el Doctor Renger a su ensayo histórico," pp. 332–33n.
12. BNRJ, CRB, 1-29, 22, leg. 8, La junta al cabildo, September 16, 1811, and ANA,

sh, leg. 214, La junta al cabildo, September 16, 1811, as cited in Williams, "Dr. Francia," p. 162.

13. ANA, SH, leg. 214, La junta de Buenos Aires a la del Paraguay, August 28, 1811.
14. ANA, SH, leg. 213, Instrucciones de Belgrano y Echevarria, August 1, 1811.
15. AGN, 10-1, 9, leg. 13, and ANA, SH, leg. 214, Tratado de 12 de octubre de 1811.
16. Chaves, *El Supremo Dictador*, p. 132.
17. ANA, SH, leg. 214, Francia al Cabildo, December 15, 1811.
18. Ibid.
19. ANA, SH, leg. 214, La junta a Francia, December 16, 1811.
20. ANA, SH, leg. 214, Francia a la junta, December 18, 1811.
21. José Antonio Vázquez, *El doctor Francia, visto y oído por sus contemporaneos*, p. 236.
22. Williams, "Dr. Francia," p. 182.
23. Chaves, *El Supremo Dictador*, p. 136.
24. John Parish Robertson and William Parish Robertson, *Four Years in Paraguay*, 1:221.
25. Chaves, *El Supremo Dictador*, p. 144.
26. Ibid., p. 142.
27. Ibid., p. 143.
28. Wisner, *El Dictador*, p. 57.
29. AGN, 10-1, 9, leg. 13, La Junta de Buenos Aires a la del Paraguay, January 13, 1812.
30. Chaves, *El Supremo Dictador*, p. 145.
31. AGN, 10-1, 9, leg. 13, La Junta del Paraguay a la de Buenos Aires, March 2, 1812.
32. For a detailed discussion of this incident, see Julio César Chaves, *Historia de las Relaciones entre Buenos Aires y el Paraguay*, chap. 13.
33. Reglamento Provincial sobre los derechos, published in the *GBA*, September 4, 1812.
34. BNRJ, RP, 2-36, 27, leg. 9 (#56), Impuestos de Santa Fee sobre La Goleta del Gobierno Paraguayo, October 6, 1812.
35. Williams, "Dr. Francia," p. 230.
36. BNRJ, CRB, 1-30, 2, leg. 80, Yegros y Caballero a Francia, November 12, 1812.
37. ANA, SH, leg. 218, Acuerdo de Francia, Yegros y Caballero, November 16, 1812.
38. AGN, 10-1, 9, leg. 13, La Junta del Paraguay a la Excelentísima Junta del Gobierno de Buenos Aires, January 27, 1813.
39. AGN, 10-1, 9, leg. 12, Herrera al Poder Executivo, July 13, 1813.
40. AGN, 10-1, 9, leg. 12, Herrera al Poder Executivo, August 19, 1813. As cited by Williams, "Dr. Francia," pp. 245, 246.
41. Williams, "Dr. Francia," pp. 248, 249.
42. BNRJ, CRB, 1-30, 2, leg. 30, La opinión de la Junta contra Fernando de la Mora, September 18, 1813, and Bando del 24 de septiembre de 1813.
43. Robertson and Robertson, *Four Years*, 2:20.
44. ANA, SH, leg. 222, La Junta al Cabildo de Pilar, August 26, 1813.
45. ANA, SH, leg. 222, Acuerdo del Cabildo de Pilar, September 4, 1813; ANA, SH, leg. 222, La Junta al Cabildo de Curuguaty, August 26, 1813; ANA, SH, leg. 222, La Junta al Cabildo de Villa Rica, August 26, 1813.
46. ANA, SH, leg. 222, La Junta al Cabildo de Pilar, August 26, 1813.
47. Robertson and Robertson, *Four Years*, 2:23.
48. Ibid.
49. Chaves, *El Supremo Dictador*, p. 159.
50. Williams, "Dr. Francia," p. 254.
51. Chaves, *El Supremo Dictador*, pp. 159, 160.

52. Gregorio Benítez, *La revolución de Mayo*, p. 79.
53. Chaves, *El Supremo Dictador*, p. 160
54. AGN, 10-1, 9, leg. 12, Herrera al Poder Executivo, October 12, 1813.
55. BNRJ, CRB, 1-29, 22, leg. 26, Bando del 21 de octubre de 1813.
56. Ibid. There is no record of the Tribunal Superior de Recursos ever having been established.
57. AGN, 10-1, 9, leg. 12, Herrera al Poder Executivo, October 13, 1813.
58. AGN, 10-1, 9, leg. 12, Herrera al Poder Executivo, October 15, 1813; Chaves, *Historia*, p. 213.
59. ANA, SH, leg. 222, Francia y Yegros a Herrera, October 29, 1813.
60. AGN, 10, 1-9, leg. 12, Herrera al Poder Executivo, November 7, 1813.
61. Decreto del Gobierno de Buenos Aires, published in *GM*, December 15, 1813.

CHAPTER 5

1. Francisco Wisner de Morgenstern, *El Dictador del Paraguay*, p. 73.
2. ANA, Colección Solano López, Francia al Ministro de Hacienda, March 23, 1815, cited in Julio César Chaves, *El Supremo Dictador*, pp. 166, 167.
3. Chaves, *El Supremo Dictador*, p. 166.
4. John Hoyt Williams, "Dr. Francia and the Creation of the Republic of Paraguay," Ph.D. diss., University of Florida (Gainesville), p. 282.
5. Johann Rudolph Rengger, *The Reign of doctor Joseph Gaspar Roderick de Francia, in Paraguay*, p. 129.
6. John Parish Robertson and William Parish Robertson, *Francia's Reign of Terror*, p. 25.
7. ANA, NE, leg. 934, Bando del Comandante del Quartel don Pedro Juan Caballero, June 12, 1811.
8. Robertson and Robertson, *Francia's Reign of Terror*, p. 21. (Italics added.)
9. Williams, "Dr. Francia," p. 274.
10. ANA, SH, leg. 223, Bando de los Consules, January 5, 1814.
11. Ibid,; Los Consules de Paraguay al Teniente Gobernador de Corrientes, January 3, 1814, found in the *Revista Nacional* (Buenos Aires), November 1, 1886, p. 253.
12. El Teniente Gobernador de Corrientes a los Consules de Paraguay, January 15, 1814, found in the *Revista Nacional* (Buenos Aires), November 1, 1886, p. 254; Chaves, *El Supremo Dictador*, pp. 168, 169.
13. Williams, "Dr. Francia," p. 275.
14. BNRJ, CAS, 4-17, 2, leg. 8, pp. 1–4, Resolución Consular del 1 de julio de 1814. For a specific example of the enforcement of this law, see the series of documents in ANA, NE, leg. 750, Castellano a Francia, October 22, 1816, and los Decretos de Francia, March 14, June 14, and September 25, 1817.
15. Wisner, *El Dictador*, p. 73.
16. ANA, SH, leg. 383 (part 1), La primera compañía de urbanos de Ybitimí a los Consules, March 2, 1814, and the Consuls' reply, March 8, 1814.
17. Rengger, *The Reign*, p. 159.
18. ANA, SH, leg. 223, Los Consules al Comandante de Villa Rica, don Francisco Aquino, July 28, 1814.
19. ANA, SH, leg. 441, El Corregidor del Pueblo de Belén, Francisco Xavier Arévalo a los Consules, February 23, 1814.
20. ANA, SH, leg. 223, Los Consules al Comandante de Villa Rica, April 18, 1814; ANA, SH, leg. 223, Resolución Consular de 8 de junio de 1814 and Resolución Consular de 4 de agosto de 1814.

21. Williams, "Dr. Francia," p. 288.
22. Chaves, *El Supremo Dictador*, p. 171.
23. Jesús L. Blanco Sánchez, *El Capitán don Antonio Tomás Yegros*, p. 23.
24. ANA, SH, leg. 223, José Artigas a Vicente Antonio Matiauda, January 26, 1814.
25. ANA, SH, leg. 71,* Matiauda a los Consules, February 12 and March 5, 1814, as cited by Chaves, *El Supremo Dictador*, p. 173. During the late 1940s the Archivo Nacional de Asunción was reorganized in a more chronological manner. Consequently, the nine documents marked with an asterisk are no longer to be found in their original *legajos*, as they are references taken from secondary works written before the reorganization.
26. ANA, SH, leg. 223, Francia y Yegros al Subdelegado del Departamento de Candelaria Don Vicente Antonio Matiauda, March 4, 1814.
27. ANA, SH, leg. 223, Francia y Yegros al Gobernador José Leon Domínguez, March 13, 1814.
28. Chaves, *El Supremo Dictador*, p. 117.
29. Wisner, *El Dictador*, p. 72.
30. Chaves, *El Supremo Dictador*, p. 177; Blanco Sánchez, *El Capitán*. p. 23.
31. Williams, "Dr. Francia" p. 281.
32. ANA, SH, leg. 223, Los Consules al Juez Comisionado de la Feligresia de Atirá, don Manuel Fierrera, September 7, 1814.
33. Wisner, *El Dictador*, p. 74.
34. Williams, "Dr. Francia," p. 297.
35. Chaves, *El Supremo Dictador*, p. 178.
36. Wisner, *El Dictador*, p. 74.
37. Chaves, *El Supremo Dictador*, p. 179.
38. ANA, NE, leg. 815, El Escribiano de la Governación General, don Jacinto Ruiz a Romualdo Aguero, September 26, 1814.
39. Wisner, *El Dictador*, pp. 78, 79; also see Rengger, *The Reign* pp. 20, 21.
40. John Parish Robertson and William Parish Robertson, *Four Years in Paraguay*, 2:202, 203. Robertson estimated that the city of Asunción was allotted between sixty and eighty delegates.
41. Wisner, *El Dictador*, p. 76.
42. ANA, SH, leg. 223, Summary of Congressional proceedings prepared by the governmental scribe Jacinto Ruiz, October 10, 1814. Unless otherwise noted, the information concerning the 1814 congress is taken from this official government summary.
43. Wisner, *El Dictador*, p. 75.
44. Ibid.
45. ANA, SH, leg. 223, Summary of Congressional proceedings . . . , as cited above, n. 42.
46. Just as the Tribunal Superior de Recursos, provided for in the 1813 "Constitution," was not established, there is no record of the Tribunal Superior de Justicia ever having been established.
47. Wisner, *El Dictador*, p. 76, and Robertson and Robertson, *Four Years in Paraguay*, 2:205.
48. ANA, SH, leg. 223, Summary of Congressional proceedings . . . , as cited above in n. 42.
49. Robertson and Robertson, *Four Years in Paraguay*, 2:205.
50. Robertson and Robertson, *Francia's Reign of Terror*, p. 27.
51. As one of his first acts as dictator of Paraguay, Francia reinforced the prohibition by the junta of July 7, 1812, upon the export of precious metal (ANA, SH leg. 218), forbidding the extraction of metallic currency by the Decreto Supremo de 13 de noviembre de 1814 (ANA, SH, leg. 223).

52. ANA, SH, leg. 223, Text of Speech of Anonymous Delegate, no date, no signature. Also see José Antonio Vázquez, *El doctor Francia, visto y oído por sus contemporaneos,* pp. 246–48.
53. Robertson and Robertson, *Francia's Reign of Terror,* p. 306.
54. ANA, SH, leg. 224, Decreto Supremo del 2 de julio de 1815.
55. Wisner, *El Dictador,* p. 81. Also Robertson and Robertson, *Francia's Reign of Terror,* p. 307.
56. ANA, SH, leg. 224, Decreto Supremo del 21 de diciembre de 1815.
57. ANA, SH, leg. 224, Decreto Supremo del 24 de diciembre de 1815.
58. Chaves, *El Supremo Dictador,* p. 236.
59. Artigas a Francia, April 21, 1815, as cited in Pedro Dupuy Lamy, *Artigas en el cautiverio,* pp. 91, 92.
60. ANA, SH, leg. 81,* Proceso a Francisco Antonio Aldao, 1822, as cited in Chaves, *El Supremo Dictador,* p. 237.
61. Chaves, El Supremo Dictador, p. 238n.
62. BNRJ, CRB, 1-29, 23, leg. 20, Francia al Subdelegado de Santiago, August 3, 1815.
63. ANA, SH, leg. 223, Francia y Yegros al Teniente Gobernador de la Ciudad de Corrientes, January 3, 1814.
64. ANA, SH, leg. 224, Francia al Comandante de Pilar José Joaquín López, October 2, 1815. For further documentation concerning this conflict, see Francia's correspondence in ANA, NE, leg. 3410, letters of August 29, September 4, and October 5, 1815; and ANA, SH, leg. 224, letters of September 16 and 26 and October 13, 1815.
65. Robertson and Robertson, *Francia's Reign of Terror,* p. 125.
66. AGN, Legato Paraguay 1811–1815 y 1819, Herrera a Robertson, March 31, 1815, as cited in Chaves, *El Supremo Dictador,* p. 241.
67. Robertson and Robertson, *Francia's Reign of Terror,* p. 241.
68. Idem, *Four Years in Paraguay,* 2:180.
69. Idem, *Francia's Reign of Terror,* p. 27.
70. AGN, 10-1, 9, leg. 13, El Gobierno de Buenos Aires a Francia, September 19, 1815. Also see AGN, 10-1, 9, leg. 13, El Gobierno de Buenos Aires a Francia, January 20 and March 15, 1815.
71. ANA, SH, leg. 224, Francia al Delegado de Pilar, November 22, 1815.
72. Mariano Velazco, *Proclama de un Paraguayo a sus paysanos,* as cited in Chaves, *El Supremo Dictador,* pp. 136, 137.
73. ANA, NE, leg. 3410, Francia al Comandante de Pilar, don José Joaquín López, May 24, 1815. (Italics added.)
74. Barbara H. Stein and Stanley J. Stein, *The Colonial Heritage of Latin America,* p. 174.
75. Chaves, *El Supremo Dictador,* p. 193.
76. AGI, ABA, leg. 322, Rivera al Rey, May 19, 1798.
77. Chaves, *El Supremo Dictador,* p. 193.
78. Ibid., p. 255.
79. BNRJ, CRB, Circular de Francia a los delegados, as cited in Chaves, *El Supremo Dictador,* pp. 194, 195.
80. ANA, SH, leg. 226, Acta del Congreso, June 5, 1816.
81. Atilio García Mellid, *Proceso a los falsificadores de la Historia del Paraguay,* 1:182.

CHAPTER 6

1. ANA, SH, leg. 226, Decreto Supremo de 17 de junio de 1816.
2. ANA, Libro de Actas del Cabildo, 1805–23, Acuerdos de Cabildo, February 4 and

8, 1819, September 10, 1821, Janaury 17, 1822, and September 10, 1822. Also see John Parish Robertson and William Parish Robertson, *Francia's Reign of Terror*, p. 307. After this decree there remained only the festivals of San Blas, Corpus Cristi, Our Lady of Asunción, and the Virgen María de Nieve.

3. ANA, NE, leg. 750, Decreto Supremo de 14 de marzo de 1817.

4. Velazco, *Poclama de un Paraguayo a sus paysanos*, as found in Chaves, *El Supremo Dictador*, pp. 185, 186.

5. Proyecto para pacificar Santa Fe, dominar Entre Ríos y Corrientes, y subyugar al Paraguay, 1817, in *Documentos del Archivo de Pueyrredón*, 3:281–83.

6. Decreto del Gobierno de Buenos Aires, January 8, 1817, published in the GBA, January 11, 1817.

7. Chaves, *El Supremo Dictador*, pp. 245, 246.

8. Johann Rudolph Rengger, *The Reign of doctor Joseph Gaspar Roderick de Francia, in Paraguay*, p. 56.

9. Artigas a Francia, July 1817, as found in Chaves, *El Supremo Dictador*, p. 244.

10. Rengger, *The Reign*, pp. 93, 94.

11. Robertson and Robertson, *Francia's Reign of Terror*, pp. 325, 326.

12. Francisco Wisner de Morgenstern, *El Dictador del Paraguay*, p. 97.

13. Ibid., p. 99.

14. Rengger, *The Reign*, p. 68.

15. Wisner, *El Dictador*, p. 99, Wisner incorrectly identified Captain Montiel as Pedro, Miguel Antonio's brother.

16. Ibid., pp. 100, 101.

17. Mario Antonio Molas, "Clamor de un Paraguayo," *Revista del Paraguay* 3(1893): 244. (Originally written in 1828.)

18. Rengger, *The Reign*, p. 57.

19. ANA, SH, leg. 100,* Francia a Fernando Acosta, November 19, 1839, as found in R. Antonio Ramos, *La política del Brasil en el Paraguay*, p. 41.

20. ANA, SH, leg. 83,* Ramírez a Francia, November 22, 1820, as found in Chaves, *El Supremo Dictador*, p. 278.

21. Wisner, *El Dictador*, p. 104; Rengger, *The Reign*, p. 63.

22. Ramón de Cáceres a Carlos Calvo, written in 1856 from Paraguay where Ramírez's former chieftain had been forced to seek asylum. As found in José Antonio Vázquez, *El doctor Francia*, pp. 490, 491.

23. ANA, SH, leg. 24,* El Delegado de Pilar a Francia, November 1820, as found in Chaves, *El Supremo Dictador*, p. 281.

24. Rengger, *The Reign*, pp. 63, 148.

25. Wisner, *El Dictador*, p. 106.

26. Rengger, *The Reign*, p. 69.

27. Ibid., p. 72.

28. Rengger, *The Reign*, p. 74. The exception being Bishop Panés, who was held for only a few hours.

29. BNRJ, CAS, 4-17, 2, leg. 8, Auto Supremo de 20 de enero de 1823.

30. Rengger, *The Reign*, p. 75. Confirming Rengger's opinion of the Spaniards' economic destruction is the fact that the government only collected 138,932 pesos. See ANA, NE, leg. 1824, Cuenta general del año 1824.

31. Wisner, *El Dictador*, p. 109; Rengger, *The Reign*, p. 64.

32. Rengger, *The Reign*, p. 65.

33. Ibid., pp. 64, 65.

34. Wisner, *El Dictador*, pp. 110–12.

35. Prudencio de la Cruz Mendoza, *El Doctor Francia en el Virreynato del Plata*, p. 58.

36. Rengger, *The Reign,* pp. 108, 142; Wisner, *El Dictador,* p. 113; Chaves, *El Supremo Dictador,* pp. 272, 273; Manuel Pedro de Peña, "Paraguay," *El Orden* (Buenos Aires), September 25, 1858, as quoted by Chaves, *El Supremo Dictador,* p. 436.

37. Chaves, *El Supremo Dictador,* p. 327; John Hoyt Williams, "Dr. Francia and the Creation of the Republic of Paraguay, p. 320.

38. BNRJ, CAS, 4-17, 2, leg. 8, pp. 11, 12, Auto Supremo de 8 de junio de 1820.

39. BNRJ, CRB, Auto de Francia de 4 de agosto de 1820, as cited by Chaves, *El Supremo Dictador,* p. 326. Although the only documentation that I could locate was the Auto Supremo de 26 de febrero de 1825 (BNRJ, CAS, 4-17, 2, leg. 8, pp. 34–36), given Francia's penchant for reaffirming major laws by subsequent decrees, the chronology of events would indicate the likelihood of this measure being enacted at the earlier date.

40. BNRJ, CAS, 4-17, 2, leg. 8, pp. 17–19, Auto Supremo de 20 de septiembre de 1824. As examples of the secularization process, see ANA, NE, leg. 783, Fray Bonifacio Segovia a Francia, November 16, 1824; ANA, NE, leg. 783, Fray Francisco Olmos y Aquilera a Francia, November 18, 1824; and ANA, NE leg. 783, Fray Lorenzo Fernandez a Francia, November 17, 1824.

41. Rengger, *The Reign,* p. 110.

42. ANA, SH, leg. 237, Decreto Supremo de 30 de diciembre de 1824; Chaves, *El Supremo Dictador,* p. 238.

43. See Appendix A, National Budgets, 1816–1823. Specific documentation is found in their respective Libros de Caja; e.g., for 1816 see ANA, LC, vol. 15, entries 128, 148, 240, and 400.

44. ANA, SH, leg. 239, Decreto Supremo de 23 de agosto de 1828, and ANA, LC vol. 30, entry for August 24, 1828 (#604).

45. See Appendix A, National Budgets, 1831–1840. Specific documentation is found in their respective Libros de Caja; e.g., for 1831 see ANA, LC, vol. 34, entries for May 6 (#266) and November 11 (#631). The seventy-peso-a-year increase beginning in 1834 is the salary of the cathedral's sexton. Specific documentation is found in their respective Libros de Caja; e.g., for 1834 see ANA, LC, vol. 37, entries for June 30 (#290) and December 31 (#546).

46. Notes for table 2. Unless otherwise indicated, the figures are taken from their respective Libros de Caja. See list accompanying Appendix A.

   a. These sums were voluntarily willed to the State.

   b. This sum is actually a forfeited bond.

   c. These sums were collected from the merchants and used for public works. The figures for 1816–20 and 1827 are found in ANA, SH, leg. 235, Cuentas de contribuciones . . . 1816, 1817, 1818, 1820, and 1827. The figures for 1823 and 1824 are found in their respective Libros de Caja. The figure for 1825 is found in ANA, NE, leg. 2922, Cuenta General de dinero efectivo desde el año de 1825 hasta el de 1827.

   The figures for 1821, 1822, and 1826 are approximations as, although the actual figures are not available, these contributions were levied during this entire period.

   d. ANA, NE, leg. 750, Invoice submitted by Francisco Diaz de Bedoya, July 30, 1817. This figure represents the confiscation of the property of Juan B. Carisimo and his godfather, the Spaniard Domingo Mareque, for violation of the 1814 marriage ban.

   e. ANA, NE, leg. 1119, Cuenta General de la Tesorería General de abril 16 hasta diciembre 31, 1816.

   f. ANA, NE, leg. 1230, Cuenta General . . . año 1818.

   g. ANA, NE, leg. 1844, Cuenta General . . . año 1824.

   h. This figure represents the collective fine of the Spaniards as ordered by the decree of January 22, 1823.

   i. ANA, NE, leg. 2922, Cuenta General . . . desde el año de 1825 hasta el de 1827.

   j. ANA, LC, vols. 24 and 25, Libros Manual de la Tesorería de Guerra . . . desde enero 1 hasta el fin de julio de 1826, and Libro Manual de la Tesorería de Guerra . . . desde julio 31 hasta el fin de diciembre de 1826.

k. This fine was levied against a ring of individuals for smuggling precious metals out of Paraguay.

l. These figures are found in their respective Dinero Efectivo en Depósito ledgers (see Appendix B). The figure for 1818, the first year that documentation is available, represents the accumulated sum to that date.

m. This money was confiscated from the Cuartas de Curas (see Apprendix B). Initially 6,636 pesos were confiscated, but 1,658 pesos were parceled back before 1840.

n. Initially, 14,473 pesos were confiscated from foreigners in 1829 and 1830, but 406 pesos were returned in 1832 and 1833.

p. These "contributions" were collected from the owners of "*casas grandes.*"

q. ANA, NE, leg. 1871, Cuaderno . . . Contribución de los Negociantes. These sums were collected as a special tax on merchants engaged in the Itapúa-Asunción trade. All but 48 pesos were held in Depósito until 1840 (see Appendix B).

r. This figure represents the confiscation of goods of fourteen merchants for engaging in commerce without the proper licenses.

s. This fine was levied against Señora Machaín because her dog bit and killed a poor woman passing by her house.

t. This figure represents the personal wealth of Francia which, as El Dictador had no heirs, was confiscated by the state when he died.

47. Rengger, *The Reign*, p. 171.
48. Wisner, *El Dictador*, p. 136, and Rengger, *The Reign*, pp. 173 and 174.
49. ANA, SC, leg. 81,* Auto de Francia, 3 de agosto de 1833, as quoted by Chaves, *El Supremo Dictador*, pp. 455, 458. Cavaãs died sometime prior to 1828.
50. ANA, SC, leg. 81,* Auto de Francia, 22 de julio de 1839, as cited by Chaves, *El Supremo Dicator*, pp. 457, 458.
51. Rengger, *The Reign*, p. 191.

CHAPTER 7

1. John Hoyt Williams, "Dr. Francia and the Creation of the Republic of Paraguay," p. 282.
2. John Parish Robertson and William Parish Robertson, *Francia's Reign of Terror*, p. 19.
3. Johann Rudolph Rengger, *The Reign of doctor Joseph Gaspar Roderick de Francia, in Paraguay*, pp. 107–8. For a specific example of Francia reprimanding and overruling a judge who had used his position to vent a personal jealousy, see the series of documents found in ANA, NE, leg. 769, Doña Maria Juana Notario a Francia, May 23, 1818; Manuel Antonio Rodríguez a Francia, May 25, 1818; and Orden Supremo de 26 de mayo de 1818.
4. For examples, see ANA, LC, leg. 37, entry for January 1834; ANA, LC, leg. 40, entries for October 9 and December 9, 1837; and ANA, LC, leg. 43, entry for February 29, 1840.
5. Francisco Wisner de Morgenstern, *El Dictador del Paraguay*, p. 150, 131.
6. ANA, SH, leg. 241, Francia a José Leon Ramírez, January 1832. From 1833 to 1840 this sum was held in the government's cash reserves for the English merchant, who, evidently, did not return; see Appendix B, *Cash Held in Deposit*.
7. ANA, Sh, leg. 240, Francia al Delegado de Itapúa, August 22, 1830.
8. Unfortunately, there exists no public source for this fascinating document, although it still can be located in several private collections. For published sources, see Justo Pastor Benítez, *La vida solitaria de Dr. José Gaspar de Francia*, pp. 152, 153, and Julio Cézar Chaves, *El Supremo Dictador*. p. 198, 199.

9. ANA, SH, leg. 223, Francia y Yegros al Comandante de Villa Rica, August 18, 1814.

10. ANA, SH, leg. 223, Francia al subdelegado de Santiago, don Juan Antonio Montiel, November 20, 1814; José Antonio Vázquez, *El doctor Francia, visto y oído por sus contemporaneos,* p. 45.

11. ANA, NE, leg. 1862, Comprobantes . . . año 1816.

12. ANA, NE, leg. 729, Resolución Consular de 9 de julio de 1814, and ANA, SH, leg. 223, Decreto Consular de 4 de agosto de 1814.

13. Váquez, *El doctor Francia,* p. 46; see Appendix A, Paraguayan National Budgets. Based upon the available documentation, 1823 was the last year that the government constructed vessels.

14. Vázquez, *El doctor Francia,* pp. 45, 46.

15. Wisner (*El Dictador,* p. 162) noted that in 1839 Francia reinforced the southern frontier due to Corrientes's involvement in the civil war against Buenos Aires. See chapter 9 for further details.

16. Robertson and Robertson, *Francia's Reign of Terror,* p. 220, and Rengger *The Reign,* p. 154.

17. The monthly tax on *tenerías públicas* was established by the Auto Supremo de 25 de junio de 1826, ANA, SH, leg. 238. The last documentation of its collection (see Appendix A, Paraguayan National Budgets, 1828), corresponds closely in time to the first documentation of the state monopolization of the exportation of shoe soles, the major product of the tanneries (see Appendix F, State Exports, Pilar, 1831).

18. BNRJ, CAS, 1-9, 2, leg. 18, pp. 12–14, Auto Supremo de 10 de enero de 1823. The last documentation available concerning taxes on livestock is the elimination of the Ramo de Cuatropea y Ganado, ANA, SH, leg. 11,* Auto Supremo de 26 de abril de 1832, as cited in Chavez, *El Supremo Dictador,* p. 443n, which corresponds to the last year that the Derecho de Ventage was collected (see Appendix A, Paraguayan National Budgets, 1832).

19. ANA, NE, leg. 1862, Decreto Supremo de 24 de octubre de 1830. In addition to the tax reductions mentioned above, this decree also abolished the *ramo de guerra* (a tax on yerba collecting) and the *estanco* (a municipal tax on yerba brought to Asunción).

20. ANA, NE, leg. 1880, Decreto Supremo de 26 de octubre de 1835.

21. ANA, SH, leg. 242, Decreto Supremo de 5 de noviembre de 1837.

22. Rengger, *The Reign,* pp. 173, 174.

23. Carlos Pastore, *La lucha por la tierra en el Paraguay,* pp. 103, 105; Rengger, *The Reign,* pp. 185, 186. BNRJ, CAS, 1-9, 2, leg. 18, pp. 17–19, Auto Supremo de 20 de septiembre de 1824.

24. Vázquez, *El Doctor Francia,* p. 42.

25. Wisner, *El Dictador,* p. 135.

26. Rengger, *The Reign,* pp. 173, 174; Wisner, *El Dictador,* p. 136.

27. ANA, SH, leg. 226, Francia al comandante de Concepción, March 13, 1817.

28. For examples of such confiscations, see ANA, SH, leg. 393, Gill a Francia, November 7, 1825, and June 22, 1826.

29. ANA, SH, leg. 226, Francia al Juez Comicionado de Capiatá, October 27, 1816.

30. Rengger, *The Reign.* p. 176, and Wisner, *El Dictador,* p. 131. Numerous such reports are to be found scattered throughout the Sección Nueva Encuadernación of the Archivo Nacional de Asunción. For examples, see ANA, NE, leg. 2974, Informe del Capataz de la Estancia de Capelania, Antonio Tomás Yegros, August 28, 1837, and ANA, NE, leg. 2982, Informe del Capataz de la Estancias de Isla Alta, Majon y Capelania, Antonio Tomás Yegros, Janaury 14, 1840.

31. ANA, SH, leg. 240, Francia a Ramírez, September 3, 1830. The distribution of state livestock and other materials will be discussed below.

32. Rengger, *The Reign,* p. 175. Also see Appendix A, Paraguayan National Budgets.

33. Rengger, *The Reign*, p. 49, and Mariano Antonio Molas, *Descripción histórica de la antigua provincia del Paraguay*, p. 34, as cited in Atilio García Mellid, *Proceso a los falsificadores de la Historia del Paraguay*, 1:209.

34. For examples of the inventory of the state store in Asunción, see ANA, NE, leg. 1880, Razón de las herramentas y otros efectos del Estado que he recibido . . . para vender . . . a los precios siguientes, December 17, 1835; and ANA, NE, leg. 1900, Efectos recibidos . . . para vender . . . a los precios siguientes, August 5, 1839.

35. For examples, see ANA, LC, leg. 38, año 1835, Hacienda en Comun entries for December; and ANA, LC, leg. 41, año 1838, various Hacienda en Comun entries.

36. For an example, see ANA, NE, leg. 1874, Cuenta que yo, Luis Mazano, presento de los Sompreros que he trabajado, y entregado en la Tesorería General desde septiembre 5 a diciembre 14, 1834.

37. See Appendix A, Paraguayan National Budgets. For the years that documentation is available during the 1816–23 period, total revenue income was 983,884 pesos, while total sales were 122,166 pesos, with 109,242 pesos in sales to the military and 12,924 pesos in sales to the public.

38. See Appendix A, Paraguayan National Budget. For the years that documentation is available during the 1816–23 period, the expenses of the state works were 91,293 pesos.

39. See Appendix A, Paraguayan National Budgets. For the years that documentation is available during the 1828–40 period, total revenue income was 1,240,827 pesos and total sales amounted to 623,415 pesos.

40. Sales to the army rose on the average from 21,848 pesos (1816–23) to 27,063 pesos (1828–40), for an average annual increase of 5,215 pesos. See Appendix A, Paraguayan National Budgets.

41. Sales to the public rose from an annual average of 2,586 pesos (1816–23) to 29,611 pesos (1828–40), for an average annual increase of 27,025 pesos. See Appendix A, Paraguayan National Budgets.

42. See Appendix A, Paraguayan National Budgets. For the years that documentation is available during the 1816–23 period, total taxes amounted to 540,165 pesos. See n. 37 for sales figures.

43. See Appendix A, Paraguayan National Budgets. For the years that documentation is available during the 1828–40 period, total tax revenue amounted to 240,424 pesos. See n.39 for sales figures.

44. ANA, NE, leg. 1232, Cuenta . . . Mayordomo de proprios . . . Asunción, 1818. The principal municipal taxes were upon property and a 3 percent tax paid on yerba brought to Asunción. This latter tax, the *estanco*, was abolished in 1830.

45. ANA, NE, leg. 1852, Cuenta . . . Mayordomo de proprios . . . Asunción, 1817.

46. El Cabildo de Asunción a Francia, March 26, 1816, as quoted in José Antonio Vázquez, *El doctor Francia*, pp. 316–19. This document is found in ANA, SH, leg. 225, but is now in such deteriorated condition that not all of it can be deciphered.

47. Robertson and Robertson, *Francia's Reign of Terror*, p. 166.

48. José Antonio Vázquez, *El doctor Francia*, p. 32.

49. Rengger, *The Reign*, p. 103.

50. ANA, LC, leg. 19, 1821, numerous entries. Also BNRJ, CRB, Auto Supremo de Francia, June 16, 1828, as cited in Chaves, *El Supremo Dictador*, p. 309.

51. Rengger, *The Reign*, p. 103.

52. José Antonio Vázquez, *El doctor Francia*, pp. 43, 44.

53. Rengger, *The Reign*, p. 104.

54. José Antonio Vázquez, *El doctor Francias*, p. 34; Los Ciudadanos de Luque a Francia, May 2, 1815, as reproduced in Vázquez, pp. 278, 279.

55. José Antonio Vázquez, *El doctor Francia*, p. 38. Also see Juan Natalicio González, *Proceso y Formación de la cultura paraguaya*, p. 331.

56. ANA, NE, leg. 1821, Maestro de Primeras Letras de San Estanislao, don Mateo Vicente Frutos a Francia, February 3, 1816; BNRJ, RP, 2-36, 28, leg. 36, Resolución de Francia, January 1, 1819.
57. Rengger, *The Reign*, p. 186; Grandsire a Baron von Humboldt, Itapá, September 20, 1825, as found in Juan F. Pérez Acosta, *Francia y Bonpland*, p. 27.
58. Wisner, *El Dictador*, p. 137.
59. ANA, NE, leg. 3412, Francia al comandante de Concepción, June 6, 1831. Also see José Antonio Vázquez, *El doctor Francia*, pp. 39, 40, for examples of the central government sending clothes to the students of Concepción.
60. Rengger, *The Reign*, p. 186.
61. José Vázquez, *El doctor Francia*, p. 40.
62. For examples of such acquisitions, see ANA, NE, leg. 1855, Autos Supremos de 2 de junio de 1835, 5 de julio de 1837, y 21 de marzo 1838.
63. César Famín, *Chile, Paraguay, Uruguay y Buenos Aires*, as cited in José Antonio Vázquez, *El doctor Francia*, p. 712.
64. For examples of Argentine and Brazilian deserters seeking asylum in Paraguay, see ANA, NE, leg. 1224, Comprobantes del Ministro de Hacienda, 1818, entry for August 18; ANA, NE, leg. 1839, Delegado de Pilar a Francia, August 18, 1820; ANA, LC, leg. 30, entry 729, September 30, 1828; and ANA, NE, leg. 1276, Comandante de Olympo a Francia, May 28, 1832.
65. Rengger, *The Reign*, pp. 35, 149. For an example of early immigration, see ANA, SH, leg. 229, Comandante Fernando Acosta a Francia, May 11, 1819. With the intensification of the Farroupilho revolt in Rio Grande do Sul, large numbers of Brazilian refugees fled to Paraguay; all were freely admitted. For examples, see ANA, NE, leg. 1890, Roxas a Francia, August 18, 1837; and ANA, SH, leg. 377, Roxas a Francia, September 9 and 21, 1837.
66. Williams, ("Dr. Francia," p. 325) estimates that by 1840 almost half the population of the far north was immigrant.
67. AGI, ABA. leg. 322, Gobernador Rivera al Rey, May 19, 1798.
68. For examples, see ANA, SH, leg. 100,* Francia al Delegado de Concepción, October 31, 1820, as cited in Chaves, *El Supremo Dictador*, p. 254; Comandante de Itapúa a Francia, October 21, 1837, as cited in José Antonio Vázquez, *El doctor Francia*, p. 753; Roxas a Francia, September 3, 1838, as cited in José Antonio Vázquez, *El doctor Francia*, pp. 762, 763; and ANA, LC, leg. 41. entry #642, December 11, 1838.
69. For examples of the *defensor de pobres* defending slaves, see José a Francia, October 30, 1814, as found in José Antonio Vázquez, *El doctor Francia*, pp. 261–63, and ANA, NE, leg. 186, series of nine documents from the *defensor de pobres* to Francia, July 1832–March 1833. Also see Wisner. *El Dictador*, pp. 135, 136.
70. Rengger, *The Reign*, p. 175, and Wisner, *El Dictador*, pp. 130, 131.
71. ANA, NE, leg. 2968, Cuentas . . . Arrendamientos de Exidos . . . año 1832, records 160 homesteads leased for a total of 395 pesos, or an average of 2.5 pesos each. ANA, NE, leg. 2983, Cuentas . . . Arrendamientos de Exidos . . . año 1839, records 174 homesteads leased for a total of 359 pesos, or an average of 2.1 pesos each. The average of these two yearly total rents, 377 pesos closely corresponds to the yearly average of 385 pesos for the ten-year period 1827–36 found in ANA, NE, leg. 2968, Cuenta . . . Arrendamientos de Exidos . . . de 1827 hasta 1836. ANA, NE, leg. 1898, Cuentas . . . de las temporales de Colegio Seminario de la Capital . . . 7 de mayo de 1839 hasta 22 de noviembre de 1840 . . . por arrendamientos . . . de las tierras pertenecientes al Estado, records 876 homesteads leased for a total of 5,018 pesos for the eighteen-month period, or a yearly average of 3.81 pesos. ANA, NE, leg. 2982, Cuenta . . . Arrendamientos recaudados de los Terrenos de la Estancia de Tabapí y los parages nominados Chuarí y Diarte . . . año 1839, records 420 homesteads leased for a total of 10,114 pesos, or an

average of 24 pesos each; ANA, NE, leg. 2983, Lista . . . cobrada a los arrendamientos de los campos del Estado en la Estancia del Salado . . . año 1839, records 9 homesteads for a total of 85 pesos, or an average of 9.4 pesos; ANA, NE, leg. 2982, Nomina y razon . . . arrendaminentos anual at Estado por los terrenos . . . Partido de Lambaré . . . parages de Mbachio y Ysaty . . . año 1840, records 76 homesteads for a total of 147 pesos, or an average of 1.9 pesos. These last 505 homesteads, with a total of 10,346 pesos rent, average 20 pesos each.

72. The 876 homesteads found in the fourteen locations of the lands of the Colegio Seminario, cited in n. 71, which include estancias, *parajes*, and *partidos*, average 62.6 homesteads per location. The 505 homesteads, found in the seven locations cited in the last three references of n. 71, which also include estancias, *parajes*, and *partidos*, average 72.1 homesteads per location. The combined 1,381 homesteads found in these twenty-one locations average 65.8 homesteads per location. After subtracting the estancias of Paraguarí (which is listed as one of the locations of the lands of the Colegio Seminario) and Tabapí because they are duplicated in the seventy-five locations listed in Appendix I, there remain seventy-three estancias and *puestos*. Using the average of 65.8 homesteads per location as determined above, these seventy-three locations would have an additional 4,803 homesteads for a total of 6,184 homesteads. (It should be noted that Appendix I is not complete; it does not include estancias, such as that of Salado, mentioned in n. 71, and the estancia of Gonzáles, mentioned in ANA, SH, leg. 244, Comandante de San Joaquín a Francia, June 2, 1839, which were established after the compilation of the document on which Appendix I is based.) To these 6,184 homesteads the 174 *ejidos* cited in n. 71, plus an additional 125 homesteads corresponding to the estancias of Salado and Gonzáles cited above, are added to give a total of 6,484 homesteads.

73. Using the 1838 census data, a sampling of five interior towns establishes the average Paraguayan family at 7.6 people. Thus, as homesteads were granted only to heads of families, the 6,484 homesteads would have supported 49,278 people. The five towns and the archival location of their respective census data are: Pirayo, ANA, NE leg. 3286; Piribebuy, ANA, NE leg. 3287; Santiago, ANA, NE leg. 3284; Santo Tomás, ANA, NE leg. 3286; and Ybitimí, ANA, NE leg. 3284.

74. For examples, see ANA, SH, leg. 235, Francia a Acosta, October 23, 1821, in which the government sent 100 ponchos, 100 pieces of cloth, and 150 shirts to be distributed among the needy people of the district of Concepción; and ANA, SH, leg. 79,* Francia al comandante de Concepción, April 27, 1831, as cited in Garcia Mellid, *Proceso*, 1:244, in which the government sent money and clothes to the needy people of Concepción.

75. For an example, see Comandante de San Isidro a Francia, September 2, 1830, as found in José Antonio Vázquez, *El doctor Francia*, p. 676, in which the commander reports distributing steel adzes, machetes, and axes among the needy people of San Isidro, San Joaquín, San Estanislao, and some Caaiguás Indians who had asked him for aid.

76. AGN, 10-1, 9, leg. 12, Herrera al Poder Executivo, July 13, 1813.

77. ANA, SH, leg. 224, Francia al comandante de Concepción, April 11, 1815.

78. For examples, see ANA, SH, leg. 226, Francia al comandante de Concepción, September 12, 1817, and ANA, SH, leg. 232. Francia al comandante de Concepción, October 31, 1820.

79. Rengger, *The Reign*, p. p. 49.

80. See Appendix E. Partial statistics for 1830 and 1831 are found in ANA, NE, leg. 2929, Cuaderno del derecho de Extración . . . Itapúa, año 1830, and ANA, NE, leg. 2936, Cuaderno del derecho de Extración . . . Itapúa, año 1831.

81. ANA, NE, leg. 2569, 2570, Cuaderno . . . Receptoría de Itapúa, año 1829.

82. Wisner, *El Dictador*, p. 143.

83. ANA, SH, leg. 393, El Juez y Alcalde, Juan Bautista Falcón a Francia, Pilar, December 29, 1825; and ANA, SH, leg. 383, Gill a Francia, December 29, 1825.

84. ANA, SH, leg. 239, Auto del Alcalde y Juez, Fernando Antonio Meza, Asunción, January 10, 1827.

85. ANA, NE, leg. 2569, 2570, Cuaderno . . . Receptoría de Itapúa, 1829; ANA, NE, legs. 2583–85, Cuaderno . . . Receptoría, de Itapúa, 1832; ANA, NE, leg. 977, Comprobantes de la Receptoría de Itapúa, 1833; ANA, NE, leg. 1062, Cuaderno . . . derecho de Alcabala . . . Quiquio, 1832, 1833; ANA, NE, legs. 2592, 2593, 2596–99, Cuaderno . . . Receptoría de Itapúa, 1835; ANA, NE, legs. 2969–73, Cuaderno . . . Receptoría de Itapúa, 1837; ANA, NE, legs. 1304–7, Cuaderno . . . Receptoría de Itapúa, 1838; ANA, NE, leg. 1299, Cuenta . . . derecho de Alcabala . . . Santiago, 1838; ANA, NE, leg. 1302, Cuenta . . . derecho de alcabala . . . San Isidro, 1838; ANA, NE, legs. 1308, 1309, Cuaderno . . . Receptoría de Itapúa, 1839; ANA, NE, leg. 1311, Cuaderno . . . derecho de Alcabala . . . Yhû, 1840.

86. García Mellid, *Proceso*, 1:214.

87. Rengger, *The Reign*, pp. 46, 47. Also see Wisner, *El Dictador*, pp. 131, 132, who erroneously dates the locust invasion in October 1826, but concurs with Rengger on all other aspects.

88. The winter crops are largely limited to wheat and tobacco.

89. Rengger, *The Reign*, pp. 47, 48; *Anais do Itamarati*, 4:85, Informe de Correa de Cámara, May 1, 1829.

90. Wisner, *El Dictador*, pp. 143, 147, 148.

91. Grandsire a Baron von Humbolt, Itapúa, September 20, 1825, as found in Pérez Acosta, *Francia y Bonpland*, p. 25.

92. *Anais do Itamarati*, 4:86, Informe de Correa da Cámara, Calculo aproximade do effeitos e producçoes do Paraguai, May 1, 1829. Also see Wisner, *El Dictador*, pp. 143–47, and Rengger, *The Reign*, pp. 47, 48. Not until the mid 1820s was enough cotton produced that it was no longer imported. See ANA, SH, leg. 393, Gill a Francia, July 16, July 21, and August 4, 1826.

93. Wisner, *El Dictador*, pp. 156, 157.

94. Ibid., p. 147.

95. ANA, SH, leg. 244, Auto de Francia de 30 de abril de 1839.

CHAPTER 8

1. John Hoyt Williams, "Dr. Francia and the Creation of the Republic of Paraguay." p. 285.

2. For examples of the armed conflict suffered by the Missions during this period, see the firsthand accounts of an unsuccessful defense of Candelaria and the defeat of a small Brazilian army at the Pueblo of Apostoles found in BNRJ, CRB, 1-29, 23, leg. 20, Juan Antonio Mora a Francia, September 13, 1815, and ANA, SH, leg. 277, José Antonio Guerrero a Francia, July 17, 1817, respectively.

3. John Parish Robertson and William Parish Robertson, *Francia's Reign of Terror*, p. 91.

4. ANA, SH, leg. 255, Francia al Subdelegado Norberto Ortellado, November 23, 1821.

5. Julio Cesar Chaves, *El Supremo Dictador*, p. 337.

6. Robertson and Robertson, *Francia's Reign of Terror*, p. 276.

7. Johann Rudolph Rengger, *The Reign of doctor Joseph Gaspar Roderick de Francia, in Paraguay*, pp. 80–81.

8. BNRJ, CRB, 1-29, 23, leg. 28, Ortellado a Francia, December 1821; Rengger, *The Reign*, p. 82.

9. Grandsire al Baron de Damas, September 6, 1826, as found in Juan F. Pérez Acosta, *Francia y Bonpland*, p. 29; BNRJ, CRB, 1-30, 6, leg. 91, Francia a Ortellado, September 10, 1824.
10. Grandsire al Baron de Damas, September 6, 1826, in Pérez Acosta, *Francia y Bonpland*, pp. 27, 28.
11. Rengger, *The Reign*, p. 82.
12. José Antonio Vázquez, *El Doctor Francia visto y oído por sus contemporaneos*, p. 685.
13. Bonpland a Roquin, February 14, 1831, as found in José Antonio Vázquez, *El doctor Francia*, p. 684.
14. Robertson and Roberston, *Francia's Reign of Terror*, p. 289.
15. BNRJ, CRB, 1-29, 23, leg. 28, Ortellado a Francia, December 17, 1821.
16. Ibid.
17. BNRJ, CAS, 4-17, 2, leg. 8, Auto Supremo de 20 de enero de 1823.
18. ANA, NE, leg. 1844, Cuenta General del año 1824, entry for December 31.
19. Instrucciones de García Cossío, *Documentos para La Historia Argentina*, 13:256–60.
20. Chaves, *El Supremo Dictador*, pp. 347–50.
21. BNRJ, CRB, 1-30, 21, leg. 86, José Pedro César a José Norberto Ortellano, San Borja, February 1, 1823, as cited in R. Antonio Ramos, *La política del Brazil en el Paraguay*, p. 46.
22. BNRJ, CRB, Francia al Delegado e Missiones, March 1823, as cited in Chaves, *El Supremo Dictador*, p. 298.
23. BNRJ, CRB, 1-29, 23, leg. 28, El Subdelegado de Santiago a Francia, September 4, 1823.
24. BNRJ, CRB, 1-29, 23, leg. 28, Ortellado a Francia, July 27 and August 7, 1823; and BNRJ, CRB, 1-29, 23 leg. 28, Moringo a Ortellado, September 2 and 4, 1823.
25. ANA, NE, leg. 1188, Cuenta de Mayordomo de Proprios . . . Ascunción, año 1813.
26. ANA, SH, leg. 237, Decreto Supremo de 12 de septiembre de 1823; BNRJ, CRB, 1-29, 23, leg. 28. Ortellado a Francia, March 8, 1823.
27. ANA, NE, leg. 1871, Cuaderno . . . Contribuciones de los Negociantes, 1834–37.
28. BNRJ, CRB, 1-29, 23, leg. 28, Ortellado a Francia, March 8, 1823.
29. Rengger, *The Reign*, p. 177.
30. For examples of the pueblos' production, see ANA, SH, leg. 242, Francia a Ramírez, October 8, 1834; and ANA, SH, leg. 378, Roxas a Francia, July 12, 1840.
31. ANA, SH, leg. 241, Francia al Administrador de Yutí, October 9, 1832.
32. ANA, NE, leg. 1854, Comprobantes del Libro de Caxa, November 9, 1829; ANA, NE, leg. 1865, Comprobantes del Libro de Caxa, February 1832; and ANA, SH, leg. 242, Francia a Ramírez, November 6, October 8, and December 13, 1834.
33. ANA, SH, leg. 223, Decreto Supremo de 12 de diciembre de 1814.
34. ANA, SH, leg. 223, Decreto Supremo de 8 de septiembre de 1816.
35. For examples, see ANA, NE, leg. 1825, Razón del Cargamento de Nuestra Señora del Rosario, March 21, 1825; ANA, NE, leg. 1845, Razón del Cargamento de Nuestra Señor del Rosario, October 17, 1825; ANA, NE, leg. 1849, Razón del Cargamento de la Goleta perteneciente a Don José Manuel Isara, January 3, 1827; and ANA, LC, vol. 27, Los derechos de Introdución y Alcabala corespondientes a los efectos que ha introducido por el Rio en esta Ciudad, June 7, 1827.
36. For examples, see ANA, SH, leg. 238, Francia al Comandante de Pilar, May 8 and September 15, 1826; and ANA, SH, leg. 394, Francia al Comandante de Pilar, August 8, 1827.
37. ANA, SH, leg. 241, Francia al Delegado de Itapúa, August 12, 1832.

38. ANA, NE, leg. 2568, Gill a Francia, July 4, 1827.
39. ANA, SH, leg. 242, Francia a Ramírez, May 14, 1834.
40. ANA, SH, leg. 241, Francia a Ramírez, May 19, 1832.
41. ANA, SH, leg. 241, Francia a Ramírez, April 12, 1831.
42. ANA, NE, leg. 1894, Ramón Leon a Francia, March 4, 1827.
43. BNRJ, CRB, 1-29, 23, leg. 8, Francia al Subdelegado de Santiago, April 17, 1823.
44. Instrucciones para Antonio Manuel Correa da Cámara, June 30, 1824, as found in Ramos, *La política del Brasil en el Paraguay*, p. 190.
45. For a lengthy summary of Paraguayan grievances against Brazil, see ANA, SH, leg. 240, Francia al Delegado de Itapúa, José Leon Ramírez, June 8, 1829.
46. ANA, NE, leg. 1860, Ramírez a Francia, December 17, 1831.
47. ANA, SH, leg. 241, Francia a Ramíez, December 22, 1831.
48. Ibid.
49. ANA, SH, leg. 241, Francia a Ramírez, December 30, 1831.
50. ANA, SH, leg. 240, Francia a Ramírez, February 24, 1830.
51. ANA, SH, leg. 241, Francia a Ramírez, March 27, 1832.
52. ANA, SH, leg. 241, Francia a Ramírez, July 8, 1832.
53. ANA, SH, leg. 241, Francia a Ramírez, March 17, 1832.
54. ANA, SH, leg. 241, Francia a Ramírez, April 25, 1832.
55. Aimé Roger al Ministerio de Relaciones Exteriores, August 10, 1836, as found in Justo Pastor Benítez, *La vida solitaria de Dr. José Gaspar de Francia*, p. 266.
56. Chaves, *El Supremo Dictador*, p. 418.
57. ANA, SH, leg. 241, Francia al Delegado de Pilar, August 11, 1832.
58. Chaves, *El Supremo Dictador*, p. 418.
59. ANA, SH, leg. 241, Francia a Ramírez, September 8, 1832.
60. Proclama de Ferré, October 6, 1832, in *Memorias del Brigadier Pedro Ferré*, p. 412.
61. AGPC, CO, EA, leg. 2, Pasqual Exhagües a Ferré, September 26, 1832.
62. For examples of Paraguayan military inexperience, see ANA, SH, leg. 242, Francia a Ramírez, June 12, November 14, and November 21, 1833.
63. ANA, NE, leg. 2951, Entradas de alcabala para el año 1833.
64. ANA, SH, leg. 242, Francia a Ramírez, December 10, 1833.
65. Rafael Atienza a los Gobiernos de los Provincias Unidas, January 22, 1834, in *Memorias de Ferré*, pp. 453–61.
66. Aimé Roger al Ministerio de Relaciones Exteriores, August 10, 1836, as found in Justo Pastor Benítez, *La vida solitaria*, p. 267.
67. Aimé Roger al Ministerio de Relaciones Exteriores, August 10, 1836, as found in Justo Pastor Benítez, *La vida solitaria*, p. 267.
68. Ibid.
69. *Documentos para la Historia Argentina*, 17:214, as cited by Chaves, *El Supremo Dictador*, p. 428.
70. Baron de Astrada a Ferré, January 7, 1834, in *Memorias de Ferré*, p. 461.
71. ANA, SH, leg. 242, Francia a Ramírez, June 12 and July 26, 1834.
72. *GM*, April 4, 1834.

CHAPTER 9

1. BNRJ, CRB, 1-30, 7, leg. 38, Parish a Francia, July 17, 1824.
2. BNRJ, CRB, 1-30, 7, leg. 38, Francia a Parish, January 26, 1825.
3. Johann Rudolph Rengger, *The Reign of doctor Joseph Gaspar Roderick de Francia, in Paraguay*, p. 78.

4. BNRJ, CRB, 1-30, 7, leg. 38, Parish a Francia, April 14, 1825.
5. Ibid.
6. ANA, SH, leg. 240, Francia al Delegado de Itapúa, May 9, 1830.
7. BNRJ, CRB, 1-29, 23, leg. 28, Orden del Dictador de la República, August 30, 1823; and ANA, SH, leg. 237, Decreto Supremo de 4 de noviembre de 1825.
8. ANA, SH, leg. 223, Decreto Supremo de 13 de noviembre de 1814.
9. ANA, SH, leg. 241, Francia a Ramírez, January 9, 1832.
10. For examples, see ANA, LC, vol. 38, February 19, 1835; and ANA, LC vol. 40, September 30, 1837.
11. ANA, SH, leg. 223, Decreto Supremo de 4 de noviembre de 1814; Rengger, *The Reign*, p. 151. For a discussion of the reasons determining export prices, see ANA, SH, leg. 240, Francia a Ramírez, June 14, 1829. In addition, as Rengger reported, the government also established maximum prices on retail sales; see José Antonio Vázquez, *El Doctor Francia*, pp. 555–60, for specific examples.
12. Rengger, *The Reign*, p. 192.
13. BNRJ, CRB, 1-29, 23, leg. 27, Francia al Comandante de Pilar, August 31, 1825.
14. Ibid.
15. Ibid.
16. ANA, SH, leg. 228, Francia al Comandante de Concepción, Fernando Acosta, June 23, 1818.
17. ANA, SH, leg. 393, Gill a Francia, December 4, 1825.
18. ANA, NE, leg. 708, Francia al Delegado de Pilar, December 12, 1825. (Italics added.)
19. José Antonio Vázquez, *El doctor Francia*, p. 70.
20. ANA, SH, leg. 235, Francia al Comandante de Concepción, August 12, 1822.
21. ANA, NE, leg. 1252, Comerciantes Brasileros a Francia, October 2, 1829.
22. Woodbine Parish to the Earl of Aberdeen, September 28, 1828, Woodbine Parish Papers, Rublic Record Office, Foreign Office no. 354, London, as quoted in John Hoyt Williams, "Woodbine Parish and the 'Opening' of Paraguay," *Proceedings of the American Philosophical Society* 16 (1972):348.
23. Mr. Hope to Mr. Parish, Corrientes, March 17, 1827, Woodbine Parish Papers, as quoted in Williams "Woodbine Parish," p. 348.
24. Chaves, *El Supremo Dictador*, p. 405.
25. *British Packet and Argentine News* (Buenos Aires), no 117, October 1, 1828.
26. ANA, SH, leg. 239, Francia to unidentified commander, November 12, 1828. Although this document does not name its recipient, as Francia used the familiar form—a liberty he took only with a handful of his closest officials—it is most likely directed to José Leon Ramírez, who at that time was serving as the Commander of Salta. Also see figure 4.
27. Informe de Correa da Cámara, January 20, 1829, as found in the *Anais do Itamarati*, 4:63.
28. Francisco Wisner de Morgenstern, *El Dictador del Paraguay*, pp. 139, 140.
29. For a summary of relations between Buenos Aires and Paraguay during the rule of Rosas, see Chaves, *El Supremo Dictador*, chapter 30. For a more detailed account, see idem, *Historia de las Relaciones entre Buenos-Ayres y el Paraguay*.
30. For examples, see ANA, NE, leg. 1886, Miguel Sampayo do Comercio de Brasil a Tesoureria do Estado, Itapúa, December 12, 1836; ANA, SH, leg. 377, Roxas a Francia, February 10, 1837; ANA, SH, leg. 377, Roxas a Francia, February 19, 1838; ANA, SH, leg. 378, Roxas a Francia, December 1, 1839; and ANA, SH, leg. 378, Roxas a Francia, June 21, 1840.
31. For examples of conversions for gold to *pesos fuertes*, see ANA, NE, leg. 2922, Cuenta General de dinero efectivo 1825–26, entry for December 8, 1825; ANA, LC, vol.

34, entry 477, September 1, 1831; ANA, LC. vol. 41, entry 24, January 4, 1838; and ANA, LC, vol. 43, entry 378, July 19, 1840.

32. BNRJ, CRB, 1-30, 2, leg. 6, Ramírez a Francia, October 23, 1830. Ramírez cites as the customary exchange rate 17 *pesos fuertes* and 6 reales, or 17.75 *pesos fuertes*, per ounce of gold. As a point of clarification, it should be noted that 8 reales equaled one peso.

33. Since at the established price of 180 pesos per ton, 17.3 pesos equals .0961 ton and 17.75 pesos equals .0986 ton, the difference of .0025 ton represents an increase of 2.6 percent.

34. ANA, NE, leg. 1890, Roxas a Francia, April 4, 1837, in which the Delegate of Itapúa noted that Francia had refused an offer to exchange 120 ounces of gold for 12.5 tons of yerba, insisting instead upon 146 ounces—an effective price of 202 pesos per ton.

35. For examples, see ANA, SH, leg. 377, Roxas a Francia, April 19, 1837, in which the delegate informed Francia that his demand of 220 ounces of gold for 18.75 tons of yerba—an effective price of 203 pesos per ton—was accepted by the Brazilian merchant; and ANA, SH, leg. 377, Roxas a Francia, February 27, 1838, in which the delegate informed Francia of another transaction in which 80 ounces of gold was exchanged for 6.75 tons of yerba—an effective price of 205 pesos per ton.

36. ANA, NE, leg. 1871, Cuaderno . . . Contribución de los Negociantes.

37. ANA, NE, leg. 1900, Libro de Receptor de yerba, 1838.

38. For examples, see ANA, SH, leg. 377, Roxas a Francia, June 30, 1837; ANA, SH, leg. 243, Roxas a Francia, October 27, 1838; ANA, SH, leg. 378, Roxas a Francia, March 12, 1839; and ANA, SH, leg. 244, Francia a Roxas, August 3, 1840.

39. ANA, NE, leg. 1900, Informe del Delegado de Concepción a Francia, December 16, 1839.

BIBLIOGRAPHY

Accioly, Hilderbrando. *Límites do Brasil (a frontera com o Paraguay)*. Rio de Janeiro: Companhia Editora Nacional, 1938.
Aguirre, Juan Francisco. *Diario de capitán de fragata . . . , 1781–1798*. Anales de la Biblioteca, no. 4. Buenos Aires, 1909.
Alberdi, Juan Bautista. *Grandes y pequeños hombres del Plata*. Paris: Garnier Freres, 1912.
———. *El Imperio del Brasil ante la democracia de América*. 1919. Buenos Aires: Ediciones ELE, 1946.
Anais do Itamarati. 4 vol. Rio de Janeiro: Ministério das Relações Exteriores, 1938.
Arquivo Diplomatico da Independencia, vol. 5. Rio de Janeiro: Litho-Typo, Fluminesse, 1922.
Arreguine, Victor. *Tiranos de América: El dictador Francia*. Montevideo, 1898.
Asambleas Constituyentes Argentinas (1813–1898). 7 vol. Buenos Aires: Casa J. Peuser, 1937–40.
Audibert, Alejandro. *Los límites de la antigua provincia del Paraguay*. Buenos Aires, 1892.
Avilés, Marques de. "Informe sobre la variación del sistema del Gobierno en Comunidad de los Indios de los treinta Pueblos." In *Documentos para la Historia Argentina*, vol. 3. Buenos Aires, 1912.
Ayala, Elías. *El Dr. Francia*. Asunción: Imprenta Nacional, 1942.
Azara, Félix de. *Descripción e historia del Paraguay y del Río de la Plata*. 1847. Buenos Aires: Editorial Bajel, 1943.
———. *Geografía física y esférica de las provincias del Paraguay y Missiones Guaraníes*. Montevideo: Talleres A. Barreiro, 1904.
———. *Memoria sobre el estado rural del Río de la Plata*. Buenos Aires: Editorial Bajel, 1944.
Baez, Cecilio. *Ensayo sobre el Doctor Francia y la Dictadura en Sud-América*. Asunción: H. Kraus, 1910.
———. *Historia colonial del Paraguay y Río de la Plata*. Asunción: Imprenta Zamphiopolos, 1926.
———. *Histoira diplomática del Paraguay*. 2 vols., Asunción: Imprenta Nacional, 1930 and 1931.
———. *Resumen de la historia del Paraguay desde la época de la conquista hasta el año 1880*. Asunción: H. Kraus, 1910.
Baliarda Bigaire, Luis. *El Dr. Francia, primer dictador perpetuo sudamericano*. Buenos Aires: Editorial Urbe, 1943.
Bazán, José S., *El Dictador Francia y otras composiciones*. Madrid, 1887.
Belgrano, Manuel, "Autobiografía." In *Memorias y Autobiografías*. Buenos Aires: Museo Histórico Nacional, 1910.
Benítez, Gregorio. *La revolución de Mayo*. Asunción, 1906.
Benítez, Luis G. *La junta superior gubernativa*. Asunción: El Arte, 1964.
———. *Historia diplomática del Paraguay*. Asunción: El Arte, 1972.
Benítez, Justo Pastor. *Carlos Antonio López*. Buenos Aires: Editorial Ayacucho, 1949.
———. *Formación del pueblo paraguayo*. Asunción: América-Sapucai, 1955.

———. *La vida solitaria de Dr. José Gaspar de Francia.* Buenos Aires: El Ateneo, 1937.
Blanco Sánchez, Jesús L. *El capitán don Antonio Tomás Yegros.* Asunción: Instituto Paraguayo de Investigaciones Históricas, 1961.
Box, Pelham Horton. *The Origins of the Paraguayan War.* Urbana: University of Illinois Press, 1930.
Brunel, Louis Adolphe. *Biographie de Aimé Bonpland.* Paris, 1871.
Burgin, Miron. *The Economic Origins of Argentine Federalism, 1820–1852.* Cambridge, Mass.: Harvard University Press, 1946.
Burns, E. Bradford. *A History of Brazil.* New York: Columbia University Press, 1970.
Burton, Richard Francis. *Letters from the Battle-Fields of Paraguay.* London, 1870.
Cabanellas, Guillermo. *El Dictador del Paraguay, El Doctor Francia.* Buenos Aires: Editorial Claridad, 1946.
Cabrera, Pablo. *Universitarios de Córdoba, Los del Congreso de Tucumán.* Cordoba: La Elzeviriana, 1916.
Caillet-Bois, Ricardo R. *La América Española y la Revolución Francesa.* Buenos Aires: Talleres Rodríques Giles, 1940.
Calvento, Mariano. *Estudios de la historia de Entre Ríos.* Paraná: Imprenta de la provincia, 1938.
Cardozo, Efraím. *Afinidades entre el Paraguay y la Banda Oriental en 1811.* Montevideo, 1963.
———. *Apuntes de historia cultural del Paraguay,* vol. 2. Asunción, 1963.
———. *Bolívar y el Paraguay.* II Congreso Internacional de Historia de America, vol. 4. Buenos Aires, 1949.
———. *El Imperio del Brazil y el Río de la Plata.* Buenos Aires: Librería del Plata, 1961.
———. *El Paraguay colonial.* Buenos Aires: Ediciones Nizza, 1959.
———. *El Paraguay independiente.* Barcelona: Salvat, 1949.
———. *El plan federal del Dr. Francia.* Buenos Aires, 1941.
———. *La politica del aislamiento durante la dictadura del Dr. Francia.* Asunción: Imprenta Nacional, 1931.
Carlyle, Thomas. "Dr. Francia." In *Carlyle's Complete Works, Critical and Miscellaneous Essays,* vol. 4. Boston, 1884.
Catálogo da Coleção Visconde de Rio Branco. 2 vols. Rio de Janeiro: Ministério das Relações Exteriores, 1950–51.
Centurión, Carlos. *Historia de la cultura paraguaya.* 2 vols. Asunción: Talleres Gráficos Lumen, 1961.
———. *Precursores y actores de la independencia del Paraguay.* Asunción, 1950.
Charlevoix, Pedro Francisco Jacier de. *Historia de Paraguay.* 6 vol. Madrid: V. Suarez, 1910–16.
Chaves, Julio César. *Belgrano y el Paraguay.* La Plata, 1960.
———. *Descubrimiento y conquista del Río de la Plata y el Paraguay.* Asunción: Ediciones Nizza, 1968.
———. *El Supremo Dictador.* 4th ed. Madrid: Ediciones Atlas, 1964.
———. *La Revolución del 14 y 15 de Mayo.* Buenos Aires: Ediciones Nizza, 1957.
———. *Historia de las relaciones entre Buenos Aires y el Paraguay: 1810–1813.* Asunción: Ediciones Nizza, 1959.
Comte, Auguste. *Appel aux conservateurs.* Paris, 1855.
Corona Baratech, C. E. "Notas para un estudio de la sociedad en el Río de la Plata durante el virreinato." *Anuario de Estudios Americanos* 6 (1953): 59–167.
Corrales y Sánchez, Enrique. *El Dictador Francia, Semblanza.* Madrid, 1898.
Corrêa Filho, V. *As Raias de Mato Grosso,* vol. 3. São Paulo: Estado de Sô Paulo, 1925.
Creydt, Oscar. *Formación histórica de la nación paraguaya.* Montevideo, 1963.
Darwin, Charles. *The Voyage of the Beagle.* New York: Bantam Books, 1958. Originally

published as *The Journal of Researches into the Geology and Natural History of the Various Countries Visited by H.M.S. Beagle*. London. 1839.

Decoud, Diógenes. *La Atlántida, Estudios de historia*. Paris, 1885.

Decoud, José Segundo, *Homenaje a los próceres de la independencia paraguaya*. Asunción, 1894.

Demersay, Alfred L. *Le docteur Francia, dictateur du Paraguay: su vie et son gouvernement*. Paris, 1856.

———. *Histoire phisique, economique et politique du Paraguay et des établissements des Jesuites*. Paris, 1860.

Dobrizhoffer, Martin. *An Account of the Abipones, an Equestrian People of Paraguay*. 3 vols. London, 1822.

Documentos del Archivo del Belgrano. 7 vols. Buenos Aires: Imprenta Coni, 1913–17.

Documentos del Archivo de Pueyrredón. 4 vols. Buenos Aires: Imprenta Coni, 1912.

Documentos para la Historia Argentina. Buenos Aires: Universidad Nacional de Buenos Aires, 1912–.

Documentos para la historia del virreynato del Río de la Plata. 3 vols. Buenos Aires: Universidad Nacional de Buenos Aires, 1912.

Du Graty, Alfredo M. *La República del Paraguay*. Besanzón, 1862.

Dwerhagen, Herman. *La Topografía de los rios Plata, Paraná, Paraguay, Bermejo y Pilcomayo*. Buenos Aires, 1831.

Eyzaguirre, José Ignacio Victor. *Los Intereses Católicos en América*. Paris, 1859.

Famín, César. *Chile, Paraguay, Uruguay, Buenos Aires*. Paris, 1834.

Frankel, Victor. *Espíritu y camino de Hispanoamérica*. Bogotá, 1953.

Fúrlong, Cárdif G. "Las Misiones Jesuíticas." *Historia de la Nación Argentina* 3 (1939): 408–29.

———*Los jesuítas y la cultura rioplatense*. Buenos Aires: Impresores Urta y Curbelo, 1933.

———*Misiones y sus pueblos de Guaraníes, 1810–1813*. Buenos Aires, 1962.

Gandia, Enrique de. *Francisco de Alfaro y la condición social de los Indios*. Buenos Aires: El Ateneo, 1939.

Garay, Blas, ed. *Descripción de las honras fúnebres que se hicieron al Exmo. Señor Dr. José Gaspar Rodríguez de Francia, Supremo Dictador Perpetuo de la República del Paraguay, primera de la América del Sud*. Asunción, 1898.

———. *El Comunismo de las Misiones*. Madrid, 1897.

———. *La revolución de la independencia del Paraguay*. Madrid, 1897.

———. *Tres ensayos sobre Historia del Paraguay*. Asunción: Editorial Guarania, 1942.

García Mellid, Atilio. *Proceso a los falsificadores de la Historia del Paraguay*. 2 vols. Buenos Aires: Ediciones Theoría, 1963.

Gelly, Juan Andres. *El Paraguay: lo que fue, lo que es y lo que será*. Paris: Editorial de Indias, 1926.

Gil Navarro, Ramón. *Veinte años en un calabozo o sea la desgraciada historia de veinte y tantos argentinos muertos o envejecidos en los calabozos del Paraguay*. Rosario, 1863.

Gilson, Etienne. *La Filosofía en la Edad Media*. Buenos Aires: Ediciones Sol y Luna, 1940.

Gómez, Hernán F. *El General Artigas y los hombres de Corrientes*. Corrientes: Imprenta del Estado, 1929.

González, Juan Natalicio. *Proceso y formación de la cultura paraguaya*. Asunción: Editorial Guarania, 1948.

Graham, R. B. Cunninghame. *A Vanished Arcadia: Being Some Account of the Jesuits in Paraguay*. New York: Dial Press, 1924.

Guido, Tomás. *Los Dictadores del Paraguay*. Buenos Aires, 1879.

Hernández, Pablo P. *Organización social de las doctrinas Guaraníes de la Compañía de Jesus*. 2 vols. Barcelona: Editorial G. Gili, 1911.

Herrera, Luis Alberto de. *La clausura de los ríos.* Montevideo, 1920.
Ibarra, Alonso. *José Gaspar de Francia el supremo defensor del Paraguay.* Asunción: Editorial Trujillo, 1961.
Irala Burgos, Adriano. *La ideología del Doctor Francia.* Asunción, 1975.
Kanki, Vicente Pazos. *A Narrative of Facts connected with the change Effected in the Political Condition and Relations of Paraguay under the Direction of Dr. Thomas Francia by an Individual who witnessed many of them, and Obtained Authentic Information Respecting the Rest.* London, 1826.
Kroeber, Clifton B. *The Growth of the Shipping Industry in the Río de la Plata Region: 1794–1860.* Madison: University of Wisconsin Press, 1957.
Lafuente Macháin, R. de. *La Virgen de la Asunción y su Oratorio.* Buenos Aires: Amorrortu é hijos, 1940.
———. *Los Macháin.* Buenos Aires, 1926.
———. *Muerte y exhumación del supremo dictador perpetuo del Paraguay.* Buenos Aires: Amorrortu é hijos, 1943.
Lamy, Pedro Dupuy. *Artigas en el cautiverio.* Montevideo: J. M. Serrano, 1912.
Lecuna, Vicente. *Cartas del Libertador.* Caracas: Tipografía de comercio, 1929.
Llanos, Julio. *El Doctor Francia.* Buenos Aires: A. Moen y hermano, 1907.
López, Carlos Antonio. *La emancipación del Paraguay.* Asunción: Editorial Guarania, 1942.
Lynch, John. *Spanish Colonial Administration, 1782–1810: The Intendant System in the Viceroyalty of the Río de la Plata.* London: University of London Press, 1958.
Machuca Martínez, Marcelino. *Mapas históricos del Paraguay gigante.* Asunción: El Arte, 1951.
Malthus, Thomas Robert. *Essay on the Principle of Population.* London, 1798.
Mariluz Urquijo, José M. *El Virreinato del Río de la Plata en la época del Marqués de Avilés (1799–1801).* Buenos Aires: Taller Gráfico San Pablo, 1964.
———. "Los Guaraníes después de la expulsión de los Jesuítas." *Estudios Americanos* 6 (1953), no. 25.
Massare de Kostianovsky, Olinda. *El Vice Presidente Sánchez.* Asunción: Escuela Fenica Salesiana, 1972.
Masterman, Jorge Federico. *Siete anos de Aventuras en el Paraguay.* Buenos Aires, 1870.
Medina, Anastasio Rolón. *Al margen de nuestra Historia.* Asunción: La Humanidad, 1955.
Memorias del Brigadier General Pedro Ferré, Buenos Aires: Editorial Coni, 1921.
Memorias de los Virreyes del Río de la Plata, Buenos Aires: Editorial Bajel, 1945.
Mendoza, Prudencio de la Cruz. *El Doctor Francia en el Virreynato de la Plata: Antecedentes universitarios y politicos del dictador del Paraguay.* Buenos Aires: Talleres Porter, 1936.
———. *Militarismo en el Paraguay.* Buenos Aires, 1916.
Ministerio del Interior (del Paraguay). *Los restos mortales del Doctor José Gaspar Rodríguez de Francia.* Asunción, 1962.
Mitre, Bartolomé. *Historia de Belgrano.* Buenos Aires, 1858.
Molas, Mariano Antonio. *Descripción histórica de la antigua provincia del Paraguay.* Buenos Aires, 1868.
———. "Clamor de un Paraguayo." *Revista del Paraguay* 3, nos. 7 and 8 (1893): 240–62 (originally written in 1828).
Molinari, Diego Luis. *¡Viva Ramírez!* Buenos Aires: Editorial Coni, 1938.
Moreno, Fulgencio R. *Estudio sobre la independencia del Paraguay.* Asunción: H. Kraus, 1911.
———. *La Ciudad de la Asunción.* Asunción: H. Kraus, 1926.

Mörner, Magnus. *The Expulsion of the Jesuits from Latin America.* New York: Alfred A. Knopf, 1965.
Murgel de Rezende, Octavio. *O Dr. Francia Ditador do Paraguay.* Rio de Janeiro: Imprenta Nacional, 1941.
Neruda, Pablo. "El Doctor Francia." In *Obras Completas.* 2d ed. Buenos Aires: Editorial Lusada, 1962.
Nogues, Alberto. *La iglesia en la época del Dr. Francia.* Asunción: El Gráfico, 1962.
Oddone, Rafael. *Esquema político del Paraguay.* Buenos Aires: Editorical Asunción, 1948.
Outes, Félix. *Los restos atribuídos al Dictador Francia.* Buenos Aires: Casa J. Peuser, 1925.
Page, Thomas J. *La Plata, The Argentine Confederation and Paraguay.* New York, 1873.
Palomeque, Alberto. *El General Rivera y la Campaña de Missiones.* Buenos Aires: Editorial A. E. López, 1914.
Parish, Woodbine. *Buenos Ayres and the Provinces of the Rio de la Plata.* London, 1852.
Pastells, Pablo. *Historia de la Compañía de Jesus en la Provincia del Paraguay.* 8 vols. Madrid: V. Suárez, 1912–49.
Pastore, Carlos. *La lucha por la tierra en el Paraguay.* Montevideo: Editorial Antequera, 1972.
Pelliza, Mariano A. *Ensayo Histórico sobre la revolución del Paraguay.* Buenos Aires, 1833.
Pérez, Manuel Antonio, "Oración." *La Gazeta Mercantile de Buenos Aires,* July 22, 1846.
Pérez Acosta, Juan F., *Francia y Bonpland,* Publicaciones del Instituto de Investigaciones Historicas, 79. Buenos Aires: Casa J. Peuser, 1942.
———. *Gaspar Rodríguez de Francia y Pedro Ferré.* Buenos Aires: Casa J. Peuser, 1942.
Plá, Josefina. *Hermano Negro. La esclavitud en el Paraguay.* Madrid: Paraninfo, 1972.
Puiggros, Rodolfo. *Historia Económica del Río de la Plata.* Buenos Aires: Editorial Futuro, 1946.
Quesada, Ernesto. *La Política Argentino-Paraguaya.* Buenos Aires: Editorial Brédahl, 1902.
Raine, Philip. *Paraguay.* New Brunswick, N.J.: Scarecrow Press, 1956.
Ramos, R. Antonio. *Correa da Cámara en Asunción.* Buenos Aires: Ediciones Nizza, 1942.
———. *La política del Brasil en el Paraguay: bajo la dictadura del Dr. Francia.* 1943. Buenos Aires: Ediciones Nizza, 1959.
Ramos Mejía, Francisco. *El federalismo argentino.* Buenos Aires, 1889.
Ramos Mejia, José M., *Las neuroses de los hombres celebres en la historia argentina.* 2 vols. Buenos Aires, 1878–82.
———. *Rosas y el Doctor Franica.* Madrid: Editorial América, 1917 (?).
Rengger, Johann Rudolph. *The Reign of doctor Joseph Gaspar Roderick de Francia, in Paraguay; being an account of a six years' residence in that Republic.* 1827. London: Documentary Publications, 1970.
Ricardo, David. *The Principles of Political Economy and Taxation.* London, 1817.
Riquelme, Andrés. *Apuntes para la historia política y diplomática del Paraguay.* 2 vols. Asunción: Editorial Toledo, 1960, 1961.
Riquelme García, Benigno. *El Ejército de la Independencia.* Asunción, 1973.
Roa Bastos, Augusto. *Yo el Supremo.* Buenos Aires: Siglo XXI, 1975.
Robertson, John Parish, and Robertson, William Parish. *Four Years in Paraguay: Comprising an Account of that Republic, Under the Government of the Dictator Francia.* 2 vols. Philadelphia, 1838.

———. *Francia's Reign of Terror, Being the Continuation of Letters on Paraguay*. London, 1839.
Rousseau, Jean Jacques. *Le Contrat Social*. Paris, 1762.
Rubio, Julián María. *La Infanta Carlota Joaquina y la política de España en América*. Madrid: Imprenta de E. Maestre, 1920.
Saguier Aceval, Emilio. *La lucha por la libertad*. Asunción, 1940.
Saint-Simon, Count Henri de. *Nouveau Christianisme*. Paris, 1825.
Saldias, Adolfo. *Papeles de Rosas*. 2 vols. La Plata: Imprenta de J. Roldán, 1904–7.
Sánchez, Quell H. *Estructura y función del Paraguay Colonial*. Asunción: Casa América, 1973.
———. *La diplomacia paraguaya de Mayo a Cerro Corá*. 5th ed., rev. Asunción: Editorial Nacional, 1973.
Scobie, James R. *Argentina: A City and a Nation*. New York: Oxford University Press, 1971.
Smith, Adam. *An Inquiry into the Nature and Causes of the Wealth of Nations*. London, 1776.
Somellera, Pedro, "Notas del Doctor don Pedro Somellera a la introducción que ha puesto el Doctor Rengger a su ensayo histórico sobre la revolución del Paraguay." 1841. In *Documentos del Archivo de Belgrano*, vol. 3. Buenos Aires, 1914.
Sosa Escalada, J. M. *Caballero*. Buenos Aires: Jordan y Villamil, 1911.
Stein, Barbara H., and Stein, Stanley J. *The Colonial Heritage of Latin America*. New York: Oxford University Press, 1970.
Susnik, Branislava. *El indio colonial del Paraguay: Los trece pueblos Guaraníes de la Misiones (1767–1803)*, 3 vols. Asunción: Museo Etnográfico Andrés Barbero, 1965–71.
Techo, Nicolas del. *Historia de la provincia del Paraguay*. 5 vols. Madrid, 1897.
Temperley, Harold W. V. *The Foreign Policy of Canning, 1822–1872*. London: G. Bell and Sons, 1925.
Tobal, Federico. *El Dictador Francia ante Carlyle*. Buenos Aires, 1893.
Trías, Vivian. *El Paraguay de Francia el Supremo a la Guerra de la Triple Alianza*, Cuadernos de CRISIS, no. 19. Buenos Aires, 1975.
Vargas Peña, Benjamin. *Paraguay-Argentina: Correspondencia Diplomática, 1810–1840*. Buenos Aires: Editorial Ayacucho, 1945.
———. *Vencer o morir*. Asunción: La Colmena, 1933.
Vásquez, Genaro V. *Doctrinas y realidades en la legislación para los Indios*. Mexico City: Departamento de asuntos indígena, 1940.
Vázquez, Anibal S. *Caudillos entrerrianos—Ramírez*. Paraná: Casa Predassi, 1928.
Vázquez, José Antonio. *El doctor Francia, visto y oído por sus contemporaneos*. Asunción: Pariguariae, 1962.
Velazco, Mariano. *Proclama de un Paraguayo a sus paysanos*. Buenos Aires, 1815.
Velázquez, Rafael Eladio. *El Paraguay en 1811*. Asunción, 1966.
Vittone, Luis. *El Paraguay en la lucha por su independencia*. Asunción: Imprenta Militar, 1960.
Volney, Constantin François, Chasseboeuf. *Les Ruines, ou méditations sur les révolutions des empires*. Paris, 1791.
Warren, Harris Gaylord. *Paraguay*. Norman: University of Oklahoma Press, 1949.
Washburn, Charles A., *The History of Paraguay*. 2 vols. Boston, 1871.
White, Edward Lucas, *El Supremo*. 1916. New York: E. P. Dutton & Co., 1967.
Wilgas, Curtis, ed. *South American Dictators During the First Century of Independence*. New York: Russell and Russell, 1937.
Williams, John Hoyt. "Dr. Francia and the Creation of the Republic of Paraguay: 1810–1814." Ph. D. dissertation, University of Florida, Gainesville.

———. "Woodbine Parish and the 'Opening' of Paraguay." *Proceedings of the American Philosophical Society* 116 (1972).
Wisner de Morgenstern, Francisco. *El Dictador del Paraguay: José Gaspar Francia.* 1923. Buenos Aires: Editorial Ayacucho, 1957.
Zavala, Francisco B. "Un informe del gobernador de Misiones, don Francisco Bruno de Zavala, sobre el estado de los treinta pueblos" (1784). *Boletín del Instituto de Investigaciones Históricas* (Buenos Aires) 25 (1941): 159–88.
Zinny, Antonio. *Historia de los gobernantes del Paraguay: 1535-1887.* Buenos Aires, 1887.
Zorraquín Becú, Ricardo. *El federalismo argentino.* Buenos Aires: Bernaoé y cía., 1939.

INDEX

Abreu, José de, 40, 42
administrative reform, 61, 78, 99–101
agrarian reform. *See* land reform
agriculture, regulation of, 123–24. *See also* yerba
alcabala, 108
Alfaro, Juan, 89
Alós, Joaquín de, 27–28
Alvarez, Juan Manuel, 106*n*
appropriations, state, 95–97
Argentina, 4. *See also* Buenos Aires
Aripí, Nicolás, 133
Arístegui, Juan, 91
armed forces: dominance of, 46, 49–50; economic effect of, 19; expansion of, 87; officer corps of, 107–8; reform of, 63; size of, 107–8, 150; spending on, 104–7; state sales to, 111; subjugation of, 54
arms: acquisition of, 64; Buenos Aires' control of, 52; manufacture of, 102; trade in, 142–43
Artigas, José: asylum granted to, 86; and Francia, 82; occupies Candelaria, 72–73; popularity of, 64
Asunción, street construction in, 116
Asunción cabildo, 46; abolition of, 8, 97–98
autarky, 143–46
Avilés, Viceroy, 27, 28
Azara, Felix de, 18, 27, 28

Babeuf, François Noël, 169
Baldovinos, Marcos, 85, 91
Banda Oriental, 37, 39
bando of October 21, 1813, 57–58
Belgrano, Manuel, 37, 38
Bogarín, Frey Francisco Javier, 44; expulsion of, 47
Bogarín, Juan, 86
Bolívar, Simón, 136*n*
Bonpland, Aimé Jacques Alexandre, 133–36
Brazil, 2; trade with, 140, 146
British Packet and Argentine News, 161
Bucareli, Francisco de Paula, 26
budget, 102, 103
Buenos Aires: annexation attempt by, 54–56; blockade by, 37, 81, 82*n*, 139; British invasion of, 33; control of arms traffic by, 52; creole attitude toward, 43; dictatorship in, 60; 1810 revolt in, 34–35; importance of, 2, 4; Paraguayan opposition to, 35–38; relations with, 49, 51–53, 74–75, 137–38, 162

Caballero, Pedro Juan: and anti-Francia coups, 66, 67, 85, 90; appointed to junta, 44; in 1813 assembly, 57; and levy of "contributions," 61–62; in May 14 and 15 Revolution, 41; suicide of, 91
cabildo, 46; abolition of, 8, 97–98
cabildo abierto, opposition of porteños to, 35–37
Cáceres, Ramón de, 87, 89, 90, 133
Cádiz-Panama-Lima merchants' guild, 2
Carlyle, Thomas, 12
cattle raising, 121–23
Cavañas, Manuel Atanasio, 37, 72, 97
Cerda, Gregorio de la, 50, 51, 55
Cespedes, Roque Antonio, 72, 93
Chaves, Julio César, 13
church: control of, 8, 80; lands of, 110; nationalization of, 69–72; weakening of, 93–94
Cisplatine War, 2, 139, 149
"civil death," 63
class confrontation, 77
Comte, Auguste, 12–13
congress of 1813, 56–58
congress of 1814, 65–69
congress of 1816, 78–79
Congress of Vienna, 154*n*
consular executive, 58
contribución fructuaria, 108
Córdoba: battle of, 88; customs barrier at, 2
Correia da Cámara, Antônio Manuel, 146, 161
credit, Spanish, 96
creoles: attitude toward Buenos Aires of, 43; dominance of, 1; expulsion of British by, 33; military leadership of, 37, 38; power struggles among, 2; and Spanish, 61. *See also* elite

Darwin, Charles, 11
defense, priority of, 102–4. *See also* armed forces
democracy, 76–77
dependence, 17; and cattle raising,

293

121–22; dismantling of, 171–72; and economic crises, 163; effects of, 19, 22–23; and foreign policy, 129; Francia on, 137–39; and trade, 20–21, 155, 156, 160
"dictator," defined, 6–7n
diezmo, 26, 108

economy: diversification of, 121–24; monocultural, 18–19, 28–29; state control of, 159–60, 164–65. *See also* dependence
education, public, 117–18
elite: control over, 7–8; weakening of, 92–93, 96–98. *See also* creoles; Spaniards
England: domination of Brazil by, 39; invasion of Buenos Aires by, 33; relations with, 152–54; sympathy of, 73–74
Espinola, José, 34–35
estancias, state, 110–11
exports: importance of, 18; level of, 144, 164; regulation of, 123, 140–42, 154–56

Famín, César, 118–19
Farroupilho Revolt, 106, 162
Ferdinand VII, 33–34
Ferré, Pedro, 149, 150, 151
fines, 80–81, 97
France, 135; blockade of Buenos Aires by, 162
Francia, José Gaspar Rodríguez de: ascendance of, 60–61; body of stolen, 12; call for independence by, 35, 36; and church, 69, 70; on dependence, 137–39; dictatorship of, 6–7, 67–69, 79; education of, 4–6; in 1811 assembly, 43–45; on free trade, 157–58; historical accounts of, 8–14; identification with masses of, 75–76; legal career of, 6; military strength of, 65; opposition to, 7, 66–67, 80–81, 82–85; on popular government, 76–77; popularity of, 66; resignations of, 46–47, 49–50; returns to government of, 47–48, 53–54; selected as deputy, 41–42
Francia, Pedro, 100
Free Commerce regulations, 20
free navigation, 74, 152, 154n, 156–57
free trade, 157–59
fuero eclesiástico, 93–94

general assembly of June 17, 1811, 43–45
government: class composition of, 99; organization of, 99–100. *See also* administrative reform

Gracia, Pedro, 36
Grandsire, Jean Etienne Richard de, 117, 135
Great Conspiracy, 7, 72, 81, 85–86, 88–92, 98
Guaraní Missions. *See* Missions

Herrera, Nicolás de, 55–56, 58–59, 121

immigration, 119
imports, regulation of, 144–46
industry, development of, 111
Inheritance Law of 1812, 62
Itapúa: prices at, 159–60; trade at, 140, 144, 162
Iturbe, Vicente Ignacio, 41, 65

Jesuits, 24–26
João, Prince Regent, 38–39
junta of 1811, 44–45; royalist plot against, 48

labor, shortage of, 19
Lagle y Rey, Vicente, 115
land, state expropriation of, 97
land reform, 8, 94, 110, 120
latifundia. *See* land reform
liberalism, economic, 158–59
library, public, 118
licensing: of doctors, 114n; of merchants, 141–42, 155
Liniers, Santiago, 33
literacy, 117
Locke, John, 166
López, Carlos Antonio, 106n
loyalty oath, for clergy, 93

Malthus, Robert, 168
Matiauda, Vicente Antonio, 64–65
May 14 and 15 Independence Revolution, 40–42
medical care, regulation of, 113–14
military. *See* armed forces; defense
Missions: civil administration of, 26–28; control of, 129–32, 137, 147–51; economy of, 141; impoverishment of, 28–29; Jesuit administration of, 24–25
monasteries, expropriation of, 94. *See also* church
monocultural economies, 18–19, 28–29, 124
Montiel, Miguel Antonio, 85, 91
Mora, Fernando de la, 44, 51, 55

nationalism, 56–57, 160, 170–71
Neruda, Pablo, 13
nonintervention, 43, 51, 64–65, 82, 125, 162

oligarchy. See elite

Panés, Pedro García de, 71, 93
Paraguarí, battle of, 37
"Paraguayan-Correntine War," 148–51
Parish, Woodbine, 152–53, 154, 160–61
peons, exploitation of, 20–21, 22
Pérez, Father Manuel Antonio, 12
physiocracy, 167
Pilar, 34; prices at, 159–60; rebuilding of, 116; trade at, 143, 144, 162
Pinedo, Agustín Fernando, 18, 19, 20, 21, 22
"Political Catechism," 101–2
Popham, Sir Home, 33
Portugal, 42–43; invasions by, 48, 51
prison system, 99
Provisional Junta of the Río de la Plata, 34–35
public works, 114–17
Pueblo of Santo Tomé, 43
Pueyrredón, Juan Martín de, 81–82

Quesnay, François, 167

Ramírez, Francisco, 131; and Bonpland, 133, 134; death of, 91; invasion planned by, 86–88
reform: administrative, 61, 78, 99–101; land, 8, 94, 110, 120; military, 63
relief programs, 120–21
Rengger, Johann Rudolph, 9, 11n
Republic of Paraguay, founding of, 57–58
revenue, sources of, 80–81, 95–97, 110–14. See also taxation
Río de la Plata, geography of, 2
roads, construction of, 115–16, 116–17
Robertson, John Parish, 9, 73–74
Rodríguez, Martín, 88
Rosas, Juan Manuel de, 59, 149, 162
Rousseau, Jean Jacques, 166
Royal Seminary of San Carlos, 94, 110, 118

Saguier, Pierre, 133–34
Saint-Simon, Henri de, 169
Sánchez, Domingo Francisco, 106–7n
shipbuilding, 104
slavery, 119–20
Smith, Adam, 167–68
Sobremonte, Rafael de, 33

social justice, 78
Souza, Diego de, 39, 40, 42
Spain, 1; military policy of, 36—37; Napoleon's invasion of, 33–34
Spaniards: appropriations from, 96–97; arrest of, 89; opposition to, 61–63
specie, 154–55, 163–64
stability, economic, 102, 164–65
staples, shortages of, 19

Tacuarí, battle of, 38
taxation, 62, 108–10, 114, 139, 140–41; by Buenos Aires, 53
torture, 90–91
trade: with Brazil, 140, 146; British, 33; control of, 159–60; decline of, 82–85; and dependence, 20–21, 155, 156, 160; problems of, 146; state, 142, 144. See also exports; imports
Treaty of October 12, 1811, 48–49; nullification of, 57
El Tribuno (Buenos Aires), 10

Uruguay, 37, 39, 162

Vargas, Juan Baltazar, 81–82
Vázquez, José Antonio, 13
Velasco, Bernardo de, 129; deposition of, 42, 44; in May 14 and 15 Revolution, 34–35, 37, 38, 39–40, 41
Velazco, Frey Mariano, 9–10
Vertiz, Juan José de, 26
Viceroyalty of the Río de la Plata, creation of, 4
Volney, Constantin François, 169

War of the Triple Alliance, 161
Whitelocke, John, 33
Wisner de Morgenstern, Enrique, 11

Yegros, Antonio Tomás, 47, 64, 65
Yegros, Fulgencio: arrest of, 86; and Artigas, 64; as consul, 58, 61, 66; in 1811 junta, 44, 46; execution of, 91; as officer, 37, 40; and opposition to Francia, 85
yerba: export of, 124; importance of, 18–19; Mission production of, 24–25, 28–29, 131–33; price of, 164; taxation of, 19–21; thefts of, 148

Zevallos, Juan Valeriano de, 41, 42, 43